POLITICAL THINKERS FOR OUR TIME

People for Our Time

A collection of books from Northern Illinois University Press

A list of titles in this collection is available at cornellpress.cornell.edu.

POLITICAL THINKERS FOR OUR TIME

WILLIAM T. REDDINGER

NORTHERN ILLINOIS UNIVERSITY PRESS
AN IMPRINT OF CORNELL UNIVERSITY PRESS
Ithaca and London

Copyright © 2026 by Cornell University

All rights reserved. Except for brief quotations in a review, this book, or parts thereof, must not be reproduced in any form without permission in writing from the publisher. For information, address Cornell University Press, Sage House, 512 East State Street, Ithaca, New York 14850. Visit our website at cornellpress.cornell.edu.

First published 2026 by Cornell University Press

Librarians: A CIP catalog record for this book is available from the Library of Congress.

ISBN 9781501785542 (hardcover)
ISBN 9781501785559 (paperback)
ISBN 9781501785573 (pdf)
ISBN 9781501785566 (epub)

To my father, who taught me to love liberty

Contents

Introduction: The Principles of the
Anglo-American Political Tradition   1

1. Brief Biographies   8
2. Edmund Burke and the Meaning
   of Liberty   25
3. Alexis de Tocqueville and
   the Meaning of Equality   47
4. Abraham Lincoln and the American
   Republic   67
5. The Federalist Papers and
   the US Constitution   85
6. George Washington and
   Religious Liberty   110
7. Friedrich Hayek and the Free Market   125
8. Wilhelm Röpke and the Cultural
   Conditions of the Free Market   143

Conclusion: Anglo-American
Principles and the US Constitution   159

Acknowledgments   165
Notes   167
Selected Bibliography   197
Index   201

POLITICAL THINKERS FOR OUR TIME

Introduction
The Principles of the Anglo-American Political Tradition

After the guns fell silent at Yorktown, George Washington reflected that "the establishment of Civil and Religious Liberty was the Motive which induced me to the Field."[1] He believed that no one was above the law, that government derives its authority from the consent of the people, and that monarchy ought to have no place in America. Like his countrymen, he claimed the historic rights of Englishmen, including constitutional limits on government power and a right to be taxed only by one's own consent. He also believed in natural rights, to life, liberty, and property, and to what he called "liberty of conscience." To summarize his wishes for the American political order, he often quoted a line from the Old Testament prophet Micah: "But they shall sit every man under his vine and under his fig tree; and none shall make them afraid, for the mouth of the LORD of hosts hath spoken it."[2] To Washington, the lines symbolized an America that would be a safe haven wherein people might enjoy those ideals for which he led the Continental Army into the crucible of war.

Such principles—the rule of law, property rights, religious liberty, limited government—are foundational to what has been called the Anglo-American political tradition. Scholars have used other terms to signify the same strain of modern political thinking that values these principles, often contrasting this tradition with "continental" political thought associated with abstract reason, central direction of political and economic activity, and secular society. Samuel Gregg, for example, distinguishes between different "Enlightenments," observing that while all manifestations valued reason, leading figures of the French Enlightenment and those like them showed less humility in their assessment of the powers of reason than did those associated with the British and Scottish Enlightenments.[3] Friedrich Hayek used the terms *Anglican* and *Gallican* to refer to different traditions of political thinking.[4] Russell Kirk distinguished between conservatism and radicalism to make much the same point.[5]

Washington and subsequent generations used reason (and, if necessary, force) to defend the principles of this tradition. In the twenty-first century some have wondered whether the Anglo-American political heritage is really something worth preserving.[6] This book outlines the principles that are foundational to the American political tradition by looking at leading thinkers who thought carefully about them.

This book differs in form and scope but not in purpose from a short book from the last century. In the early years of the Cold War, the public intellectual and conservative author Russell Kirk wrote *The American Cause*, which he called a "little book" that was "a statement of the moral and social principles that the American nation upholds in our time of troubles." The standoff with the Soviet Union made it such a time, but so too did the fact that many people at the beginning of the Cold War era were "badly prepared for their task of defending their own convictions," with the result that they were "ignorant of those ideas and institutions which nurture our culture" and "political liberty."[7] In the spirit of Kirk, this book presents essential principles using leading figures from the Western intellectual tradition to inform our thinking about important issues in contemporary American politics.

What is liberty? What is the best form of government? How should religion relate to politics? The men of the past examined in this book can inform our thinking about these and other important political issues in our own time. Rather than seeking to apply abstract theories without taking into account real people and circumstances, these thinkers considered prudently how foundational principles could, if used wisely, make our world freer and more just. The very best political thinkers follow the example of the nineteenth-century French thinker Alexis de Tocqueville, who used reason "to see, not differently," from the parties of his day, but to see "further."[8] If we wish to see further like Tocqueville, we must do the difficult work of reasoning through the political matters that are of pressing importance in our day.

Western political thought, in particular the Anglo-American political tradition, is a tradition that is predominantly white and male. It goes without saying that there are limits to the perspectives of these Western political thinkers and that what a woman or a person of color from the same time period thought about, say, political liberty might have differed in at least some respects from Edmund Burke's understanding. Others, as Frederick Douglass observed of Abraham Lincoln, had many of the prejudices of similar people of their time. Even so, the men discussed in this book share with us, as they shared with others of their own day whatever their differences, a common humanity, and the principles they thought and wrote about are universal.

To understand the ideas of people from the past, it is helpful to know something of the historical context in which they lived. Before considering what each political thinker can teach us about the ideas and institutions of modern liberty, the first chapter provides brief biographies. A chapter each is given to Edmund Burke, Alexis de Tocqueville, Abraham Lincoln, Publius (the shared pseudonym of Alexander Hamilton, James Madison, and John Jay, the authors of *The Federalist*), George Washington, Friedrich Hayek, and Wilhelm Röpke.

Chapter 2 examines Edmund Burke, the eighteenth-century statesman and political thinker who was arguably the greatest defender of a sound, cogent conception of liberty. In his *Reflections on the Revolution in France*, he predicted the collapse of the French Revolution's high ideals of liberty, equality, and fraternity into a violent maelstrom that terminated in tyranny. Burke understood liberty as that state of society in which one has the freedom to do what is right and good, not an absolute freedom to realize all our desires, which is a liberty more appropriate to an animal than to a human being. An examination of Burke's writings and speeches reveals that he believed that self-regulation was necessary to enjoy political liberty This chapter considers Burke's uneasiness with what has been called "rights talk," which is the manner in which most people in the modern world tend to speak of liberty. Burke suspected that assertions of rights are often merely angry demands for desires. The chapter also looks at the two primary means by which Burke thought that people might enjoy liberty: through the "little platoons" of society—social entities like families, churches, local communities, and the like—and as a kind of inheritance from past generations.

In chapter 3, we consider the work of Alexis de Tocqueville, whose *Democracy in America* has been called the greatest book ever written on democracy and the greatest book ever written on America.[9] Tocqueville taught that the characteristic feature of democratic societies is love of equality, and he thought deeply and wrote eloquently about what this means for liberty. He made a powerful argument that the magnitude of the passion for equality in democratic times puts countries at greater risk of tyranny. Tocqueville wanted a society in which modern democratic equality coexisted with liberty, and for this reason, he understood equality in liberty to be equality before the law because of equal human dignity. He thought carefully about the possibility of democratic life descending into tyranny, and this chapter considers three modes of tyranny that appear in his writing—namely, the "tyranny of Caesars," the "tyranny of the majority," and "soft despotism."

Chapter 4 looks at Abraham Lincoln's understanding of republican government, by which he meant a political regime in which the people govern themselves. Lincoln showed that Stephen Douglas's defense of "popular sovereignty" perverted the very meaning of that idea, not to mention liberty itself. How could enslaving another human being be properly called popular sovereignty? How could a republican government "of the people" truly be of the people if some had no say in the laws that governed them? This chapter highlights three implications of the republican phenomenon of popular self-government: No person may enslave another; people must have the freedom to work and to enjoy the fruits of their labor; and the people must be the source of the laws because they are the ultimate political authority.

Chapter 5 reviews *The Federalist*, popularly referred to as the Federalist Papers—the greatest contribution to political thought produced in the American political tradition. Coauthored by James Madison, Alexander Hamilton, and John Jay, *The Federalist* is a goldmine of political thought and wisdom. This chapter explains the thesis in *The Federalist* that the US Constitution represents the true, long-term will of the American people and gives particular attention to the accusation that the Constitution is undemocratic. A correct understanding of the political thought of *The Federalist* shows that the US Constitution illustrates a practical implementation of the principle of popular self-government.

Chapter 6 focuses on "religious liberty." Aside from the First Amendment, perhaps the best, clearest, and most concise understanding of religious liberty in American political history appears in the writings and speeches of George Washington, who argued that religious liberty, or "freedom of religion," means the freedom to believe and the freedom to live one's life according to those beliefs. This chapter also considers lesser imitations of religious freedom in our time—ideas such as religious toleration and freedom of worship, for example.

Chapters 7 and 8 address the idea of the free market, which this book suggests is a necessary part of a good society, but only if the free market is understood rightly. In chapter 7, we consider the twentieth-century Austrian economist Friedrich Hayek's understanding that a free market is an economic system that preserves individual economic liberty through certain structural conditions—namely, private property, the rule of law, and free prices. Chapter 8 examines the same topic from a different angle, focusing on the twentieth-century German economist Wilhelm Röpke. Röpke supplemented Hayek's understanding, arguing that a truly free market is one that depends not only on necessary structural conditions but also on necessary cultural conditions, without which the free market cannot survive.

In the course of this book, several secondary themes emerge that are helpful for understanding what political thinkers can tell us about the principles and institutions conducive to political liberty. These themes are as follows: First, political debate is fitting for our nature and is a way of avoiding conflict. In this, I take the position of the classical philosopher Aristotle against that of the modern Thomas Hobbes, for whom rights were claims founded on nothing more than individual will and who thought animals were more peaceful than human beings because they do not use speech but instead communicate only to signal to others what they desire.[10] According to Hobbes, human beings err by using speech to debate good and evil, categories that have no real existence and are only names for imaginary notions that cause conflict.[11] As in so many other matters, this was Hobbes's way of attacking Aristotle, for whom the unique feature of our humanity is our ability to use reason and speech to debate what is just and unjust.[12] Violence is not properly political insofar as political people use rational language to try to persuade others in a community about what is good for them. This book highlights thinkers whose facility with the written and spoken word fostered a political order that contributes to the reconciling of competing interests through language and debate.

Second, political language is subject to distortion, especially during times of social instability. In his record of the revolution that spread to the entire Greek world during some of the years of the ancient Peloponnesian War, Thucydides observed that people were worked up into a fit of virtual madness, with language itself being rendered the slave of white-hot passion rather than a symbol to reflect what our minds believe to be real. "Words," Thucydides explained, "had to change their ordinary meaning and to take that which was now given them. Reckless audacity came to be considered the courage of a loyal supporter; prudent hesitation, specious cowardice; moderation was held to be a cloak for unmanliness; ability to see all sides of a question incapacity to act on any."[13] The thinkers in this book observed something similar in their time, and their reflections on these matters can help us to navigate political debate in our own day.

Third, reasoned deliberation befits political liberty, but impatience accompanies tyranny. Thucydides's history presaged a recurring danger in the history of Western civilization—namely, impatience and disgust for collective deliberation. Words and the thoughts they convey stand in the way of a strong man who would impose his will on a people. It was for this reason that it was foundational to fascist dogma to oppose deliberation and the reconciliation of competing interests. The fascist legal theorist Carl Schmitt, who for a time was legal counselor to the Third Reich, advocated a doctrine sometimes called "decisionism" in which every political order required a single leader who must decide when to wage war against enemies. In this, Schmitt opposed modern liberal democracy and its neutral state in which the interests of various groups are reconciled into a workable community.[14]

Fourth, the political thinkers of the Anglo-American political tradition were careful to distinguish theory and practice. Much of the time, distortion of the proper understanding of a political principle happens when someone infuses a word with meaning that is conceptually false in proportion as it is too abstract. A basic feature in Aristotle's ethical and political thought was his insistence on distinguishing theory and practice. One must consider the degree of precision appropriate to a particular field of study.[15] Politics is less precise than geometry. There is no equation that determines the correct answer for constantly shifting political circumstances, and the consequences of a failure to distinguish theory and practice include, at best, an accompanying failure to realize some political good (e.g., liberty) and, at worst, an active undermining of that political good.

Fifth, free speech is an essential part of political liberty. Not long ago, most people in the West regarded as sacrosanct John Stuart Mill's argument that "the peculiar evil of silencing the expression of an opinion is that it is robbing the human race; posterity as well as the existing generation; those who dissent from the opinion, still more than those who hold it. If the opinion is right, they are deprived of the opportunity of exchanging error for truth; if wrong, they lose, what is almost as great a benefit, the clearer perception and livelier impression of truth produced by its collision with error."[16] As political polarization proceeds apace, these ethical commitments without which the center cannot hold become increasingly precarious. Some viewpoints increasingly appear beyond the pale—virtual thought crimes with no place for expression, even in that place seen historically as the locus of free thought and expression, the university, where insistence on uniformity and compliance even apart from reasonable arguments threatens to void the very purpose of the academy and to break out into American society generally.[17] There are some who would say that freedom of speech should not include the right to be offensive. Still others like Herbert Marcuse believe that freedom of speech is an illusion; in this view, elites may enjoy a liberty of speech, but those who wish to speak words at odds with elite opinion have no such liberty because they have no real social power.[18] For such thinkers, freedom of speech is a freedom for me but not for thee, and we would be better off abandoning the charade. Why play by the rules if the rules are rigged so that the house always wins? In contrast to those suspicious of freedom of speech, this book affirms with George Washington that "if men are precluded from offering their Sentiments on a matter, which may involve the most serious and alarming consequences, that can invite the consideration of Mankind, reason is of no use to us; the freedom of Speech may be taken away, and, dumb and silent we may be led, like sheep to the Slaughter."[19]

Chapter 1

Brief Biographies

To understand political thinkers well, one must read their political writings carefully, but an understanding of the historical context of their thoughts and the major events and turning points of their lives can be helpful as well. This brief chapter contains portraits of the political thinkers whose ideas are addressed in detail in subsequent chapters. Their lives span three centuries—the eighteenth, nineteenth, and twentieth.

Edmund Burke

One of Britain's great orators and parliamentarians, Edmund Burke was a statesman who used careful reasoning even as he spurned abstract philosophical speculation as out of place in legislative halls and chambers. Burke never wrote anything like a systematic treatise in political philosophy, and he lived his adult life not in an ivory tower but in political debate. Consequently, some see him as someone who only barely deserves a place in college classes or books about political theory. But this is to misunderstand that Burke's political *reflections*, to allude to the title of his most famous work, were never divorced from a deeply sophisticated grasp of theory. The ideas that constitute a Burkean political theory are available for those willing to draw them out from the particular speeches and writings on his political ideas.[1]

Born in Dublin in 1730, Burke was raised the son of a Protestant father and a Catholic mother. He was raised in the Church of England and held Christian beliefs throughout his life. His religiously mixed parents gave him an early loathing of unjust intolerance that would stay with him throughout his political career. Another early factor that produced a disdain for intolerance was his schooling that began in 1741 under the tutelage of a Quaker named Abraham Shackleton, whose religion and manner encouraged a tolerant spirit in the young Burke.

In 1744, Burke entered Trinity College, Dublin, graduating in 1748. He moved to London two years later, taking up the study of law at London's famous Middle Temple. An able student, he nevertheless found the study of law to be somewhat restrictive to a mind that was attracted more to a broad study of things not only legal but also historical and philosophic. His first published work indicates as much: After his legal studies, he finished a project that he had begun during his time at Trinity College—his 1756 book titled *A Philosophical Inquiry into the Origin of Our Ideas of the Sublime and Beautiful*, an influential treatment of aesthetics. The same year saw the publication of his *Vindication of Natural Society*, a satirical work that critiqued the views of Jean-Jacques Rousseau and others who had as of late taken to arguing that political laws and social customs are antithetical to what is natural. In contrast to Rousseau and those like him, Burke had an understanding of political liberty that depended on a conception of nature that was incomplete if understood without the salutary augmentations of just laws and healthy social customs. Another indicator of Burke's capacities as a thinker appears in the company he kept. In 1764, he became one of the first members of "The Club," a group of intellectuals who famously met at the Turk's Head Inn in London and included writer Samuel Johnson, painter and aesthetic philosopher Joshua Reynolds, moral philosopher and economist Adam Smith, and historian Edward Gibbon.

But it was during his political career that Burke produced the great speeches and writings for which he is most well known. He entered politics in 1765, occupying a seat for Wendover in Buckinghamshire. He quickly distinguished himself by his oratory and skill in debate. Aligning himself with the opposition Rockingham Whigs, in 1770, he penned *Thoughts on the Cause of the Present Discontents*, which became a sort of Rockingham Whig party creed. More well-known are Burke's two famous speeches that addressed the growing tensions with the American colonies: his speech on American taxation in 1774 and the speech on conciliation in 1775.

In these speeches we first see the themes that he developed in greater detail in his most important and famous work, his *Reflections on the Revolution in France*, published in 1790: suspicion of abstract ideas of rights that, far from promoting any political good, could destabilize government and society; defense of prudence and caution rather than a stubborn, and potentially counterproductive, insistence on political principles; and cautious deference to tradition in most cases, for which Burke became known as the intellectual father of modern conservatism. The *Reflections* appeared during the early years of the French Revolution, which began in 1789 and which many of Burke's contemporaries welcomed as a great moment in the historical progress of liberty. He weighed the developing evidence for about a year after the French Revolution began, until over three hundred moderate deputies of the French National Assembly fled, in October, leaving that body under the control of the Jacobins, who would soon get to work doing away with all aspects of the ancien régime. He was then convinced that the Revolution was an evil that should be opposed. In stark contrast to many in Britain, even former friends and members of his own party, Burke criticized the French Revolution, its leaders, and its defenders. He even predicted that the Revolution may well terminate in chaos and tyranny, an assertion that alienated friends and foes alike until chaos and, eventually, Napoleonic tyranny proved him right.

While Burke is rightly remembered for his prudent approach to the American crisis and for his opposition to the French Revolution, it would be improper not to observe two additional features of Burke's political life: his defense of Irish Catholics and of those who were in British subjection in India. Both illustrate Burke's hatred of tyranny, no matter where it would be found. His first public political work was his *Tract Relative to the Laws Against Popery in Ireland* (1765), a caustic tract that critiqued the deprivation of Irish Catholics of civil rights related to politics, economics, and religion. His work related to India occurred mostly in the later years of his career and focused on his (failed) effort to impeach Governor General Warren Hastings for abuse of power and mistreatment of people in India. While Burke mostly failed in his reform efforts for those in Ireland and India, many of his policies for both were realized in the nineteenth and twentieth centuries.

Alexis de Tocqueville

Alexis de Tocqueville (1805–1859) lived, as he put it, in "a world altogether new," its novelty the product not only of the French Revolution but of centuries of development toward greater social equality.[2] He was born into an aristocratic family with deep ties to the French monarchy. A maternal great-grandfather to Tocqueville, Guillaume-Chrétien de Malesherbes, was a member of the administration of the old regime who pushed Louis XVI unsuccessfully to reform destabilizing tax and penal laws. Later, Malesherbes would defend, again unsuccessfully, Louis XVI at his trial. After Malesherbes's tearful, passionate closing statement, the Jacobin leader Maximilien Robespierre announced that he forgave him for crying but that the king had to die. Malesherbes himself was guillotined in 1794. Tocqueville's father, Hervé de Tocqueville, supposedly went gray at age twenty-one as a result of the strain of fearing execution after having been put in prison in 1793, though he was released after ten months of incarceration following Robespierre's arrest in July 1794.

The Tocqueville family was firmly of the Legitimist (royalist) persuasion, and their opponents did little to change their affections. But it would be Tocqueville's suspicion of unchecked power that would be more enduring than any partisan allegiance, and that conviction was strengthened also by instruction as a youth. His tutor, Abbé Le Seuer, saw Alexis's potential early on and encouraged him in his studies; these included the Christian teaching on original sin, which encouraged a suspicion of unchecked, concentrated power. Tocqueville's reading augmented this teaching: Blaise Pascal's *Pensées* taught him to expect human wickedness as much as virtue, while Charles Baron de Montesquieu's *Spirit of the Laws* instructed him in the importance of political moderation, of checks on power, and of habits and social customs as a key to understanding any given political situation. The writings and public lectures of the liberal thinker and politician François Guizot, author of *The History of Civilization in Europe*, would also influence Tocqueville's political thinking, although he became somewhat disillusioned after finding that Guizot the politician was less impressive than Guizot the thinker.

In 1826, Tocqueville received his law degree; the next year holding the post of *juge auditeur*, a minor magistrate; it was at this position that Tocqueville would meet his dear traveling companion and intellectual friend Gustave de Beaumont, with whom he would make the voyage to America beginning in 1831. They crossed the Atlantic with an assignment from the French government to study the American penitentiary system (which they thought terrible), but both were interested in studying America as a whole as well. When he first arrived in New York, Tocqueville found Americans to be a vulgar people who cared only for money, and he complained about American food (it "represented the infancy of the art. . . . In a word, complete barbarism"[3]); his concerns about unrestrained pursuit of money and physical comfort would be prominent in *Democracy in America*. The people of Boston and New England were more to his liking: more aristocratic, educated, and generally moderate in their appetites. He also traveled west through what was then still largely a frontier wilderness, visiting the Great Lakes and traveling the Ohio and Mississippi Rivers all the way to the Gulf of Mexico before returning north by land. By the time he made the trip back to France, he had a robust hatred for American slavery and for the mistreatment of American Indians.

A year after returning to France, Tocqueville had still not started writing, so he went to his parents' attic in Paris, where he stayed for the next year, researching, making outlines, remaking them, and finally, writing *Democracy in America*. Its lessons about the ills of modern democracies, and about how healthy democratic life would look, often seem as relevant for our own time as for Tocqueville's. Volume 1 of *Democracy in America* appeared in 1835 to great commercial and critical success. For it, he won the prestigious Montyon Prize, with a significant monetary award, from *L'Académie Française*. With important exceptions, the first volume is rather optimistic and full of praise of American political life, and the book soon appeared in American schools so that young Americans could learn from a Frenchman about their own political system. Volume 2 appeared in 1840. It is more philosophic, darker, and more critical of democracy. Most editions today combine both volumes in a single book, one worth returning to time and again to find lessons about America's past and about the future of modern democracies everywhere.

Like Burke, Tocqueville was not only a thinker but active in politics. Unlike Burke, he was, with some exceptions, not especially skilled in political dealing and debating, although the same mind that produced *Democracy in America* at times showed an impressive ability to size up some current predicament, to prescribe the appropriate remedy, and to defend political liberty with eloquence. Tocqueville first ran for office in 1837 but lost. In 1839, he ran again, this time winning office to the Chamber of Deputies, the French legislative assembly during the Bourbon Restoration (1815–1830) and July Monarchy under the reign of

Louis Philippe (1830–1848). During this time, he was at times socially awkward and not always impressive in oratory. He was above all a political thinker, and where others ran for office with campaign messages about petty local concerns, Tocqueville spoke of preserving liberty and avoiding another revolution. He once observed of himself that his "true worth is above all in works of the mind" and that he was "worth more in thought than in action."[4]

This gave him an uncanny ability to predict the future, observing in *Democracy in America* over a hundred years before the Cold War that "there are two great peoples on the earth today who, starting from different points, seem to advance toward the same goal: these are the Russians and the Anglo-Americans . . . [and] each of them seems called by a secret design of Providence to hold the destinies of half the world in its hands one day."[5] This same clairvoyance also gave him his greatest hour as a politician, which he recorded in his fascinating posthumous book *Recollections*, which appeared in print in 1893. During his time in the Chamber of Deputies, he observed an ominous decline in public morality and a corresponding increase in nascent socialist sentiment and in the number of fellow legislators who cared only for the perquisites of office and but little for service to the public good.[6] From this, he concluded that "the time will come when the country will find itself once again divided between two great parties."[7] In other words, a new revolution was brewing. In a courageous speech to a nonreceptive audience in the Chamber of Deputies on January 29, 1848, Tocqueville made this "gloomy prediction," as he called it, to his colleagues, earning only their scorn. (A "nasty little man," one parliamentary colleague labeled him after the speech.[8]) But after events soon proved Tocqueville right, his colleagues viewed him in another light, and he was on a committee to draft a new constitution, which briefly established the Second French Republic. It was not an especially good constitution, Tocqueville observed, for there were still people rioting in the streets, pressuring the committee with threats while the drafting was going on. "Taking the Committee as a whole," he wrote, "it was easy to see that no very remarkable result was to be expected from it." Indeed, "all this bore very little resemblance to the men, so certain of their objects and so well acquainted with the measures necessary to attain them, who sixty years before, under George Washington's presidency, so successfully drew up the American Constitution."[9] For a short time, Tocqueville served as foreign minister, but he resigned five months later when the president of the French Republic pronounced himself emperor in 1852.

Throughout his adult life, Tocqueville pondered the means by which modern democracies might avoid the twin perils of tyranny and revolutionary chaos. Before the end of his life, he wrote one final book—or at least the first major section of a book that he never quite finished before his death in 1859—*The Old Regime and the Revolution*, which appeared in 1856. It is a penetrating book that sought out the true causes and effects of the French Revolution. It might be said of *The Old Regime and the Revolution* what he said of his masterpiece, *Democracy in America*: While others calculated their next political maneuver, Tocqueville was contemplating grand ideas and long-term history. In writing *Democracy in America*, he said, he wrote a book that was "not precisely in anyone's camp." Rather, he "undertook to see, not differently, but further than the parties; and while they are occupied with the next day," Tocqueville "wanted to ponder the future."[10]

Abraham Lincoln

Abraham Lincoln's life was a quintessentially American one in that he was a self-made man, and his status as thinker fits much the same description. Born in a log cabin in Kentucky on February 12, 1809, Lincoln grew up in poverty, and his youth was one of hard work and austere religious practice (if not belief). Lincoln recalled that his grandfather, also named Abraham, "emigrated from Rockingham County, Virginia, to Kentucky, about 1781 or 2, where, a year or two later, he was killed by Indians," and reaching farther back still, he noted that his grandfather's ancestors, "who were Quakers, went to Virginia from Berks County, Pennsylvania." When Lincoln was eight years old, his father, Thomas, "removed from Kentucky to . . . Indiana," where Lincoln grew up in a frontier wilderness, "with many bears and other wild animals, still in the woods."[11] Thomas Lincoln trained his son in farmwork—planting, tending to animals, and splitting wood with an ax.

Lincoln's father sought also to develop Abraham's mind through education, but only so far as might be relevant to manual labor. Thomas, who seemed never to have shown much affection to his son, was at times annoyed with Abraham's insatiable hunger for reading, for the father thought Abraham's time should be better spent in labor. It is probably accurate to say that while the future president was a self-made man, he seemed to be the beneficiary of a large stock of natural intellectual potential that was apparently denied to his father. Lincoln had a minimum of formal elementary education, but that which he lacked, he taught himself. Soon, the autodidact expanded well beyond the elementary level, and according to Allen Guelzo, Lincoln came to see in the reading of books a means "for self-transformation, for joining the ranks of the revolutionary soldiers" or of other great actors on the pages of history.[12]

The Lincoln family moved to New Salem, Illinois, in 1830. At about that time, Lincoln had a life-changing experience: He worked a job on a flatboat, for which he was paid a dollar. Material gain now joined reading as another means of advancement. He recalled the moment years later in his 1860 speech at New Haven, observing that he achieved what was possible only in a free republic: "When one starts poor, as most do in the race of life, free society is such that he knows he can better his condition; he knows that there is no fixed condition of labor, for his whole life. I am not ashamed to confess that twenty five years ago I was a hired laborer, mauling rails, at work on a flatboat—just what might happen to any poor man's son."[13]

In the intervening years between his first dollar and his 1860 campaign, Lincoln worked his mind on the anvil of politics, law, and more reading. He ran for office, unsuccessfully, for the Illinois legislature in 1832. (He did, however, win his first election later that year—in the Black Hawk War. He did not see action in battle, but he did succeed in being elected captain by his fellow soldiers.) In a campaign message to local voters for the seat in the Illinois House of Representatives, Lincoln stated his policy proposals for Sangamon County, Illinois, and he was strikingly candid in his aspirations: "Every man is said to have his peculiar ambition. Whether it be true or not, I can say for one that I have no other so great as that of being truly esteemed of my fellow men, by rendering myself worthy of their esteem."[14] We can see in this message a theme that he would repeat in his magnificent Lyceum Address of 1838: Many people in politics satisfy their ambition with, say, a seat in Congress, but *"such belong not to the family of the lion, or the tribe of the eagle.* What! Think you these places would satisfy an Alexander, a Caesar, or a Napoleon? — Never! Towering genius disdains a beaten path."[15] Lincoln saw, perhaps because he could see in himself, that those of immense ambition would be discontent with a mere seat in Congress. It is to the benefit of posterity that he wished to be "truly esteemed of [his] fellow men, by rendering [himself] worthy of their esteem"[16] rather than by malevolent means.

He succeeded in winning election in 1834 to the Illinois House of Representatives as part of the Whigs. He made his first public statement of opposition to slavery three years later when he joined a small contingent of other representatives in that body to draft a resolution stating that "the institution of slavery is founded on both injustice and bad policy,"[17] something of which we will have more to say in a later chapter. He was elected as an Illinois representative to the US House in 1846, where he quickly became a Whig critic of the Mexican-American War; he did not seek a second term.

As we will see in a later chapter, Lincoln felt obliged to reenter politics in 1854, after he became convinced that the Kansas-Nebraska Act effectively derailed the historical trajectory of the nation, taking it off a course that would naturally lead to the end of slavery. After the passage of the bill, Lincoln would spend much of the summer sifting through books, studying the policy history of slavery in the United States. The result would be his 1854 speech at Peoria, in which he laid out the case for why slavery was an injustice fundamentally at odds with the legal and moral principles of the American polity. Themes from this speech would recur in nearly all his well-known addresses in the years to come: the Lincoln–Douglas debates of 1858, the Cooper Union address that rocketed him to the Republican nomination in 1860, and his critical wartime addresses.

Among those wartime speeches, his second inaugural deserves attention here, for it reveals an important feature of Lincoln the political thinker: At the same time that he was unwavering in his commitment to some political principle after having decided on it, he also showed understanding and patience with those with whom he disagreed. More open to the Christian religion of his youth by 1865, he reflected in the second inaugural that "if God wills" that the Civil War continue "until every drop of blood drawn with the lash, shall be paid by another drawn with the sword, as was said three thousand years ago so still it must be said 'the judgments of the Lord, are righteous altogether.'"[18] There was no mistaking Lincoln's condemnation of slavery. Yet he also concluded the speech not with condemnation but with a very different flavor: "With malice toward none; with charity for all; with firmness in the right, as God gives us to see the right, let us strive on to finish the work we are in."[19] This kind of humility of mind was an echo of the conclusion to his first inaugural: "We are not enemies, but friends. We must not be enemies. Though passion may have strained, it must not break our bonds of affection."[20]

Publius: Alexander Hamilton, James Madison, and John Jay

Publius was the collective pseudonym of Alexander Hamilton, James Madison, and John Jay used in 1787-1788 for their drafting of the eighty-five papers that made up *The Federalist*. ("Publius" was the Roman "who, following Lucius Brutus's overthrow of the last king of Rome, established 'the republican foundation of the government.'"[21]) *The Federalist* was the single greatest contribution to political philosophy in the American political tradition. After the framers drafted a new Constitution in the summer of 1787 to replace the anemic Articles of Confederation, some Americans, keen to preserve their liberty lately won in the American Revolution, opposed ratification of the new charter, arguing variously that it was too monarchic, too aristocratic, too national, too centralized, or too complex.

While influential figures like George Washington, John Dickinson, and Roger Sherman were convinced of the need for such a change and gave their approval to the Constitution, none was intellectually so rigorous, and politically so pivotal, as that which Publius gave it. Article VII of the US Constitution stipulates that nine of thirteen states must vote to ratify the proposed charter for it to become law. In practice, however, without the support of Hamilton's New York, the Constitution would lack the necessary support and the Union the necessary cohesion. When in October 1787 the first major opposition emerged in New York in the form of a series of essays under the pseudonym Centinel, Hamilton went to work. The first of the *Federalist* essays appeared on October 27, and his coauthors Madison and Jay soon joined in. In the end, the trio produced eighty-five essays, and in July 1788, the New York Ratifying Convention voted in favor of the Constitution by a vote of 30-27.[22]

The Federalist was a work of political philosophy of the first order. Alexander Hamilton (1757-1804), a founding father whose reputation received a boost from Ron Chernow's *Alexander Hamilton*,[23] as well as from a popular musical based on the book, was an intellectual heavyweight. Born on the Caribbean Island of Nevis, Hamilton was an illegitimate child who by his teenage years was also an orphan. In spite of these early challenges, he soon revealed himself to be a precocious and capable intellect, and with the benefaction of wealthy patrons, he made his way to the American colonies, where he studied at King's College (now Columbia) in New York City. There, he read John Locke, David Hume, William Blackstone, and others of the English-speaking Enlightenment.[24]

When the War for Independence erupted, Hamilton joined up, soon distinguishing himself for his cool in battle as an artilleryman, and in March 1777, George Washington invited him to join his staff.[25] His close friendship and working relationship with Washington boosted his reputation, but so did his intellectual prowess. During the war, Hamilton could be seen reading one of the many books that he lugged about the countryside: six volumes of Plutarch's *Lives*, two large volumes of Malachy Postlethwayt's *Universal Dictionary of Trade and Commerce*, and more.[26] And before the end of the conflict, he had written six essays titled *The Continentalist*, in which he laid out a national vision for the American states.[27] In 1782, the New York Assembly elected Hamilton to the Confederation Congress and then sent him to the Constitutional Convention in 1787. In the new US government, Washington appointed him to be secretary of the treasury in 1789, and in 1790-1791, he made one of his greatest contributions to the nascent republic: his four reports to Congress (on credit/taxes, on a national bank, on a mint, and on manufactures).[28] Hamilton knew probably more than anyone in America about fiscal and monetary questions, and his efforts made it possible for the United States to have the kind of credit and financial standing that would stabilize the country in its early years and make growth possible in future ones. Hamilton died in 1804 hours after a duel with Aaron Burr. "Thus has perished one of the greatest men of this or any age," said friend and fellow founder Oliver Wolcott.[29]

James Madison (1751-1836) is one of the few people of the time who could claim to match Hamilton's mind. Madison was a child born into a well-to-do family of Orange County, Virginia. While, according to historian Douglass Adair, Madison, "through the mysterious alchemy of the genes, was endowed with a capacity for extraordinary intellectual accomplishment"[30] in contrast to his apparently average family, he nevertheless had little opportunity in early childhood to nurture his mind. That changed in 1762, when he came under the tutelage of one Donald Robertson, a Scottish immigrant who taught the young James for five years. His subjects in those days included Latin, Greek, French, algebra, geometry, and geography, as well as various kinds of literature. In 1767, a Rev. Thomas Martin became his teacher, and it was Martin, a recent graduate of Princeton, who first interested Madison in studying there. Madison arrived in Princeton in 1769, graduated in 1771, and stayed for a time to study under the influential John Witherspoon, a Scottish immigrant who wore the various hats of college president, Enlightenment philosopher, Presbyterian minister, and, if the reports of the loyalists are to be believed, a troublemaker with few parallels in the American colonies.[31]

When the American Revolution began, Madison's weak constitution prevented him from fighting, but he soon entered into political life. By May 1776, he was in Williamsburg to serve as a delegate from Orange County to the convention tasked with drafting a new government for an independent Virginia. He soon moved on to the Virginia governor's cabinet (1777) and then to the Continental Congress (1779–1783). In 1784, he was elected to the Virginia House of Delegates, but it was in his service in the Constitutional Convention of 1787 that his intellectual greatness shone brightest.[32] He also had the advantage, in his drafting of his many contributions to *The Federalist*, of having been present for the entire Constitutional Convention, while Hamilton was present for comparatively few sessions. Madison's work there as one of the leading legislators earned him, said Adair, "the right to be called the philosopher of the American Constitution."[33] During the debates, said one of Madison's fellow delegates, he "took the lead in the management of every great question."[34] He also took detailed notes of the proceedings, and his *Records of the Federal Convention of 1787* remains a key source for anyone wanting to understand America's fundamental law. Like many great political thinkers, Madison had a mind that far outshone his ability as a practitioner, as his underwhelming performance as US president—especially in the War of 1812—illustrates, but his contributions as a political thinker are beyond question.

After writing *The Federalist*, Madison's and Hamilton's political views would famously drift apart. In one illustrative episode in 1791, Madison and Hamilton would pen competing interpretations of the necessary and proper clause of Article I, Section 8, of the US Constitution as part of their larger disagreement about the constitutionality of a national bank and about the powers of the federal government. They also took opposing sides in one of the most important debates about executive power in American history in the Pacificus-Helvidius debates of 1793–1794.[35] Hamilton wanted to build America into a modern fiscal-military state, whereas Madison did not.[36] Indeed, at times, Madison and Thomas Jefferson were even convinced that Hamilton represented a threat to the republican order itself.[37]

But in *The Federalist*, the two combined with John Jay (1745–1829) to produce a great work of political theory. Jay wrote comparatively few *Federalist* papers, but his early contributions (Federalist Nos. 2–5) were eloquent defenses of the importance of a strong federation of the American states. Jay was a devout Christian who viewed the American republic through the lens of God's providential guidance of the new country,[38] a theme that appeared in Federalist No. 2: "This country and this people seem to have been made for each other, and it appears as if it was the design of Providence" that the American states "should never be split into a number of unsocial, jealous, and alien sovereignties."[39]

Later, Jay would go on to serve in the Washington administration as a foreign diplomat and as the first chief justice of the US Supreme Court. He was also a governor of New York.[40]

George Washington

George Washington (1732–1799) may seem a fitting name to include in a political history of the United States or of the modern world, but does he deserve to keep company in a volume about political thinkers? Although he never had a formal college education like other famous founders—a fact that haunted him throughout his life—he was not only a great statesman but also a serious political thinker. For many years, it was fashionable for scholars to argue that Washington was merely a self-interested man of action, but by the early twenty-first century, scholars have given greater attention to Washington's political intelligence and his status as a thinker in his own right.[41] A later chapter will give attention to Washington's mind, especially as it relates to his contributions to religious liberty in America. An introductory overview of his life is our concern here.

Washington was born in 1732 near the Potomac River in Westmoreland County, Virginia. Although his father, Augustine Washington, was rich in land, he was cash-poor, and when Augustine died in 1743, George then had even less opportunity to receive a formal education. That which he did receive occurred before his father's death and consisted of instruction from an in-house tutor and in a schoolhouse. Even so, Washington early developed a habit of reading for purposes of moral and intellectual self-improvement, his studies ranging from mathematics, history, and rhetoric to geography, astronomy, and surveying. Washington achieved fame as an officer in the Virginia militia. Between 1753 and 1755, he was part of a series of actions in the frontier wilderness that is now western Pennsylvania, and in 1754, he was involved in the pivotal Jumonville Affair, in which he and his fellow soldiers killed a group of Frenchmen in what is now western Pennsylvania, an event that led directly to the French and Indian War (1756–1763).[42]

In 1758, Washington's military exploits helped him to win a seat in the Virginia House of Burgesses, and his political career moved quickly until it culminated in war with Britain. After Parliament passed the hated Townshend Acts of 1767, Washington responded by writing in 1769 to George Mason that he was willing to use arms to defend America if necessary; he also took part that year in assisting Mason in the drafting of a plan to boycott British goods. As tensions continued to mount with Britain, he again joined Mason in authoring the Fairfax County Resolves of 1774, which among other things asserted the right to colonial self-government. In 1774–1775, he was elected as a Virginia delegate to the First and Second Continental Congresses, and in June 1775, he accepted his commission as commander-in-chief of the Continental Army. When the fighting was over, he returned his commission to Congress in December 1783, an act for which King George III called him the "greatest character of the age."[43] Of course, it would not be the final time that Washington gave up power.

During the war, he scrupulously observed deference to congressional, and therefore popular, authority, but that was not always easy. Disputes among the states, mismanagement of funds, and unwillingness to make outlays where necessary convinced Washington of the necessity of some greater central authority. He therefore agreed in 1787 to serve as a Virginia delegate to the Constitutional Convention in Philadelphia. He was soon elected president of that assembly, and his mere presence added a necessary ethos of legitimacy to the deliberations, even as he contributed little to the debates as such. He served as president of the United States from 1789 to 1797. Both as commander of the Continental Army and later as president, Washington displayed a mind that was important in his drafting of public documents that were foundational to the American political order. His wartime "Circular to the States" was typical of his careful statesmanship, as were his private letters and addresses that secured the American experiment in self-government and civil supremacy from the temptations of monarchism and militarism. His Farewell Address of 1796—a document sometimes incorrectly thought simply to be ghostwritten by Hamilton and Madison with a rubber stamp from Washington—was partly written by Washington himself, with final editorial changes coming from his own hand; it remains one of the most important writings in American political history. His actions as statesman and his writings that effectively served as tutor of the young American republic reveal a mind that had been in conversation with many of the hundreds of volumes in his personal library. His letters, speeches, and public documents reveal the thinking of a man familiar with ancient sources like Cicero and the Bible, as well as modern sources like John Locke and others in the British Enlightenment.

Washington declined to run for a third term out of fear that he would not live to see its end, an outcome that would have robbed him of the opportunity to teach the young republic that American presidents would not be like kings, wielding power till the end of their days. This would turn out to be a well-placed fear. Washington died in December 1799 after having contracted a respiratory infection.[44]

Friedrich Hayek

Friedrich Hayek was one of the most important economists of the twentieth century, although it seems appropriate to call him as much a political thinker as an economist. He also was politically influential, though he was no politician. Political leaders and academics of his time who read and were influenced by his work tended to espouse ideas that we have come to think of as part of the Anglo-American political tradition, although he was himself an Austrian.

Hayek was born in 1899 in Vienna.[45] His paternal lineage was a scientific one: His father was a medical doctor and part-time lecturer in botany at the University of Vienna, while his grandfather was a high school teacher and student of biology and ornithology. Hayek had a lifelong interest in biology and psychology, something that appears interwoven in his later writing in political philosophy. Hayek's children would include an entomologist and a microbiologist.

However, economics was his first love, but before he was able to go to university, Hayek went to war. He joined the Austrian army in 1917 and spent a year as part of a field artillery unit on the Italian Front in the Great War. After the Armistice, he went to study law and economics at the University of Vienna. Like many bright young students of that time, Hayek was a socialist, and it was at the university that he first encountered the Austrian school of economics, known for its advocacy of free markets and its laissez-faire approach to the economy; it was at this time that he read Carl Menger, father of the Austrian school. Yet it was not Menger but his first boss (and mentor), Ludwig von Mises, who would steer him away from a socialist approach to economics. Hayek graduated from the University of Vienna in 1921 and went to work for Mises as a legal assistant. Then, for a year in 1923, he went to New York, where he saw a robust capitalist economy and where he continued thinking and reading about economics. Upon his return to Vienna, he again went to work for Mises, whose books *Economic Calculation in the Socialist Commonwealth* and *Socialism* were pivotal in shaping his thinking.

Soon, Hayek would come into his own as a scholar. He joined Mises in developing the Austrian school's approach to business cycles; for

Hayek, the ups and downs of modern economies were attributable not to inherent pathologies of capitalism but to governmental intervention (especially monetary interventions) into the economy. Owing to his growing notoriety, Hayek secured a professorship at the London School of Economics in 1931. In the 1940s, he would write two of his most important works. The first, a journal article titled "The Use of Knowledge in Society," appeared in 1945. This article, brief but seminal, will play an important part in our later chapter on Hayek. In 1944, he published *The Road to Serfdom*, a book that argued that Nazism was made possible by government intervention and planning, a thesis that outraged many contemporary academics, for whom the economics of authoritarian regimes was based not so much on planning but on the wrong kind of planning. More bluntly, Hayek argued that socialism and fascism were not opposites so much as collectivist cousins. The book sent Hayek's reputation among many academics to the gutter, although it became wildly popular with some. Winston Churchill read it and made it part of his failed reelection attempt against Clement Atlee after the war, and eventually the book would be critical as a primary intellectual source of the Reagan Revolution and Thatcher government in the 1980s.

In 1950, Hayek took a position at the University of Chicago on its Committee for Social Thought; there, in 1960, he published *The Constitution of Liberty*, a lengthy work of political philosophy. In, 1962, he took a professorship at the University of Freiburg in Germany, and in 1968, a position at the University of Salzburg in Austria. In the 1970s, he would publish another work of political and legal thought, titled *Law, Legislation, and Liberty*. Hayek died in 1992.

Wilhelm Röpke

Wilhelm Röpke (1899-1966) was born and raised in Schwarmstedt, Germany. He served on the front lines in the Great War, earning the Iron Cross for valor in combat, an experience that instilled in him a lifelong hatred for war. He later studied law and economics at three universities in Germany: Tübingen, Göttingen, and Marburg. As a young man, Röpke blamed the Great War on capitalistic imperialism, but as with Hayek, the writings of Ludwig von Mises changed his mind, and he became more open to free enterprise. He graduated with a doctorate in economics in 1921. After his studies, he became a professor in economics at age twenty-four at the University of Jena, which made him the youngest professor in the German-speaking world. In 1928, he took a position at Marburg University.

A professor in Germany at the time that Hitler came to power, he believed that he had a moral duty to "speak a word of warning," so he wrote and distributed a leaflet in which he tried to show his fellow Germans "how appallingly they were being deceived," but he was "laughed at and abused."[46] Soon after, in February 1933, on the morning before the burning of the Reichstag, he delivered a public lecture warning that the Nazis were "proceeding to turn the garden of civilization into fallow land and to allow it to revert to the primeval jungle."[47] The Nazis noticed, and Röpke fled to Amsterdam and then to the University of Istanbul, where he taught economics, before taking a professorship at Geneva's Graduate Institute of International Studies in 1937. His writing influenced German economist Ludwig Erhard, architect of the *Wirtschaftswunder*—the German economic miracle that saw West Germany move rapidly out of the destruction of total war to being the most robust economy in Europe in only a few decades. He remained at Geneva till his death in 1966.

During his career, Röpke became associated with the Freiburg school and its corresponding economic philosophy "ordoliberalism," which holds that free markets are good and government intervention undesirable but that nevertheless government and especially culture must provide a necessary environment conducive to optimal functioning of the market. This concern with culture is evident in his most well-known and influential works: *The Solution of the German Problem* (1946), *The Social Crisis of Our Time* (1950), and *A Humane Economy* (1960).[48]

CHAPTER 2

Edmund Burke and the Meaning of Liberty

> As to the right of men to act anywhere according to their pleasure, without any more tie, no such right exists.
>
> —Edmund Burke, *Letters on a Regicide Peace*

The United States is a self-governing republic in which the will of the people sooner or later appears in law. As such, law will always be better in proportion as the people be of sound judgment. This requires that people think, speak, and debate, using intelligible language that signifies that which is real and true. In times of social unrest when people are worked into a froth by their own passions and the words of demagogues, the public discourse atrophies to a condition like the screeching of animals.

Few people understood this more than Edmund Burke. While many people of Burke's time looked at what was happening in revolutionary France and thought of it as another American Revolution that would produce the latest world-historical development in the long march for freedom, Burke warned that the French were undermining institutions that were necessary for social stability.[1] Burke thought that basic social order might flee before the revolutionaries. In this sense, Burke was merely observing what other great thinkers have noticed throughout history: During periods of temporary passion, otherwise rational people tend to set aside their reason, with the resulting linguistic laxity.

Of "all the loose terms in the world," wrote Burke, "liberty is the most indefinite."[2] In his day, just as in ours, the meaning of liberty and of rights was contested and ambiguous. Most will admit that no one is free to harm another person, but with that caveat, many seem to understand liberty to mean something like an absolute and unqualified license to act in any way. But is this really liberty? Too often, says Burke, people understand themselves as having a "solitary, unconnected, individual, selfish liberty, as if every man was to regulate the whole of his own will."³ This unqualified sense of liberty tolerates no restraint and, at its extreme, opposes the limits of our nature. If this is what we understand liberty to mean, Burke would have us know that we misunderstand it.

In this chapter, we will see that liberty is not absolute and that it is not a licentious expression of raw will and desire. Instead, liberty rightly understood is the freedom to do what is right and good. Perhaps no one in the history of political ideas thought as seriously about liberty as did Edmund Burke. There are two main sections in this chapter. The first explains the meaning of liberty as Burke understood it: the freedom to do what is right and good. The view that self-regulation is necessary to avoid the loss of political liberty is by no means unique to Burke, although he arguably voiced it with better arguments and better prose than anyone in the history of political philosophy. His view of liberty is that which political theorists and statesmen sometimes call "ordered liberty." In his exposition of this phrase, the twentieth-century writer and conservative intellectual Russell Kirk argued, following Burke's lead, that "our American polity is a regime of ordered liberty, designed to give justice and order and freedom all their due recognition and part."⁴ Without order (and justice), there can be no freedom; individual freedoms must be balanced against the need for order, without which they cannot be realized.

The second section of this chapter considers what has been called "rights talk," which is the manner in which most people in the modern world tend to speak of liberty. Burke criticized the language of rights, although as we will see, this was not so much because of an opposition to rights as such but rather because of his concern that careless assertions of rights are often merely angry demands that make true political liberty difficult to secure. This second section considers what Burke thought was the means by which liberty might be secured. In general, there are two means. First, it must be inculcated in what Burke called the "little platoons" of society—social entities such as families, churches, and local communities. In other words, liberty for Burke is a type of social freedom. Second, Burke believed that liberty is a kind of inheritance from past generations. If we want to enjoy greater liberty in our day, a good starting point would be not to tear down those social goods bequeathed to us from those who have gone before.

Any attempt to summarize or exposit Burke's political thought cannot do justice to the power of his mind and the beauty and power of his prose. Burke valued aesthetics, and it is no surprise that this comes through in his writing. As he writes in his *Reflections on the Revolution in France*, "To make us love our country, our country ought to be lovely."[5] What follows is not an exhaustive overview of Burke's political thought but rather an attempt to summarize the most important of his contributions to the idea of liberty, that dearest of all political words.

The Meaning of Liberty

The Freedom to Do What Is Right and Good

Burke believed that absolute liberty is "the worst of all slavery"—the "despotism" of one's own "blind and brutal passions." This faux liberty "transforms us into something little better than the description of wild beasts," and just as predators in zoos need cages, people for whom liberty means the absolute exercise of will soon find that "a state of strong constraint is a sort of necessary substitute for freedom."[6] Paradoxically, then, insistence on an absolute liberty that tolerates no moral limits often involves expansive state power as people unable to control themselves soon find themselves needing to be controlled by others to have some modicum of social order.[7]

Against this absolute liberty, Burke defended what he called a "rational" and "regulated" liberty more becoming of our humanity.[8] Rational liberty is that in which people are guided by their reason, which tells all who will but listen to it what is good for us. Liberty, then, does not mean merely the absence of external restrictions on free movement. In the strictest sense, that person who uses freedom of movement to, say, harm themselves or others, or to give free reign to vice, is not truly enjoying liberty. Burke joins the heritage of Western civilization in believing that "man is free *for* something."[9] Human beings are rational creatures who have a purpose they do not determine for themselves. A freedom to pursue ignoble ends is an abuse of liberty that does not merit that designation. Regulated liberty is an expression that suggests, of course, the opposite of unregulated. This is a liberty regulated first of all by reason but also by internal moral restraints, such as conscience and the cultivation of moral virtues in the communities that rear us. Without the moral teachings and habits of our local communities, Burke thinks, human beings have only their "naked, shivering nature" that leaves them cold before the harsh realities of a political world in which impassioned demands for absolute liberty threaten to sow disorder and violence, and such disorder in the case of the French Revolution terminated in Napoleonic tyranny and war.[10] Finally, a liberty worthy of the name will also be regulated by law; legal restraints on human action should be considered as among the most important rights in any political community, for without legal restraint, none can have any reasonable expectation of basic social order, of any degree of freedom of movement, and of any enforcement of justice against those who would otherwise do us harm.[11]

It is necessary to grasp that when Burke used his seat in Parliament to defend liberty, he was interested not so much in a principle alone but in the actual enjoyment of true liberty. Absolute liberty is a kind of abstraction divorced from the circumstances of political life. Talk about it all you please, but unless talk can explain how to procure political liberty in practice, it remains, at best, just talk. For this reason, circumstances are a consistent theme in Burke's writing and oratory. "Circumstances," he remarks, "give in reality to every political principle its distinguishing colour, and discriminating effect . . . Abstractedly speaking, government, as well as liberty, is good," he maintains, but abstractions mean little if they do not actually signify the practical enjoyment of some political good.[12]

Burke's most famous and influential political work is *Reflections on the Revolution in France*. The occasion for the work, aside from the revolution itself, was a letter from a Frenchman who had inquired as to Burke's opinions on it. The Frenchman seemed to have been soliciting praise, but Burke had little to offer. It becomes clear as the reader progresses through the *Reflections* that Burke could well anticipate the dangerous consequences of the French Revolution. Early in the *Reflections*, he urges caution: Let's wait to see what happens, he suggests. When the "spirit of liberty" first breaks out in some time and place, all that one can know about it is that it is, like an unstable gas, potent and powerful: "The wild *gas*, the fixed air, is plainly broke loose: but we ought to suspend our judgment until the first effervescence is a little subsided, till the liquor is cleared, and until we see something deeper than the agitation of a troubled and frothy surface. I must be tolerably sure, before I venture publicly to congratulate men upon a blessing, that they have really received one."[13] More plainly, Burke wants to be sure that the revolutionaries were acting like human beings in full possession of their faculties. "Is it because liberty in the abstract may be classed among the blessings of mankind," he asks, "that I am seriously to felicitate a madman, who has escaped from the protecting restraint and wholesome darkness of his cell, on his restoration to the enjoyment of light and liberty?" Turning to another metaphor, he asks whether he ought to "congratulate an highwayman and murderer, who has broke prison, upon the recovery of his natural rights?"[14] Salutary additions to naked concepts like freedom, things like good customs and laws, far from putting people in bondage, make it possible to enjoy liberty at all. It would therefore be premature to congratulate France on its newfound liberty immediately following the commencement of the Revolution until one could determine "how it had been combined with government; with public force; with the discipline and obedience of armies; with the collection of an effective and well-distributed revenue; with morality and religion; with the solidity of property; with peace and order; with civil and social manners."[15] Political liberty is not the acquisition of power and the effecting of some kind of absolute liberation. Instead, it means understanding how authentic goods can be enjoyed in circumstances that vary in different times and places.

The chief circumstance with which Burke is concerned is that of internal self-regulation. "The effect of liberty to individuals is," Burke says, "that they may do what they please: we ought to see what it will please them to do, before we risque congratulations, which may be soon turned into complaints."[16] Insistence on unqualified and absolute rights does not necessarily produce their enjoyment. What is more, to employ the word *liberty* to mean doing whatever people want to do is to confuse liberty with "the worst of all slavery," which is "the despotism" of one's own "blind and brutal passions."[17] In other words, constant demand for the satisfaction of one's desires is tantamount to slavery to those passions. Such a view is more appropriate to "wild beasts" than to human beings, who ought to be governed by "rational faculties," leading to a rational and regulated liberty more becoming of our higher nature.[18] As he states plainly in his *Letters on a Regicide Peace*, "As to the right of men to act anywhere according to their pleasure, without any more tie, no such right exists."[19] What is more, this subjection to one's own desires does not stay there in the soul, for it soon manifests in political consequences: "Men are qualified for civil liberty in exact proportion to their disposition to put moral chains upon their own appetites. . . . Society cannot exist, unless a controlling power upon will and appetite be placed somewhere; and the less of it there is within, the more there must be without. It is ordained in the eternal constitution of things, that men of intemperate minds cannot be free. Their passions forge their fetters."[20] Human beings control themselves or they soon find themselves being controlled by others.

Burke's conception of liberty was rejected about a half century later by John Stuart Mill; it was Mill who argued that "the only purpose for which power can be rightfully exercised over any member of a civilized community, against his will, is to prevent harm to others."[21] Known as the harm principle, Mill's effectual point was that an individual ought to be free to do anything unless that thing directly harms another. Present-day advocates of a Millian meaning of liberty sometimes say that "victimless crimes"—say, drug use or some forms of sexual activity—should not be crimes at all.[22] After all, they are not hurting anyone, right? "Wrong," Burke would reply. There are, in the Burkean view, no such things as victimless crimes, because, first, such actions often (maybe usually) hurt someone, just not directly and not right away; and second, if people are in fact free to do what is right and good because human beings have a purpose, then acting contrary to that purpose is, strictly speaking, not reconcilable with liberty rightly conceived.

Burke's understanding of liberty, while expressed in uniquely powerful prose, is in itself by no means unique. It was shared by many of his contemporaries in America. His career in the House of Commons coincided with the great events of the American founding, and virtually no one in America during that time understood liberty in an absolute sense. Nearly all Americans who thought seriously about it understood by it not an unrestrained demand for the satisfaction of one's desires but instead a freedom to do what one ought.[23] This is what George Washington meant when in his Farewell Address he said that "virtue and morality is a necessary spring of popular government,"[24] and it is the sort of reasoning that John Adams had in mind when he said that "our Constitution was made only for a moral and religious people. It is wholly inadequate to the government of any other."[25] Mercy Otis Warren, the literary figure and friend of Washington and Adams, shared those men's views, writing in her *History of the Rise, Progress, and Termination of the American Revolution* of her concern that there "had indeed been some relaxation of manners" after the conclusion of the Revolution—a concerning observation insofar as "a violation of manners has destroyed more states than the infraction of laws." Her prescription was that "every American" must "endeavour to stop the dissemination of principles evidently destructive of the cause for which they have bled," adding that "it must be the combined virtue of the rulers and of the people to do this, and to rescue and save their civil and religious rights from the outstretched arm of tyranny."[26]

The US Constitution sought to protect American liberty, and while that document established the institutional means by which Americans might enjoy that liberty, it nevertheless rested on a deeper foundation of virtue becoming of self-governing citizens. In 1775, Burke advised Parliament to pursue a policy of conciliation with the American colonies: The Americans loved liberty too much for the British to be able to suppress a rebellion without the greatest possible effort and expense. Among the Americans, Burke wrote, "a love of freedom is the predominating feature which marks and distinguishes the whole," and this "spirit of liberty is stronger in the English colonies probably than in any other people of the earth." But this spirit of liberty was not, in general, understood as the complete absence of restraint. This ultimately was what differentiated the American Revolution from the terror and excess of the French. Burke's view of liberty is also the view of the great political thinkers of the ancient world, and in some respects his political thought sounds more classical than modern. Plato wrote in *The Republic* of a correlation between the condition of a people's souls and the condition of the civil government under which they live. Those who love money will be ruled by the rich, for example, and people for whom nothing matters more than military glory will be ruled by Spartan kings. Similarly, people who refuse to submit to any moral laws in their personal lives are slaves to their passions, and they are more likely to be subject to tyrannical slavery in politics. As with Burke, Plato warned that if a people have disordered souls, they will have disordered politics, and order must then be imposed from without. Plato's assessment of democracy, far from being the kind of flattering portrayal that a modern reader might hope for, was an eerie description of people so addicted to absolute liberty and to the law of equality that they refuse to submit to anyone but are in reality the unhappy slaves of their own desires. For such people, the political order most likely to develop after democratic culture runs its course is tyranny.[27]

The political theorist Patrick Deneen observes that many of the leading thinkers of political modernity achieved their ends "by redefining shared words and concepts" from the classical and medieval eras. "Liberty," Deneen explains, "was fundamentally reconceived, even if the word was retained." Recalling Plato and others in the history of political philosophy, Deneen writes that "liberty had long been believed to be the condition of self-rule that forestalled tyranny, within both the polity and the individual soul."[28] While Deneen probably overstates the extent to which this modification of liberty applies to the whole of political modernity— George Washington and the framers of the Constitution would have been surprised to learn that they were unconcerned with internal self-rule—he nevertheless captures a very real trend in the modern world that Burke refuted in his famous writings on the French Revolution. In opposing the absolute liberty of the French revolutionaries in favor of a conception of liberty nested within the limits of unchanging standards of justice and morality, Burke was trying to restore an older, truer conception of the word *liberty*.

A close companion of absolute liberty is what philosophers and sociologists nowadays call "expressive individualism"—that is, "the freedom to define oneself anew in a plethora of identities."[29] By contrast, Burke's view of liberty presupposes that human beings are born into a world in which right and wrong, just and unjust, duty and obligation, and liberty and rights exist regardless of whether we consent to any of those things.[30] It also presupposes that what it means to be a human being is a given rather than a blank canvas for the self-expression of each individual. In contrast to this view of things, the eighteenth-century philosopher Jean-Jacques Rousseau insisted that freedom was absolute. Rousseau is of particular interest here because of his influence on the French Revolution and more generally on the modern view of liberty as an absolute freedom of will.[31] Burke quipped that Rousseau was the "insane Socrates of the National Assembly," referring to his influence on the initial representative body following the outbreak of the Revolution.[32] The political theorist Pierre Manent explains that for Rousseau, "it is natural for man to change his nature because man, at bottom, is not nature but *liberty*. And liberty [for Rousseau] is that power by which man gives orders to his own nature, or changes his nature, or is a law unto itself."[33] Man has no nature; if you want to be someone, make yourself.[34] This power to fashion one's nature after the blueprint of one's own feelings comes in Rousseau's political thought (and arguably in modern political practice) to be married to robust state power: If the absence of internal restraint requires the presence of an external restraint, liberty as self-definition means that political power now requires a government that facilitates the realization of one's innermost feelings and desires. In contrast to the limited governmental function of protection of a limited number of rights so that Americans may otherwise be free, the growth of state power accompanies the protection of, as well as the consequences of, unqualified and absolute liberty.[35]

The political imprimatur for self-definition in modern America appears most conspicuously in the American context in US Supreme Court decisions of the last several decades. In 1992, the Supreme Court waxed philosophical: "At the heart of liberty is the right to define one's own concept of existence, of meaning, of the universe, and of the mystery of human life."[36] Later, the Supreme Court divined that "the Constitution promises liberty to all within its reach, a liberty that includes certain specific rights that allow persons, within a lawful realm, to define and express their identity."[37] Some Americans are still looking for the clause in the Constitution that promises such a liberty, although the court maintained that it appears in the Fourteenth Amendment, which also allegedly codifies "fundamental liberties" such as "certain personal choices central to individual dignity and autonomy, including intimate choices that define personal identity and beliefs."[38] Liberty as self-definition is sometimes so broad that it seems to break out of the political to alter reality itself, if that were possible. Rather than an authentic birthright as a human being or the civic entitlement of a political community, such a conception sees liberty to be rooted less in a given reality and more as the creation of each individual. In 2022, the Supreme Court shifted course, suggesting in a more Burkean manner that its 1992 philosophizing may have been inadequate: "While individuals are certainly free to think and to say what they wish about 'existence,' 'meaning,' the 'universe,' and the 'mystery of human life,' they are not always free to act in accordance with those thoughts. License to act on the basis of such beliefs may correspond to one of the many understandings of 'liberty,' but it is certainly not 'ordered liberty.'"[39] The point is that unrestrained liberty falls inevitably back on the political realm in a heap of disastrous consequences. A moment's consideration reveals the incoherence of liberty as self-definition. If the Supreme Court were correct that "liberty is the right to define one's own concept of existence, of meaning, of the universe, and of the mystery of human life," it is not clear why the Constitution does not also protect a right, say, to self-identify as a wild animal, which then would have a right to consume human beings for its sustenance. While this may seem a ridiculous or sensational way to assess the merits of the court's philosophizing, it is not entirely clear why the Constitution would not protect such a notion if what the Supreme Court stated about the nature of liberty in 1992 were true. As Burke wrote in 1782, "There is an extreme in liberty, which may be infinitely noxious to those who are to receive it, and which in the end will leave them no liberty at all."[40] Indeed, we ought to see what people are pleased to do before we congratulate them on their freedom to do as they please. Insistence on the liberty to define one's own concept of existence turns out to be an insistence on acting quite like a wild animal after all, and among animals, the most powerful and the most vicious win. The good news is that this definition of liberty is a false one, and politics is not merely a power struggle. Human beings are rational creatures of a higher order than the animals. The simple fact is that the universe, like human nature, is what it is, and one's feelings have no bearing on the question.

What About Rights?

If liberty means the freedom to do what is right and good rather than the ability to do whatsoever you please or even to define oneself, what does this mean for rights? Does it mean that Burke thought that there was no such thing? The short answer is that he certainly did affirm rights, but just because one claims that one has a right to something does not necessarily make it so. This, of course, follows plainly from the foregoing discussion of the meaning of liberty. Could it really be true that one person has a right to do what is quite wrong? (We will see more of this point later in the chapter on Lincoln, who objected to those who said that they did not think slavery to be morally right but that they thought that people had a right to own slaves. Lincoln responded that one cannot logically say that one has a right to do what is wrong.) Stated plainly, Burke's view of liberty as the freedom to do what is right and good means that people do have a right to that which is right and good. However, he cautioned against careless assertions of rights, which he regarded as an unhelpful or even dangerous deterioration of political discourse.

Some of the most well-known portions of Burke's *Reflections* contain his objection to modern natural rights language in political discourse, something he attacked so viciously that some scholars have concluded that Burke rejected belief in natural rights entirely.[41] "The pretended rights" of the leaders of the French Revolution, said Burke, "are all extremes; and in proportion as they are metaphysically true, they are morally and politically false."[42] At one point, he groaned that he "hate[d] the very sound" of rights.[43] While Burke was no advocate for modern conceptions of natural right, a careful reading of his writings and speeches reveals that he did not so much oppose actual rights as false claims of rights that had the paradoxical effect of undermining liberty. He affirmed the existence of natural law and sought to defend actual natural rights, not (usually) by appealing to those natural rights in political debate, but instead by appealing to the *civil* rights to which people in particular political communities were legally entitled. Rebuking in advance those on the New Right who claim Burke as one of their own while showing suspicion of free enterprise, he was clear that people have a "right to the fruits of their industry, and to the means of making their industry fruitful. They have a right to the acquisitions of their parents. . . . Whatever each man can separately do, without trespassing upon others, he has a right to do for himself." As he wrote in the *Reflections*, "Far am I from denying in theory, full as far is my heart from withholding in practice . . . the *real* rights of men. In denying . . . false claims of right, I do not mean to injure those which are real, and are such as their pretended rights would totally destroy."[44] Bald appeals to natural rights without consideration of circumstances often lead to radical measures that undo actual civil rights that people do enjoy and that are tangible manifestations of natural rights in particular political communities.

The modern distillation of political rhetoric into a high-proof spirit of rights has harmed public discourse in our time. Many rights claims are mere expressions of will, simple declarations that gild some desire with a veneer of moral rectitude rather than legitimate claims to authentic entitlements. Burke believed that the modern language of rights perverted language and threatened to undo the laws and customs that cultivated human beings into a condition suitable for political society and that prevented a descent into injustice, tyranny, and barbaric violence. To the extent that the word *liberty* fell into disuse in modern times in favor of its reduction to rights, political debate itself increasingly gave way to each individual's expression of raw desire, though it often lies beneath a thin façade of ostensibly moral speech.

Kirk observed that the problem with talk of rights is not so much with rights themselves but rather with alleged rights, which are too often mere expressions of will and desire; often, such expressions neglect "the correspondent duty that is married to every right."[45] By forgetting that all rights claims imply duties (e.g., a right to life implies a duty to preserve life), alleged rights claims conceal the fact that the realization of a right will often involve force. What is more, the fact is that many such alleged rights are not realized, claimants to them inevitably grow displeased with the current state of political affairs, leading to greater instability and more widespread discontent. Mary Ann Glendon has made much the same point in her *Rights Talk*: "A tendency to frame nearly every social controversy in terms of a clash of rights (a woman's right to her own body vs. a fetus's right to life) impedes compromise, mutual understanding, and the discovering of common ground. A penchant for absolute formulations ('I have the right to do whatever I want with my property') promotes unrealistic expectations and ignores both social costs and the rights of others."[46] Kirk's and Glendon's analyses point to another of Burke's objections to modern rights claims: In contrast to the hard work of using well-reasoned arguments for what would be good for one's community, claiming rights is an easy-to-learn knack for getting what you want. Burke quipped that "the little catechism of the rights of men" is easy to learn.[47] Looking back on the early liberal tradition that had emerged in seventeenth-century thinkers such as Thomas Hobbes and John Locke, Burke feared that the reduction of political language to mere assertions of rights would have dangerous consequences, in part because theirs was a simple political language that all can pick up as easily as one can express demands for fulfillment of desire, and when competing parties make only demands and eschew debate and compromise, nothing good comes of it.

Another aspect of Burke's understanding of liberty and natural rights emerges from a consideration of his thinking about, and example of, statesmanship. The chief virtue of statesmanship is prudence, which consists in the ability to apply timeless historical truths to particular historical circumstances. That is politics. By contrast, abstract assertions of rights are the domain less of politics than of the university lecture on philosophy, and uncompromising demand for those rights is less the work of the statesman than of the naive revolutionary whose insistence on absolute principle removes the possibility of enjoying even those partially just political goods that fall short of perfection. The prudent statesman understands that while natural rights do exist, these "rights entering into common life, like rays of light which pierce into a dense medium, are, by the laws of nature, refracted from their straight line. Indeed in the gross and complicated mass of human passions and concerns, the primitive rights of men undergo such a variety of refractions and reflections, that it becomes absurd to talk of them as if they continued in the simplicity of their original direction."[48] Two significant lessons from Burke's understanding of liberty and rights are packed into these few lines. First, the responsible statesman will generally be concerned less with some abstract assertion of rights than with actual civil rights to which people do (or should) have a legitimate legal claim. It is "absurd" to insist on an abstract right while neglecting the facts of each political situation. Not only is it impossible to realize rights simply by crying loudly for them, but it sometimes may be the case that actual civil rights are harmed by that very insistence. As Burke asked, "What is the use of discussing a man's abstract right to food or medicine? The question is upon the method of procuring and administering them."[49]

Second, it is worth observing that Burke's metaphor of abstract rights entering political life like light refracting and reflecting in a watery medium is one of the few times that Burke used the word *reflections* in the *Reflections*. It suggests the importance that he placed on the distinction between political theory and political practice. The rarified air of the philosophy classroom is one thing; having the wisdom to see the way in which real human beings can enjoy actual political liberty in practice is quite another. Burke's affirmation of the existence and importance of natural rights alongside his critique of modern natural rights language in political life is a consequence of his prudential, Aristotelian distinction between political theory and political practice. In the case of political reasoning, the stakes are high: Stubborn insistence on precision and absolute demand for the realization of absolute principles threatens to undermine the very principles that one insists on preserving.

The Sources of Liberty

Little Platoons

To fully understand Burke's thought on liberty, it is necessary that one consider the means by which that liberty can be secured. Stated more plainly, if true liberty requires internal self-regulation, then where does this self-regulation originate? In general, there are two sources. First, it must be inculcated in what Burke called the "little platoons" of society—things like family, church, and local community. Liberty for Burke is best understood as emerging in a social context rather than something that each individual naturally possesses automatically until stolen away by some aspect of society. Burke saw—as does any parent with a modicum of common sense—that a child does not emerge from the womb in possession of fully developed moral aptitude. Instead, family norms, social customs, religious catechesis, civic education, and the political laws of one's community cultivate citizens into cultivators of that same community. The protection of a political order in which such communities can flourish therefore becomes essential in Burke's understanding of politics. A Millian liberty to pursue all immoral actions conceivable short of directly harming others consequently becomes a matter of public well-being insofar as immorality can have a corrosive, if indirect, effect on the well-being of local communities and associations; the examples of drug use and illicit sexual activity cited previously serve as plausible illustrations.

To fully appreciate Burke's understanding of the importance of little platoons, it is necessary to consider the alternative. In contrast to Burke, another view suggests that children are innocent; only by retaining the native goodness of the human heart can we have any hope of having peace, order, and justice. We sometimes hear that "no one is taught to hate." In this view of things, it is only the world that stains the human heart, which is otherwise pure and prepared for a moral life right from the start. Beliefs, customs, laws, and the little platoons that cultivate them are but so many chains that bind the beneficent will of human beings at some point in their development. This view was stated most famously by Rousseau. His *Discourse on the Origin of Inequality* was a kind of eighteenth-century version of the outlook of some contemporary anthropologists who naively suppose that if we could all just live in the virgin simplicity of a lost Amazonian tribe, we would be happy and at harmony with humanity and nature. Rousseau's presumption of the innocence of the human heart in its natural, presocial condition has been so pervasive in modern ways of thinking about politics that it is worth considering at some length. Doing so will also serve to better illustrate Burke's own understanding of the conditions conducive to political liberty, for it is the opposite of Rousseau's.

In the famous opening lines of *On the Social Contract*, Rousseau proclaimed that "man is born free, and everywhere he is in chains."[50] Civilization itself is a kind of conspiracy, obstructing true freedom, which is the unadulterated exercise of beneficent will. Burke regarded such a vision of society as immensely pernicious; it only serves to spread a suspicion in people that law and social norms are the tools of an oppressive cabal, and that is a recipe for social unrest if not revolution. Rousseau believed that true liberty was a natural liberty that people enjoyed prior to all society, when in a "state of nature" people followed their benign instincts and desires without interruption from laws or social pressures like prejudice and shame. While earlier social contract thinkers such as Hobbes and Locke *claimed* that they understood what people were like in a prepolitical state of nature, they did not actually go back far enough into prehistory.⁵¹ They looked at political man and wrongly said that they saw natural man. Hobbes, for example, wrote that the miserable and warlike natural state of humankind prior to political society was "solitary, poore, nasty, brutish, and short,"⁵² but in fact, said Rousseau, Hobbes had wrongly concluded that violence was the result of an absence of government when in fact it was the result of its presence and of political society, which distorts the pure, peaceable, and happy innocence of human beings in a state of nature. In their original prepolitical state, said Rousseau, people are free from conflict in part because they obey only instinct, and they can easily satisfy their limited desires: Rousseau imagined early man "satisfying his hunger under an oak tree, quenching his thirst at the first stream, finding his bed at the foot of the same tree that supplied his meal, and thus all his needs are satisfied." In such a condition, the "natural fertility" of the earth easily satisfies the desires of men, who operate according to "animal instinct."⁵³ Both survival and contentedness in this natural condition are a consequence of the negligible distinction between man and beast; humankind in this state is a "savage man" that is "left by nature to instinct alone."⁵⁴

And precisely because savage man is governed not by speech but by unadulterated instinct, he is "a free being whose heart is at peace and whose body is in good health."⁵⁵ The hearts and bodies of other people are in good shape as well, since it is only in this natural state that the self-preservation of each individual is "the least prejudicial to that of others."⁵⁶ Only in nature, says Rousseau, do people possess an *amour de soi*, a love of oneself, which allows them to live at peace with others as they paradoxically feel pity toward others—just as animals do when they operate by pure natural instinct.⁵⁷ Society itself, in particular the development of private property, distorted this idyllic Eden by destroying the easy satisfaction of desire and instinct-driven pity.⁵⁸ Acquisition of various material goods eventually led humans to various problem-inducing social inventions, ranging from family life to language, to rules of justice related to the enforcement of property rights, and ultimately to *amour propre*—a different kind of self-love that amounts to pride and vanity as everyone compares themself to others. This ultimately culminates in greater and more complex desires than people knew prior to society, and that in turn leads to conflict. To summarize, for Rousseau, our truest self is the self of subrational instinct and desire that occurs in human beings before they are exposed to any social influence.[59] Political society and its laws and customs then come to be regarded as oppressive obstacles to our true selves that appear in our unrefined desires and feelings.

Burke's response to Rousseau's belief in native innocence began with his conviction that at the most fundamental level, the problems of human life are not "out there" in the world and its social structures but are "in here" in the heart of each and every human being.[60] "You would not," Burke explained, cure social problems "by resolving, that there should be no more monarchs, nor ministers of the state, nor of the gospel; no interpreters of laws; no general officers; no public councils.... Wise men will apply their remedies to vices, not to names."[61] Burke was making the same point as that made by Alexsandr Solzhenitsyn, who wrote about the horrors of Soviet communism in *The Gulag Archipelago*. Solzhenitsyn remarked that "the line separating good and evil passes not through states, nor between classes, nor between political parties either—but right through every human heart—and through all human hearts."[62] For Burke and for Solzhenitsyn, the political struggle for justice and liberty must first and foremost happen inside each one of us—in our reason, our conscience, and our habits. The error of the French revolutionaries (and, we may add, the error of all revolutionaries since then) was that they sought a liberty in the abstract apart from consideration of social circumstance, as if wiping away evil institutions through riots, mob violence, or warfare would wipe away evil itself. Many of Burke's opponents supposed that humanity needed only to return to the purity of the prepolitical state of nature, existing before notions of law and private property. The problem, they thought, was society—or at least other people in society.

For Burke, it is folly to forget that it is necessary to have social customs, local communities, and political laws for liberty to be enjoyed at all. This is because the most important precondition for a political community to enjoy the liberty to do what is right and good is that there must be local groups and societies—the little platoons of society.[63] Burke's view of liberty is, as Yuval Levin explains, "a freedom not only from outside constraint but also from an inner anarchy. And that kind of freedom is achieved in society, with the help of its institutions of moral formation."[64] Do we want our children to grow up acting nicely with their neighbors? Do we want them to avoid crime? To be educated? To oppose injustice and support the weak and oppressed? These are things they must be taught, or better, these are habits they pick up through the example and, if need be, the instruction, of those in their little platoon.

The first of these little platoons, as the contemporary social science literature shows clearly, is the family.[65] "To be attached to the subdivision, to love the little platoon we belong to in society," Burke said in the *Reflections*, "is the first principle (the germ as it were) of public affections. It is the first link in the series by which we proceed towards a love of our country and to mankind."[66] Indeed, "we begin our public affections in our families."[67] It takes a family to raise a child, and then when the child becomes an adult, that child is fit to contribute to a village. The French revolutionaries erred by putting the cart before the horse; insisting on the rights of humanity in the abstract, without first considering institutions in which people naturally learn to care for other, real, tangible human beings, they end up neglecting the very human beings they claim to care so much about. Many of the "democratists" who supported the French Revolution, Burke observed, "treat the humbler part of the community with the greatest contempt" while pretending to care about them and their rights.[68] The despicable irony was that the partisans of the Revolution, while lamenting the ancien régime's crimes against the Rights of Man, in fact looked on the common man and his old-fashioned morality with contempt. "Benevolence of the whole species, and want of feeling for every individual with whom the professors come in contact, form the character" of the political philosophy that drove the French Revolution. The typical leader of the Revolution was "a lover of his kind, but a hater of his kindred."[69] Following the example of Rousseau, the revolutionaries did not think much of the obligation of a father to his child, but they crowed about their own commitment to the rights of men.[70] It is, after all, much easier to use the language of rights to talk about caring for others than it is to do something for the person next door.

While Burke desired a "rational liberty" rather than an absolute liberty guided by base instinct and raw desire, his was a liberty augmented by sentiments and affections consistent with reason, and one of the chief purposes of the little platoons of society was, Burke thought, the inculcation of such affections. This was the affection lacking from the French revolutionaries who, while signaling their support for the Rights of Man, were neglecting those nearest themselves. Moral affections such as loyalty to one's own, reverence for God and for one's fellow human being, the old code of chivalry, and what one commonly thinks of as manners serve as the "decent drapery of life"; these are "superadded ideas, furnished from the wardrobe of a moral imagination, which the heart owns, and the understanding ratifies, as necessary to cover the defects of our naked shivering nature."[71] These moral affections, these "superadded ideas" that come from a "moral imagination," were for the French revolutionaries but so many old-fashioned and oppressive moral customs that prevent people from enjoying true liberty and from being their true selves. For Burke, they were sentiments to pass down from generation to generation. They are not bare natural instinct—that is what Rousseau wanted to guide us to—but rather moral sentiments that gently guide human beings to act according to their natural potential.[72] No, Burke said, the British were "not the converts of Rousseau" or "the disciples of Voltaire." They "have not yet been completely [dis]embowelled" of their "natural entrails," but instead they feel "those inbred sentiments which are the faithful guardians, the active monitors of our duty." What is more, the British still "fear God." They "look up with awe to kings; with affection to parliaments; with duty to magistrates; with reverence to priests; and with respect to nobility."[73]

The social aspect of Burke's conception of liberty shows that true political liberty "is, indeed, but another name for justice; ascertained by wise laws, and secured by well-constructed institutions."[74] But by emphasizing a natural freedom understood as a complete liberty of movement independent of any social expectation or institution, Burke's opponents attacked the very conditions within which people learn to be good. Rather than being native to the human heart, goodness must be inculcated in an ecosystem of local institutions, without which liberty itself dies. People do by nature have an awareness of right and wrong, but this lies to a great extent in a condition of potential. People are not born already meeting their potential; they must be cultivated in political communities—in their little platoon—for people are the most political of all the animals.

Liberty Is an Inheritance

It is critical for Burke's political thought that it was not only moral teaching and habits that are inherited but also political and social institutions themselves. A full treatment of this topic in Burke's political thought goes beyond the purpose of this chapter, but no account of Burke's view of liberty is complete without a consideration of his view that liberty is an inheritance.

One of the ways Burke thought that the statesman could learn how to protect liberty in practice is by a study of, and especially a reliance on, history. Burke himself was a student of history, early in his career writing a history of England that included portraits of prudent as well as imprudent leaders from past centuries.[75] Burke wrote in 1771, "My principles enable me to form my judgment upon Men and Actions in History, just as they do in current life; and are not formed out of events and Characters, either present or past. History is a preceptor of Prudence not of principles."[76] One must study in the pages of history wise examples to be followed, and one must study how past generations secured liberty so that gains once made might not be cast away by the ignorant.

Burke's suspicion of individual reason led him to defer to history and custom, which is often bound up in the laws and institutions inherited from our forebears, as well as in the affections and benign prejudices that we learn from the communities that rear us. He was confident that the collected reason of the ages can deliver wisdom in the shape of institutions and practices delivered to the present by past generations. He wrote in the *Reflections* that the British were "afraid to put men to live and trade each on his own private stock of reason; because we suspect that this stock in each man is small, and that the individuals would do better to avail themselves of the general bank and capital of nations, and of ages."[77] He said elsewhere, "The individual is foolish, . . . but the species is wise."[78] The simplest explanation for why Burke opposed the French Revolution is that he valued liberty, and mobs that tear down, rather than reform, serve only to destroy institutions, laws, and customs, which take time for many generations to construct—not through abstract reason alone but through trial and error. As such, those who truly care about liberty must realize that it is "the first and supreme necessity only, a necessity that is not chosen but chooses, a necessity paramount to deliberation, that admits no discussion and demands no evidence, which alone can justify a resort to anarchy"—that is, to violence and revolution.[79]

Besides the simple fact that after the state comes tumbling down no one really knows how to build it back again, there is also a more abstract moral consideration: No single individual, no single group of people, and no single generation has the *right* to destroy their inheritance for the simple reason that it is not theirs alone. Burke argued that there was no Lockean right to withdraw consent from a government for the simple reason that people do not give consent in the first place. On the contrary, people acquire duties to others whether they consent to them or not. It could hardly be any other way for a thinker like Burke. For him, natural law and moral obligation exist independent of human will and choice. Because justice exists, human consent is unnecessary to produce many of the duties that we incur in life. It is enough that someone enjoy the benefaction of another. Just as parents are duty bound to care for their children, children are bound (in most cases) to honor their parents, from whom they have received so much. In like manner, just as children receive much from parents, the citizens and subjects of political orders that provide some measure of protection for liberty and for the goods of social life justly give a due recompense to their political communities. For Burke, then, the origin of political obligation does not lie so much in individual consent as Hobbes and Locke had taught; it lies instead in the nature of things.

He therefore rejected Hobbes and Locke's philosophy of a social contract, at least as it was understood by those thinkers. He did affirm, however, that "society is indeed a contract," but it is not a contract that "may be dissolved at pleasure." It is not merely some kind of business partnership for the trading of "pepper and coffee." Instead, "it is to be looked on with other reverence, because it is not a partnership in things subservient only to the gross animal existence of a temporary and perishable nature." The true social contract is multigenerational: "As the ends of such a partnership cannot be obtained in many generations, it becomes a partnership not only between those who are living, but between those who are living, those who are dead, and those who are to be born."[80] As it would be unjust to cast off the precious gift of ordered liberty inherited from one's ancestors, so too would it be the greatest robbery to destroy that inheritance and thereby deny it to posterity.

Burke's rejection of modern social contract theory and his deference to history may lead a reader to conclude that Burke had no conception of an original social contract, or no concern for property rights as understood in a Lockean sense, but that is not quite accurate. He did affirm an "original contract" of political society.[81] Yet he also asserted that "there is a sacred veil to be thrown over the beginning of all government."[82] As a result, when injustice occurs, recourse must be had most of the time,[83] not to natural rights—appeals to which are often destabilizing—but instead to tangible civil rights, such as laws that effectively secure life and property, civil laws that protect authentic natural rights in particular historical and political circumstances. He regarded it as tyranny to take away lives, liberty, or property, since these are the "things for the protection of which society was introduced."[84] In fact, Burke ranked property as among the most important of social goods worth preserving. Revolutionaries may rant and rave about the evils of the rich, of capitalism, and of private property, but it is impossible to imagine how freedom of any kind can exist for anytime at all without protection of private property. As we have seen, Burke sometimes spoke of liberty as a "rational liberty," and it is significant that he usually connected that phrase with the protection of property. After Burke was well into his argument regarding the French Revolution, he was prepared to say that "of course property is destroyed, and rational liberty has no existence."[85] Because Burke is often said to be the father of modern conservatism, rather than the father of, say, classical liberalism, people sometimes overlook the importance of property in his thought, but one cannot fully understand his political thought without it. A political society that enjoys liberty will be one that is "in a perfect state of legal security, with regard to . . . life, to . . . property, [and] to the free use of [one's] industry."[86] In other words, those things in life that are more dear than material possessions cannot be enjoyed in the absence of security in property. Liberty is not some abstract notion to be enjoyed without consideration of particular circumstances; a liberty that provides no protection for the basic necessities of life and no security by which to pursue the higher goods of life is a liberty not worthy of the name.

Burke's conservatism included the recognition that preserving liberty requires deference to tradition, and also that sometimes prudence dictates a temporary deviation from tradition—for the sake of preserving what is good. Burke invites us to exercise the virtue of prudence to distinguish between the normal hardships of political life, during which time one must have fidelity to tradition, and authentic crises, during which time one must take bold action to preserve tradition by deviating from it.[87] In the convulsive moments of British history, Burke noted, the protection of the inheritance of liberty required such deviations from tradition, not to build the world anew, but to preserve the ship of state by correcting course. This was the error of the French Revolution: By abandoning a structure that needed only improvements, the revolutionaries would soon find themselves with less liberty, less equality, and less fraternity.

Revolutionaries make the mistake of thinking that right exists only in themselves, while evil exists only in the current state of things. Burke teaches us that liberty means the freedom to do what is right and good. By contrast, an absolute liberty to do as you please is incompatible with actual liberty of any kind. Just as an absolute liberty is incompatible with society, so too is absolute equality. We turn to a consideration of Alexis de Tocqueville's understanding of equality in the next chapter.

CHAPTER 3

Alexis de Tocqueville and the Meaning of Equality

> Nations of our day cannot have it that conditions within them are not equal; but it depends on them whether equality leads them to servitude or freedom, to enlightenment or barbarism, to prosperity or misery.
>
> —Alexis de Tocqueville, *Democracy in America*

Alexis de Tocqueville in *Democracy in America* suggested that it is easy to think about equality. Tocqueville explained that modern democratic societies are busy commercial places, "so practical, so complicated, so agitated, so active" that people have "little time ... for thinking."[1] They therefore tend to prefer words and ideas that are easier to use even if those words would be less clear or precise. People in democratic societies, he wrote, prefer "general ideas" because they "contain many things in a small volume and give out a large product in a little time." This preference for general ideas allows writers to pontificate about "vast objects at small cost" and to attract "public attention without trouble."[2] This preference for general ideas means that democratic people often give new meaning "to an expression already in use," a habit that "is very simple, very prompt, and very convenient." Happily, "ignorance even facilitates its employment." In the employment of convenient terminology, people often "render the expression more rapid and the idea less clear. But in the case of language, democratic people prefer obscurity to hard work."[3] Readers of democratic literature "demand facile beauties that deliver themselves and that one can enjoy at that instant"—that is, they demand books "that are quickly read." Authors in this democratic climate happily oblige, aiming "more at rapidity of execution than at perfection of details."[4]

CHAPTER 3

The several hundred pages of *Democracy in America* make clear that the general idea of equality is no exception to these observations. Tocqueville's magnum opus suggests that people in modern democracies like equality so much not only because it is easy to think about it but also because it is easy to *feel* the goodness of equality. The perpetual democratic demand for more equality emerges less out of a clear conception of what equality is than from a subrational passion for it. Modern democrats feel that more equality must obviously be a good thing, and the words *equal* and *equal rights*—and its many cognates, such as *fairness*, and *social justice*—spring forth from the lips and pens of imprecise interlocutors everywhere.

The word *equality* and the ubiquitous feeling of its desirability manifests less in a feeling of the equal worth that all people have by virtue of their personhood than in a chronic discomfort with the least distinction between persons. Tocqueville argued that in medieval and aristocratic times, people in different classes tended to look so different and to have such distinct ways of life and such separate interests that "they scarcely believe[d] themselves to be part of the same humanity."[5]

He contrasted that with democratic cultures in which people seem so similar that all people everywhere are rightly regarded as fellow humans, as one of "us."[6] "When ranks are almost equal in a people, all men having nearly the same manner of thinking and feeling," wrote Tocqueville, and "each of them can judge the sensations of all the others in a moment: he casts a rapid glance at himself; that is enough for him. There is therefore no misery he does not conceive without trouble and whose extent a secret instinct does not discover for him. It makes no difference whether it is a question of strangers or of enemies: imagination immediately puts him in their place. It mixes something personal with his pity and makes him suffer himself while the body of someone like him is torn apart."[7] In other words, it is easier to feel sympathy toward someone you can sense and with whom you can identify. It is for this reason that in twenty-first century life, we see a regular lack of sympathy in political debates on social media, in which the medium itself seems to filter out the fact of other people's humanity. An unrefined sense of equality's inherent goodness also explains why people tend to find remaining inequalities to be repugnant and shocking. As people become more equal, they become that much more repulsed by still-existing inequalities. For this reason, Tocqueville argued, "equality always becomes more insatiable as equality is greater. In democratic peoples, men easily obtain a certain equality; they cannot attain the equality they desire. It retreats before them daily but without ever evading their regard, and, when it withdraws, it attracts them in pursuit."[8]

If no one thought more deeply about liberty than did Edmund Burke, no thinker in the history of political philosophy thought more carefully about equality than did Tocqueville. Traveling to America in 1831 with help from a grant from the French government, Tocqueville had the ostensible task to study American penitentiaries, but his real passion was the study of America as a whole. He planned to examine this still-young republic to understand what made it a successful experiment in self-government, and he hoped to write a great book about it. The product of Tocqueville's travels was *Democracy in America*, a massive tome sometimes called the "best book ever written on democracy and the best book ever written on America."[9] He divided his book into two volumes, releasing the first in 1835. It was a commercial and academic success; its explanation of American social and political life combines analytical depth and beautiful prose. The second volume appeared in 1840 and reveals the degree to which Tocqueville seems to have become more critical of democracy as time went on; but when his work is read carefully, one observes that both volumes, which today appear in most editions as a single book, share the same major observations, the same goals, and the same concerns.[10] The major observation in *Democracy in America* is that the distinctive feature of American political and social life consisted of "equality of conditions," which, Tocqueville wrote, "gives a certain direction to public spirit, a certain turn to the laws, new maxims to those who govern, and particular habits to the governed." Taken together, these things constitute America's "national" character."[11]

Tocqueville was well aware that the dreadful inequality of slavery rendered some aspects of American life miserable, repugnant, and unsustainable. His extended reflection on American slavery near the end of volume 1 surely stands as one of the most thoughtful and moving commentaries on the topic that one can find anywhere, but he didn't think that slavery constituted the essence of America. Instead, slavery and other inequalities were products of an old world that was fading away, and the real character of the Americans was their ability to live in a self-governing republic in which more-or-less-equal citizens lived freely.[12] That was the true America, and it was America's future.

Looking behind him, he saw long, aristocratic ages when the predominant arrangement of society was one of inequality and of static, assigned social roles out of which people rarely wandered. Yet he also noticed that a slow development of greater equality had crept forward over the preceding seven hundred years, and as he imagined the future before him, he saw a tide of ever-increasing equality that nothing could stem.[13] So strong was the evidence for this that Tocqueville famously concluded in the introduction of *Democracy in America* that "the gradual development of equality of conditions is . . . a providential fact."[14] Because the world was changing, there must be, he argued, a "new political science . . . for a world altogether new."[15] Some naive French aristocrats wrongly imagined that it would be possible to turn back the rising tide of democracy and equality, but to Tocqueville it was folly to imagine that one generation (or more) could stop the providential drift, for there would be no going back to aristocracy, to regional kingdoms, to great nobles, and to all the medieval institutions that the French Revolution had so dramatically swept away. In contrast to the other famous sociologist of the nineteenth century, Karl Marx, Tocqueville was not convinced that greater inequality (culminating in a proletarian revolution) was the course of the future. Instead, the future was an equal one.[16]

Tocqueville's goal, therefore, was to provide a new political science that would understand the idea of equality rightly so that people could learn to steer equality of conditions in a salutary direction. He wanted his readers to realize that although they could not halt the march of equality of conditions, they could nevertheless steer it to be amenable to liberty by having a salutary idea of an equal society. The reader of *Democracy in America* must realize that there is "no legislator so wise and so powerful as to be in a position to maintain free institutions if he does not take equality for his first principle and creed," for all people should be "friends of equality."[17]

This goal, however, revealed Tocqueville's apprehensions. He was concerned that equality and the nascent democracies of the Western world would be untutored and would not be guided toward political liberty but would drift toward tyranny. In fact, concern does not adequately capture the real spirit of the book, which, Tocqueville said, "was written under the pressure of a sort of religious terror in the author's soul."[18] While people could conceivably steer equality of conditions to be compatible with liberty, the opportunity to do so would soon escape them. To avoid tyranny in this world altogether new, "those who direct society in our day" would have to "instruct democracy" appropriately, but the opportunity to do so would not last forever.[19] This was because people in modern democracies "have an ardent, insatiable, eternal, invincible passion; they want equality in freedom, and, if they cannot get it, they still want it in slavery. They will tolerate poverty, enslavement, barbarism, but they will not tolerate aristocracy."[20]

This, in turn, resulted from the ease of thinking about equality. Tocqueville explained that democratic people love equality so much because it is easier to think about equality than about liberty. More specifically, only thoughtful people can truly see the benefits of freedom and the dangers of equality, but everyone can see the dangers of liberty and the benefits of equality.[21] The person who understands equality rightly will have a passion for equality rightly understood. This kind of person feels what Tocqueville called a "legitimate passion" for equality; this, he said, is the "true spirit" of equality. This true spirit leads citizens to desire the good of their fellow citizens in such a way that they draw upward the weakest of the citizens so that all are strong and beneficial members of a free society.[22]

Yet, because everyone no matter how simple can see the dangers of liberty and the benefits of equality, democratic citizens may instead exhibit a "depraved taste" for equality that Tocqueville called "the spirit of extreme equality" in which the strong are pulled downward rather than the weak drawn upward.[23] This second, "depraved" passion for equality leads people to *feel* that greater equality must always be good. Modern democratic people are sometimes delirious with this passion. It is not even worth trying to reason with them if they are too taken with it, for they are "deaf" and "blind," perceiving "only one good in the whole universe worth longing for," the good of equality.[24] But to steer equal societies toward liberty, it is necessary to hear and to see.

Tocqueville's *Democracy in America* teaches us that equality means equality of all people before the law because of the equal dignity of all people. People who understand equality in this way will have a passion for helping and for building up the least member of society so that all may have the protection of law and the habits of a citizen rather than of a subject. They will also insist on not giving over to the modern state more power or responsibility than is fitting.

Early in *Democracy in America*, Tocqueville explains that it is Christianity that introduced the moral goodness of this kind of equality into the world, and equality was increasing "in all the Christian universe."[25] The Christian understanding of humankind's creation by God and, more specifically, humankind's having an intrinsic worth not shared by the lower animals produces a conception of every human being, from the king to the beggar, as having worth. The Christian belief in the creation of humanity also means an affirmation of humankind's unique rationality and use of rational speech, as well as moral accountability to God. In this view of things, all people are of great worth; all deserve, at minimum, equal protection of the law. A civilization shaped by Christianity would mean no more demigod emperors who claim to deserve civil obedience and even worship. Also out of the question is the repugnant belief that some are too simple to deserve protection of the law—those thought to be subhuman and fit only for slavery and subjection.[26] "Christianity," Tocqueville explained, "which has rendered all men equal before God, will not be loath to see all citizens equal before the law."[27] Equality, properly understood, is equality before the law because of equal dignity. The good democratic society is the one that seeks equality before the law because of equal human dignity.

Tocqueville regarded equality of conditions as being consistent with tyrannies that take different forms. In this respect, this chapter seeks not only to explain to the reader the true conception of equality as being a morally neutral social condition but also seeks to explain the meaning of *tyranny*. Tocqueville's vision for modern societies includes equality of conditions that support a truly free society in which people with equal intrinsic worth enjoy the equal protection of the law through the equal possession of the habits of freedom.

Equality of Conditions and the Problem of Tyranny

Equality of Conditions and the Tyranny of Caesars

Tocqueville argued that the modern world would be a place of relative equality. Material conditions would not be perfectly equal, but there would be no peasantry or formal aristocracy. In many ways, moral conditions would be equalized as well. If there would be fewer who are fabulously wealthy, there would be fewer who are desperately poor. Likewise, if there would be fewer geniuses and fewer illiterates, there would be many who had some education. If there would be fewer with saintly virtues, there would be less vice and less tribal violence. One might say that most people would be closer to average. Even if there may be an absence of certain kinds of greatness, it may well be more just in an important respect: More people would be less miserable than in medieval aristocratic ages.[28]

And yet this relative equality comes with dangers. Tocqueville suggests that some of the distinctive social phenomena that emerge under conditions of modern equality are those same conditions that tend to foster tyranny. The word *tyranny* appears throughout the history of political philosophy in volumes ranging from Plato's *Republic* to Friedrich Nietzsche's *Beyond Good and Evil*. Tocqueville wrote of three general types of tyranny that could emerge in this new, modern world.

The "tyranny of Caesars" is the first type. Not an original idea, this goes back to Aristotle, whose political thought was in some ways quite similar to Tocqueville's.[29] In his exposition of tyranny, Aristotle alluded to a story from the ancient Greek historian Herodotus.[30] In his *Histories*, Herodotus speaks of a tyrant named Periander of Corinth. To learn to rule well, Periander sends a messenger to ask for advice from "the tyrant of Miletus," a person named Thrasybulus. Thrasybulus leads the messenger into a field of corn, "breaking off and throwing away all such ears of corn as over-topped the rest. In this way he went through the whole field, and destroyed all the best and richest part of the crop; then, without a word, he sent the messenger back." The messenger returns to Periander and says that Thrasybulus has given him no advice. Upon his return to Periander, the messenger was confused at having been sent "to so strange a man, who seemed to have lost his senses, since he did nothing but destroy his own property." Periander, however, understood the message." Periander understood that "Thrasybulus advised the destruction of all the leading citizens" and "treated his subjects from this time forward with the very greatest cruelty." He "perceived that Thrasybulus had counselled him to slay those of his townsmen who were outstanding in influence or ability; with that he began to deal with his citizens in an evil manner."[31] The story illustrates how material equality could be a friendly environment for tyranny. A tyrant who wishes to be safe from threats knows, like Periander, that the best course of action for him is to exterminate the rich and the powerful, just as one cuts off the tallest ears of corn. In other words, if all are more or less equal, then none are strong enough to stop a tyrant in his tracks. This is Tyranny 101.

It is not only equality as such that can be conducive to tyranny. Under conditions of equality, Tocqueville argued, people tend to become naturally more isolated from everyone except for their immediate family or friends, as well as from their ancestors. Tocqueville's term for this was "individualism."[32] In conditions of equality, when people and their immediate social group have a stable source of income, they need not rely so much on others as a matter of survival. Instead, left to themselves, many people in modern democracies become isolated if not downright lonely, collaborating only if there is some financial incentive to do so, and while they do not have much in the way of particular obligations to particular flesh-and-blood human beings, they feel some sort of obligation to that abstraction that is humanity. By contrast, in aristocratic societies, the nobility relies on the labor of the peasantry for working the land and for rent, while the peasantry relies on the lords for security from marauders.[33] What this means is that the relatively isolated people in modern democracies are relatively easy prey. As Tocqueville explained, tyranny "sees the most certain guarantee of its own duration in the isolation of men." Indeed, "a despot readily pardons the governed for not loving him, provided that they do not love each other." In other words, trust along with the ability to mobilize makes a people dangerous to a despot. This is why "equality places men beside one another without a common bond to hold them," but "despotism raises barriers between them and separates them."[34]

Another phenomenon consequent to social equality is the relentless pursuit of more and more material well-being. While Tocqueville was no friend of the nascent socialism that was emerging in the middle of the nineteenth century in Europe,[35] he was concerned with what he called the "restive" commercial spirit of Americans: Always looking for just one more source of wealth, many Americans were never quite content with what they had. With so much of their lives consumed in the pursuit of more material prosperity, they scarcely had grabbed hold of a new source of money till they were off in pursuit of another. Tocqueville argued that it was equality more than anything that made this possible: In contrast to aristocratic ages when the lot of a person's life seemed to be an immovable fact of the universe, people in relatively equal societies tend to pursue wealth all the more diligently because almost no one is fixed to a social class.[36] With the thought of the very possibility of greater wealth, people pursue it constantly and demand swift satisfaction for their desire, although after more comforts they find that their lust remains as insatiable as before.

While there is nothing wrong with wealth as such, the regular pursuit of it can have unhealthy social by-products. Tocqueville reasoned that the relentless pursuit of material prosperity so completely absorbs modern democratic people that they can lose sight of grander realities: virtues, duties, love, beauty, religion, and so on. This all-consuming focus on material goods makes people want to enjoy those goods as soon as possible before death comes. This, too, is reminiscent of Aristotle's political thought on the nature of tyranny, which, he said, "aims at three things: one, that the ruled have only modest thoughts (for a small-souled person will not conspire against anyone); second, that they distrust one another ... [;] and third, an incapacity for activity."[37] It is the first of these that sometimes disturbed Tocqueville in his travels in America: The same equality that makes extreme poverty rarer also makes it rare to find great riches, as well as the daring plans, whether noble or nefarious, to obtain such riches. Instead, the banal habits of commercial society can sap the soul of its vigor. He observed that "what above all turns men of democracies away from great ambition is not the smallness of their fortune, but the violent effort they make every day to better it. They compel the soul to employ all its strength in doing mediocre things—which cannot fail soon to limit its view and circumscribe its power.'[38] Tocqueville feared that if such habits proliferated throughout a society, people would be not unable so much as uninterested in opposing a tyrant. These habits have the potential to render a people weak rather than wicked. Such people, he wrote, "fall into softness rather than debauchery," and a tyrant need not fear a soft subject.[39] More subtly, Tocqueville feared that the habits of commerce could so habituate society to the pursuit of material well-being that it could make people think so little of God and so much about money that in their pursuit of wealth they would soon even accept a tyrant who promises material comforts.[40] The point becomes the enjoyment of material pleasures, and so all things, including political liberty and the higher goods to which liberty is a means, must fall by the wayside.

Tocqueville's vision of the modern world was at times a somewhat dark one, but it was the Christian religion as much as anything that gave him hope that democratic societies would not be tyrannical. The same religious dogma that introduced the idea of equality into the world is the one with the power to deter its venturing into excess. He observed that it was religion, for example, that had the capacity to interrupt the habitual pursuit of material comfort by drawing the minds of the people upward to another world: "Democracy favors the taste for material enjoyments. This taste, if it becomes excessive, soon disposes men to believe that all is nothing but matter; and materialism in turn serves to carry them toward these enjoyments with an insane ardor."[41] Yet, religion, if it were in fact a religion that was not consumed with the cares of this world, had the ability to raise the mind above material concerns and thereby to temper the frantic pursuit of them.

More fundamentally, Tocqueville understood religion to be a necessary condition of a free society. Contrary to some of his contemporaries who saw free societies as places that had no need of religion—or even needed religion to go away—Tocqueville saw the inward self-restraint that comes from religion to be necessary in proportion as the outward restraints of civil magistrates were relaxed: "Despotism can do without faith, but freedom cannot. . . . How could society fail to perish if, while the political bond is relaxed, the moral bond were not tightened? And what makes a people master of itself if it has not submitted to God?"[42] Tocqueville was clear that religion's influence must be only indirect, and far from advocating some sort of established church or even theocracy, he (speaking hyperbolically) said that he "would rather chain priests in the sanctuary than allow them to leave it," but this was only because he was so insistent that religion must not interact too closely with politics, because the former would otherwise be damaged by the latter. And that would be a development that would erode the moral basis of a free society.[43]

Equality of Conditions and Tyranny of the Majority

The second type of tyranny that Tocqueville described was what he called "tyranny of the majority." College students who take an introductory course in American politics sometimes read a brief selection from *Democracy in America*, and more likely than not that brief selection will come from Tocqueville's discussion of majority tyranny. While Tocqueville certainly believed that people in democratic countries had reason to fear the possibility of the tyranny of caesars, he thought that such societies, because they are democratic, were particularly at risk of tyranny of the majority.

The idea that a majority can be tyrannical strikes some as being almost offensive in that it seems to suggest that democratic outcomes may not always be fair and just. We consider this point further in the chapter on the meaning of the US Constitution. For now, it will be helpful to consider an obvious example: Surely Tocqueville was correct that in the slaveholding states of antebellum America there was such a thing as majority tyranny! But are Tocqueville's insights on this matter still relevant today? Certainly. One reason why they still matter is that human nature does not change. If majorities could be tyrannical in the past, then they can still be today. Tocqueville argued that the rule of majorities can be just as dangerous as the rule of one individual for the simple reason that an individual does not become benevolent by being joined together with others. Anyone suspicious of the power of a king ought likewise to be suspicious of the power of a majority.

Some may think that Tocqueville went too far in his warnings about majority tyranny. This sentiment appears most often among those who presuppose the remedy of the ills of democracy to always be more democracy. The nineteenth-century historian James Bryce, for example, believed that Tocqueville's "descriptions of democracy as displayed in America" were "no longer true" and, in fact, in some respects, "they were never true." Bryce regarded one of Tocqueville's incorrect observations to be the threat of majority tyranny, which, he incorrectly said, "does not strike one as a serious evil in . . . America."[44] Theodore Roosevelt later cited Bryce approvingly on this topic, saying that Tocqueville's warning about majority tyranny "may have been true then, although certainly not to the degree he insisted, but it is not true now."[45] Others side with Tocqueville, who was as determined to oppose tyranny in monarchies as he was to ensure liberty in democracies: "If you accept that one man vested with omnipotence can abuse it against his adversaries," Tocqueville asked, then "why not accept the same thing for a majority? As for me, I cannot believe it; and I shall never grant to several the power of doing everything that I refuse to a single one of those like me."[46] Anyone who would defend liberty must support checks and limitations not only on the power of executives and courts but also on the power of majorities.

If human nature has not changed, then neither has the tendency of majorities in democratic society to exercise power over the range of acceptable thought in that society. Tocqueville argued that the majority's greatest power lay not in the halls of the legislature but in the chamber of the mind. There, Tocqueville believed, the opinion of democratic majorities on matters of truth and morality often comes to rest without examination. The majority's version of acceptable speech and the fashionable meaning of words do as well.[47] In one of the most oft-quoted lines from *Democracy in America*, Tocqueville wrote that "I do not know any country where, in general, less independence of mind and genuine freedom of discussion exist than in America."[48] To understand his meaning fully, one must first understand why there existed in America what Tocqueville called "the moral empire of the majority."[49] Above all else, Tocqueville was a sociologist, and he attributed to social structure the emergence of the moral empire of the majority. We can fairly summarize his complex and lengthy reasoning on this point by saying that democratic society tends to make people rely first on their own reason and second on the reason of the democratic multitude that is so much like oneself. Immanuel Kant famously argued in his essay

"What Is Enlightenment?" that enlightened people have the courage to rely first on their own reason rather than on the reason of another.[50] Tocqueville would say that this is good as far as it goes, but it can go only so far, because everyone from farmers to philosophers must rely on some intellectual authority for much of what they believe. Paradoxically, when a whole society protects freedom of speech, thought, and judgment, people tend to believe that truth is indeed "found on the side of the greatest number."[51] Tocqueville's reasoning on this point is worth citing at some length:

> Not only is common opinion the sole guide that remains for individual reason among democratic peoples; but it has an infinitely greater power among these peoples than among any other. In times of equality because of their similarity, men have no faith in one another, but this same similarity gives them an almost unlimited trust in the judgment of the public, for it does not seem plausible to them that when all have the same enlightenment, truth is not found on the side of the greatest number. . . . In the United States, the majority takes charge of furnishing individuals with a host of ready-made opinions, and it thus relieves them of the obligation to form their own. There are a great number of theories on matters of philosophy, morality, or politics that everyone thus adopts without examination, on the faith of the public.[52]

Undoubtedly, the size and diversity of the United States means that our nation "is partitioned among several great irreconcilable interests" such that "the privilege of the majority is often unrecognized." Yet when mobs take to the street to shout at and even threaten people who dare to have thoughts of their own, we can be sure that Tocqueville's analysis of majority tyranny remains all too relevant.[53]

In contrast to religion's deterrent effects of the more classical tyranny of caesars, Tocqueville at times gave the impression that he did not see religion as being of much assistance in countering tyranny of the majority. This was because it was not only political opinions but also philosophical and religious dogma that Americans seemed to affirm without much thought.[54] Americans were very religious, and this was required to avoid the necessity of strong legal restraints, but too often Americans affirmed religious dogmas simply out of blind deference to the latest fashion of the majority. Rather than religion, some of the deterrents to majority tyranny should include such things as administrative decentralization, which is to say, the limits of the potential area over which a majority wields its influence, something fostered by solving local political problems locally rather than from a central source of power.[55] This, in turn, will prove to be one of the necessary means of limiting the dangers associated with the third sort of tyranny that appears in Tocqueville's thought.

Equality of Conditions and Soft Despotism

Tocqueville's gloomy comments about the tyranny of caesars and tyranny of the majority notwithstanding, the "Kind of Despotism Democratic Nations Have to Fear," as he put it in a chapter title, is what he called "soft," "mild," or "democratic" despotism.[56] *Democracy in America* concludes with some rather dark passages that paint a picture of a potential plague of modern politics, in which a tired, spiritless, hopeless, and almost subhuman multitude of inept individuals live out their dull lives as helpless recipients of various forms of state assistance and protection. This, more than anything else, is what Tocqueville had in mind when he warned that modern equality could also coexist with servitude. But this would be a servitude unlike the tortured or penurious tyrannies of past ages. It would be something new. He reasoned as follows.

If left to itself, the passion for equality would lead to a despotism that would be soft as a result of its ironic gentleness. Soft despotism is therefore an oxymoronic concept: Despotism is rule by force, but soft despotism is a mild and gentle tyranny. Despotism understood in its traditional sense was the tyranny of caesars. Tocqueville wrote that under "the greatest power of the Caesars," the emperor wielded immense, awful power and yet "the details of social life and of individual existence ordinarily escaped his control." In democratic times, Tocqueville believed, rulers and subjects would look different.

Some of the same sorts of social factors already discussed here—the general weakness consequent to equality, as well as the individualism and isolation—could produce soft despotism in democratic polities. Under these circumstances, an individual has "confidence and pride among his equals," but his "debility makes him feel, from time to time, the need of the outside help that he cannot expect from any of them, since they are all impotent and cold. In this extremity, he naturally turns his regard to the immense being that rises alone in the midst of universal debasement." In this dark image, the individual's "needs and above all his desires" lead him to look up to the State as a kind of omnipotent and omnipresent deity, providing protection at every step. As a result, the subjects "show themselves proud and servile at the same time."[57]

We should not think of this "immense being" as a vicious dictator but instead as a sort of mellow schoolmaster. In the 1830s, Tocqueville saw these schoolmasters only in their historical infancy, but he imagined what may lie ahead:

> I see an innumerable crowd of like and equal men who revolve on themselves without repose, procuring the small and vulgar pleasures with which they fill their souls.... Above these an immense tutelary power is elevated, which alone takes charge of assuring their enjoyments and watching over their fate. It is absolute, detailed, regular, far-seeing, and mild. It would resemble paternal power if, like that, it had for its object to prepare men for manhood; but on the contrary, it seeks only to keep them fixed irrevocably in childhood; it likes citizens to enjoy themselves provided that they think only of enjoying themselves. It willingly works for their happiness; but it wants to be the unique agent and sole arbiter of that; it provides for their security, foresees and secures their needs, facilitates their pleasures, conducts their principle affairs, directs their industry, regulates their estates, divides their inheritances; can it not take away from them entirely the trouble of thinking and the pain of living? ... [I]t does not destroy, it prevents things from being born; it does not tyrannize, it hinders, compromises, enervates, extinguishes, dazes, and finally reduces each nation to being nothing more than a herd of timid and industrious animals of which the government is the shepherd.[58]

Many in the twenty-first century would not see this state of affairs as soft despotism or as a species of tyranny. Is it really so bad that the government provides for our security and helps us to enjoy ourselves? It may be helpful to consider that as human beings we are not "timid and industrious animals"[59] whose purpose is merely to be fed, cowlike, and to be kept safe from all danger. As we saw in the preceding chapter, children are for a time imperfect and incomplete apprentices, learning the craft of adulthood, after which time the protections of one's parents fade away to reveal the unforgiving challenges and dangers of life. To the degree that the state provides—or pretends to provide—an impersonal and overarching security from such dangers, the smaller social units tend to atrophy from disuse and children grow up only to remain children.[60] Of course, in the earlier quotation, Tocqueville was even more pessimistic: We grow up and find ourselves being cared for as farm animals. But to be cared for as livestock is beneath the dignity of a human being. It is to live in subjection to a government that takes care of the bother of living for us.

All this may still be somewhat abstract, though. What sorts of specific social phenomena did Tocqueville have in mind? The US presidents who have promised to provide Americans with freedom from fear or those who promise to eradicate poverty may come to mind. Besides being financially unsustainable in the long term, such programs can do exactly what Tocqueville feared. The idea that the government has the job of taking care of our lives so changes how citizens view the world that "if his own security or that of his children is finally compromised, instead of occupying himself with removing the danger, he crosses his arms to wait for the nation as a whole to come to his aid."[61] One perhaps can think of the way some people respond to the challenges of natural disasters. Less dramatically, one might consider any number of mundane social needs: a bridge that needs fixing, a local problem with youth crime, or regulations to protect people from such extreme dangers as unpasteurized milk or the location at which it is safe to cross the street. In the kind of paternalistic democracy envisioned in Tocqueville's comments, people effectively cease to be fully rational human beings with the ability to talk with other human beings about how to solve problems, and they are habituated to living in a state of helplessness. Just as we cannot expect great feats from a flabby athlete who never goes to the gym, we should not expect much, socially speaking, from one who has not had much practice at solving social problems. In some respects, Tocqueville's dark prophecy was a description of modern democratic welfare states, which involve governance by unelected bureaucrats who oversee programs that allegedly keep people safe, out of harm's way, and out of poverty by a great labyrinth of regulations, many of which are comical in their precision.[62]

Tocqueville was more specific about which kinds of programs could be constitutive of soft despotism: In his 1835 *Memoirs on Pauperism*, he observed that various sorts of public charity, while sometimes necessary for particularly helpless people or in times of public emergency, too often dehumanized people. He reasoned that "the right that the poor person has to obtain society's assistance is unique," in contrast to more salutary political rights that elevates "the heart of the man who exercises it," because this new right "debases him," since it is effectively a public recognition of inferiority. Besides being problematic at the level of basic outcomes—such programs rarely solve poverty—such programs therefore often dehumanize the recipients of the aid, "For what is there to hope for from a man who cannot be improved, because he has lost the respect of his fellows, which is the first condition of all progress?" In the end, such a one has little room left for "action for conscience and human activity," which "remains in a being so limited in every way, who lives without hope and without fear because he knows the future, as an animal does, because he ignores destiny's circumstances, and who is thus focused like the animal in the present and in the ignoble and fleeting pleasures that the present offers to a brutalized nature?"[63]

This hideous portrait of a possible future was one that was by no means an inevitable fate, but it was one to which democratic people would tend to drift because of a perennial preference for general ideas. If social equality can contribute, as we have seen, to general political weakness resulting from a lack of aristocracy, to impotence, to individualism, and to reliance on the judgment of the majority, one additional feature of social equality tends to put modern democratic societies in particular danger of soft despotism: The very habits of thought of democratic people drifts in the direction of centralization, so much so that at times the words *democracy* and *centralization* almost appear interchangeable in Tocqueville's thought. He argued that when people are in historical epochs of class inequality, there appears to be something like "many distinct humanities," but in modern democracies, one seems to be unable to "consider any part whatsoever of the human species without having his thought enlarge and dilate to embrace the sum," with the result that "all the truths applicable to himself appear to him to apply equally and in the same manner to each of his fellow citizens."[64] In this environment, people develop a habit of using generally applicable political ideas, since it seems only natural that if a law or an idea is good for one group of people, it must only be fair that it should be true for all. Legislation emanating from a distant, centralized authority then seems to be the natural course of things: "Every central government adores uniformity; uniformity spares it the examination of an infinity of details with which it would have to occupy itself if it were necessary to make a rule for men, instead of making all men pass indiscriminately under the same rule."[65]

This instinctive bias toward general ideas and uniform legislation from a distant impersonal force also tends to make people look instinctively to that "immense being" when a social need arises. In Tocqueville's time, it was the French who most lacked the kind of civic virtue that would have made them more inclined to do things for themselves, whereas Americans of that time were quite competent. "Everywhere," Tocqueville observed, "that at the head of a new undertaking, you see the government in France and a great lord in England," you can be sure that you will see a group of people doing it for themselves in the United States.[66] Most French people of Tocqueville's day "deem[ed] that the government acts badly; but all [thought] that the government ought to be acting constantly and to take everything in hand." The French "conceive[d] the government in the image of a lone, simple, providential, and creative power."[67] Among European nations more broadly, nearly "all the charitable establishments of old Europe" were formerly "in the hands of particular persons or corporations," but "they have all more or less fallen into dependence on the sovereign," so that the state "has undertaken almost alone to give bread to those who are hungry, aid and refuge to the ill, [and] work to the idle." Similarly, education had increasingly become a function of the state, which "receives and often takes the child from the arms of his mother to entrust him to its agents."[58]

In some measure, the same tendency to sympathize with other people that makes democratic people feel the goodness of equality also makes them more willing to help rather than wait for state aid. "Should some unforeseen accident come up on a public road," Americans "come running from all around—whoever the victim may be," and "should some great unforeseen misfortune strike a family, the purses of a thousand strangers open up without trouble."[69] In the end, soft despotism makes people unfit for citizenship. It is a kind of deformed species of equality in which people are promised equal security. But it does not view people as having intrinsic worth, and as we will see, in the end, it does not provide people with an equal protection of law either.

An Equality That Coexists with Liberty

How can equality of conditions be compatible with liberty? What are the means by which all people in a society are politically equal rather than being unequal, with some being dehumanized and put in subjection under a soft despotism? Tocqueville believed that we need a new political science for a world altogether new, so while the inward self-restraint that comes from religion would be necessary, new remedies would be needed as well. It would be necessary to understand how this new democratic world differed from the old world: The new world is a world without nobles, without regional powers, without fiefdoms, without knights. During aristocratic ages, nobles and regional rulers served as a salutary buffer between the potentially tyrannical rule of a king and the potential subjection of the common people. What made nobles salutary was not necessarily or even primarily their character or virtue, and obviously nobles could be as dastardly as any king. Instead, the nobility constituted a kind of structural limitation on the degree of centralized power that any one ruler could enjoy. In the modern, democratic world, there is no group comparable to the nobles or dukes of medieval Europe that immediately jumps to mind as the obvious pre-installed circuit breaker, so to speak, against the tyrannic shock that is a malevolent prince.

What, then, can people in democratic polities do if they have no such aristocratic class of nobles, dukes, and knights? What can be done against a caesar, against a tyrannical majority, or against a paternalistic web of state regulations that arrests the development of whole nations? Tocqueville's vision of a healthy modern democracy was one predominated by localism: In this vision, various social entities in which local problems are solved locally would tend to be a healthy society in which people would act more like people and less like helpless dependents. For starters, they would look like the Americans of the 1830s, who rather than waiting, arms crossed, for help to come from afar, would have the capacity and the tenacity to help themselves.

More fundamentally, Tocqueville argued that democratic people must have something that serves the same function as "aristocratic persons" even though they have no aristocracy in any feudal sense.[70] They must act as a kind of buffer between the people and a prince. This aristocratic person must, like an aristocrat, be able to rise to the challenge of a caesar when that caesar comes. For this purpose, Tocqueville encouraged his readers to promote various "secondary" or "intermediate" institutions. The kinds of institutions that he had in mind were an eclectic medley of people and groups, including elected officials, courts, the press, and churches.[71]

One of the most important of secondary institutions was what he referred to as "associations" of citizens, whether political associations comparable to interest groups or civil associations comparable to any number of citizen groups ranging from charitable organizations to schools to ad hoc groups formed to respond quickly in a natural disaster. When citizens of a democratic society come together in a group, "they can constitute very opulent, very influential, very strong beings—in a word, aristocratic persons."[72] Individually, democratic citizens may be weak, but when joined together, they are strong. Such associations have the particular benefit of providing the strength of a medieval aristocratic noble while not jettisoning the equality of the people that democratic citizens love so much and that we will, in any case, have with us for the foreseeable future.[73] The point here is that democratic citizens must not be so concerned with self that they neglect the freedom and duty to come together by being involved in the larger political and social life of the community, whether that means serving in public office or serving in some civic group. Such gatherings are a kind of aristocracy within democratic society. Tocqueville was less concerned about the particular solutions to particular problems than he was about the unintended byproducts of associations. Associations act as a kind of "school" at which "all citizens come to learn the general theory of associations."[74] It is in this politically collaborative gymnasium of the association that one develops the muscles needed to fight against a tyrant when he appears.

In these respects, associations serve a similar function to that of local political governments (especially townships and counties) in Tocqueville's time. There are numerous benefits to local self-governance. Rather than having people just going once every two or four years to vote in a federal election, true liberty looks like a people who decide local matters locally through the democratic process. In local governments, there will be many problems because of the weakness of the government and the lack of wisdom of some of the citizens, but local government officials will have a more intimate knowledge of the details of people's lives than a federal bureaucrat ever could. Local officials are representative of the people. Still more fundamentally, local government involvement "habituates" citizens to the spirit and practice of self-governance. A person learns to govern themself in the school of local self-government. Without this, "freedom proceeds only through revolutions."[75] To the extent that modern democracies are decentralized, associations and regional or local governments can flourish and may act as schools of liberty. To the extent that central governments take care of atrophied individuals who in times of need have no recourse to intermediate social entities, those intermediate groups will themselves atrophy.

The equal respect and dignity warranted by virtue of each person's humanity becomes weaker by the velvet shackles of a new, soft despotism in which the true potential of each person is suppressed in the interest of security. Perversely, this unequal condition is supported in the name of a more equal society. Those under the subjection of a new soft despotism also, in the end, risk turning themselves over to an older, more violent tyranny. In the name of equality, people therefore lose the protection of the law in a fundamental sense. Cared for as farm animals throughout life, developing the habits of children rather than of adults, people are then expected to go to the polls to choose their public servants, but to little purpose. A new inequality of master and subject could occur, ironically, even while exercising one's electoral rights. Tocqueville explained:

> Subjection in small affairs manifests itself every day and makes itself felt without distinction by all citizens. It does not make them desperate; but it constantly thwarts them and brings them to renounce the use of their wills. Thus little by little, it extinguishes their spirits and enervates their souls, whereas obedience, which is due only in a few very grave but very rare circumstances, shows servitude only now and then and makes it weigh only on certain men. In vain will you charge these same citizens, whom you have rendered so dependent on the central power, with choosing the representatives of this power from time to time; that use of their free will, so important but so brief and so rare, will not prevent them from losing little by little the faculty of thinking, feeling, and acting by themselves, and thus from gradually falling below the level of humanity.[76]

It would be irrational to expect an enervated person to make a good choice of who should represent them in the halls of the legislature. In contrast to a condition of actual equality in which people have equal possession of the habits of freedom and enjoy their right to the equal protection of law, such a people neither take care of themselves in cooperation with others nor govern themselves through voting wisely for their representatives. Such a scenario, if realized, would mean nothing less than the very impossibility of republican government, which is a polity in which people govern themselves.

Chapter 4

Abraham Lincoln and the American Republic

> Allow ALL the governed an equal voice in the government, and that, and that only is self-government.
>
> —Abraham Lincoln, "Speech at Peoria"

The constitutional scholar Walter Berns once wrote that Abraham Lincoln was "the greatest president this country has ever had. And much of his greatness consisted in the power and beauty of his words."[1] Berns wrote that "instead of playing the role of Caesar and destroying the American Republic, he saved it. He saved it by his actions of course.... But he also saved it, for his time and ours, with his words."[2] Lincoln was deliberate and scrupulous in his use of words, often remaining silent, often thinking long, and considering various opinions on a question before making a clear and precise statement in public.[3] Confident in the soundness of his position, he refused to waver in his commitment to truth and to the best course of action. In his speech delivered at Peoria, Lincoln reminded Americans of their republican principles when some perversely employed the term *liberty* to claim a "liberty of making slaves of other people."[4] When Senator Stephen Douglas spoke of "popular sovereignty," referring to his policy of allowing new states to have a right to decide for themselves whether to have slavery, Lincoln explained that none have the right to do what is wrong.[5] And when Douglas accused Lincoln and the Republicans of "violent resistance" to the US Supreme Court's infamous *Dred Scott* decision that falsely asserted that the US Constitution protected the right to own human beings as property, Lincoln denied it, explaining that disagreement with a decision of the Supreme Court was not violence. On the contrary, explained Lincoln, Chief Justice Taney, who wrote the majority opinion in *Dred Scott*, did "violence to the plain, unmistakable language of the Declaration [of Independence]" when he denied that Blacks were included in the Declaration of Independence's famous phrase "all men are created equal."[6] In the Gettysburg Address, Lincoln reminded Americans that their country was "conceived in Liberty, and dedicated to the proposition that all men are created equal."[7] In the Emancipation Proclamation, he proclaimed that "all persons held as slaves within" the territory in rebellion against the Union "are, and henceforth shall be, free."[8] He used his words to appeal to "the better angels of our nature," saying in his first inaugural address, "We are not enemies, but friends."[9] And in his second inaugural, he called Americans to have "malice toward none" and "charity for all, with firmness in the right as God gives us to see the right," that there may be "a just and lasting peace among ourselves and with all nations."[10] A danger that Lincoln faced in his day was that some Americans believed themselves to be fighting for liberty and republican self-government when in fact politicians and other pedants had so corrupted political discourse that some did not realize that their fight for liberty was directed to opposite ends.

Of interest in this chapter is Lincoln's definition of republican government, by which he meant a polity in which the people govern themselves. We will see that the American republic, as a republic, is a political community in which the people govern themselves through laws to which they give their consent. This political arrangement, Lincoln thought, was based on the moral truth that all people deserve to enjoy human liberty as the birthright of the human species. The American republic is therefore based on the moral claim of human equality in the Declaration of Independence. We will also see the relevance of this view of the American republic to economic freedom, or what we sometimes today call equality of opportunity; it was Lincoln's view that America should be a place where "artificial weights" are lifted from all shoulders so that all people would have an equal chance in the race of life. Part of republican self-government means the freedom of individuals to work freely and to enjoy the fruits of their labor.

We will also consider that for which Lincoln is most well known: his determination to abolish slavery. As Lincoln rightly understood, the American republic does not belong to people of just one race. In their struggle for the republic, for liberty, and for popular sovereignty, some

Americans of Lincoln's day were fighting for their opposites. Lincoln was not merely fighting to preserve the Union or to end slavery, though he was indeed doing those things. Lincoln's rhetoric and actions had as their fundamental goal the preservation of the American republic against a new revolution, understood in the precise sense of a transition from one kind of regime based on the principles of human liberty, human equality, and the idea of "government of the people, by the people, for the people," to another regime "founded upon," in the words of the vice president of the Confederate States "exactly the opposite idea," which was "the great truth that the negro is not equal to the white man."[11] In defense of liberty, popular sovereignty, and states' rights, many Americans in Lincoln's day believed not in the principles of the Declaration of Independence but instead in human inequality and in the moral rectitude of slavery. Such beliefs, Lincoln believed, undermined liberty properly understood and if left to grow and fester would render government "by the people" impossible. How could a republican government "of the people" truly be of the people if some had no say in the laws that governed them? For Lincoln, the American republic was inconsistent with slavery. He shared the position of Frederick Douglass that America is not the possession of one race. All are eligible to be self-governing citizens of the American republic by virtue of their humanity. Any claim to the contrary fundamentally misunderstands America. Lincoln's view was that a government that asserts a moral right to own another person cannot be a republican government of popular sovereignty.

The American Republic and Self-Government

Political Self-Government in the American Republic

Lincoln understood a republic to be a political community in which the people govern themselves. This self-government has two aspects: an individual, moral aspect and a political, institutional aspect. At the individual level, Lincoln's republicanism was based on the moral claims of the Declaration of Independence and its assertion of human equality. Positively speaking, Lincoln believed with the American founders that all humans are born with equal inalienable rights, especially the rights of life, liberty, and the pursuit of happiness.[12] Negatively, he believed that "no man is good enough to govern another man, *without that other's consent*," something that he called "the sheet anchor of American republicanism."[13] None deserves to rule another because of a greater allotment of natural virtues, because of a greater inheritance of wealth, because of greater scientific expertise, because of greater intelligence—whether natural or acquired, or for any other reason.

When the founding fathers said that all men are created equal, they did not, Lincoln explained, "mean to assert the obvious untruth, that all were then actually enjoying that equality, nor yet, that they were about to confer it immediately upon them. In fact they had no power to confer such a boon. They meant simply to declare the *right*, so that the *enforcement* of it might follow as fast as circumstances should permit."[14] Lincoln regarded this truth that all men are created equal as a kind of "standard maxim for free society." This insistence on equality should be a goal that though never to be perfectly attained should be a guide to political action. A careful reading of Lincoln's speeches and writings shows that he did not think that human equality meant either that all people are or that they should be equal in all respects.[15] Scholars have long debated whether Lincoln overemphasized equality relative to the American founders' emphasis on political liberty.[16] The subtleties of that debate are not of great interest here. The relevant point is that if one speaks of political liberty without speaking of equal political liberty for all, then one cannot in any true sense speak of political liberty. For Lincoln, the American republic was a nation bound together not only by ideas but also by "bonds of affection" and "mystic chords" of national memory.[17] In America, the truth that no one has the right to govern another without their consent serves as an "electric cord . . . that links the hearts of patriotic and liberty-loving" people together.[18]

The second aspect of republican self-government is the political or institutional aspect. In Lincoln's words, the fallen at Gettysburg fought for "a new birth of freedom" so that "government of the people, by the people, for the people, shall not perish from the earth."[19] Lincoln's various speeches call to mind Alexander Hamilton's sober observation in Federalist No. 1 that "it has been frequently remarked, that it seems to have been reserved to the people of this country to decide, by their conduct and example, the important question, whether societies of men are really capable or not, of establishing good government from reflection and choice [i.e. reason and consent], or whether they are forever destined to depend, for their political constitutions, on accident and force."[20] For Lincoln, republican self-government means majority rule. Through constitutional means, the people in a republic decide what the laws will be to which they will be subject until such time as they decide to change them.

If a portion of a political community dislikes the determination of the majority, leaving that community (i.e., seceding) simply shows that government by consent of the governed cannot function. If instead of agreeing to submit to the determinations of the majority a portion of the people decides to leave rather than use rational persuasion to get the majority of the community to switch sides, then republican government by consent breaks down into some other form, if not into anarchy. The Civil War, a struggle in part to preserve the Union, was also more broadly a war to preserve republican government. However, this institutional aspect of republican government—rule by majority—is not the point. This majority, and the laws that the majority decides must be in harmony with equal human liberty. Human liberty is the point. The institutional side of republicanism is critical, but it is subordinate to the individual aspect.

These ideas—majority rule, the importance of law, and the limits placed on majority rule and law by the foundational aim of human liberty—are illustrated in Lincoln's first inaugural address. When Lincoln delivered this address (March 4, 1861), tensions were high. Several states had already voted to leave the Union, and the first shots at Fort Sumter would be fired in a month. As he was about to leave Springfield, Illinois, after being elected to the presidency, Lincoln delivered a farewell address in which he said that he was setting off to meet a challenge that was even "greater than that which rested upon Washington."[21] Lincoln was conciliatory: He expressed openness to a constitutional amendment that "the Federal Government shall never interfere with the domestic institutions of the States, including that of persons held to service," and he closed with his famous words that "we are not enemies but friends."[22] He was also firm in his posture that secession was not a lawful means by which to express disagreement either with his election or with the laws of the country.

The basic reason for this was that Lincoln supported majority rule, because America was a republic. In arguing against the idea of secession in his first inaugural, Lincoln observed that secession was tantamount to minority rule: "A majority held in restraint by constitutional checks and limitations, and always changing easily with deliberate changes of popular opinions and sentiments, is the only true sovereign of a free people." In such an arrangement, "unanimity is impossible," so there will always be a minority, but in a republic, one agrees to obey the laws, even when in the minority, until a law can be changed. To secede—to leave—when in disagreement with the majority is merely the "rule of a minority," which leaves only "anarchy or despotism in some form."[23] It implies that republican self-government through law is, in the end, impossible. But Lincoln was not prepared to admit that. "This country, with its institutions, belongs to the people who inhabit it." This means in part that Lincoln recognized "the rightful authority of the people"[24] to amend the Constitution in a manner outlined in Article V of the document, but secession was not prescribed as an option in Article V or anywhere else in the document. The republican means by which to change the law when in the minority is to persuade the majority that one's position is correct. Lincoln unambiguously supported, and exercised, this option. (He made sure that he signed the Thirteenth Amendment abolishing slavery after Congress passed it, although the Constitution did not require that. Tragically, he did not live to see its ratification.[25]) In 1861, after the first shots were fired at Fort Sumter, Lincoln explained that the new challenge was to show that a republic could successfully maintain its form of government "against a formidable internal attempt to overthrow it." It had to show, Lincoln told Congress, that "when ballots have fairly and constitutionally decided, there can be no successful appeal back to bullets." Only the "people themselves, and not their servants, can safely reverse their own deliberate decisions."[26] That was why Lincoln insisted that there would be a presidential election even in 1864, at a moment when it looked quite possible that he would lose to George McClellan, who would have put an end to the war, with the result that the Union would be lost. But for Lincoln, the "election was a necessity. We can not have free government without elections; and if the rebellion could force us to forego, or postpone a national election, it might fairly claim to have already conquered and ruined us."[27]

Just as Lincoln opposed secession and the suspension of elections as procedures incompatible with the nature of republican government, so too did he insist that the legal means by which the people govern themselves is ultimately through the process of constitutional amendment. What this meant for Lincoln was that in the American republic, the American people, and not the Supreme Court of the United States, was the final court of appeal. In other words, the people in a republic are the ultimate source of, and ultimate judge of, the meaning of the fundamental law, which in the case of the American republic is the US Constitution. Popular self-government was for Lincoln incompatible with servitude, but he also thought it incompatible with blind submission to the decisions of the Supreme Court. This was a live issue as a result of the Supreme Court's decision in *Dred Scott v. Sanford* (1857), which ruled in part that slavery protected the right of some human beings to own other human beings. Lincoln and the nascent Republicans rightly believed that the US Constitution does no such thing. Instead, the Supreme Court made it up (about which more will be discussed in the next chapter). The American republic was not an oligarchy led by the Supreme Court. As Lincoln said in his first inaugural address, "If the policy of the Government upon vital questions affecting the whole people is to be irrevocably fixed by decisions of the Supreme Court, . . . the people will have ceased to be their own rulers, having to that extent practically resigned their Government into the hands of that eminent tribunal."[28] The Constitution, after all, is the will of the people and not the will of the Supreme Court. Lincoln explained that this by no means permits Americans to disregard the rulings of the Supreme Court while they are still binding, but this does not require either that Americans agree with those decisions or that American are not permitted to work to have those decisions overturned.

Economic Self-Government in the American Republic

Later, we will consider Lincoln's argument that all people know, or rather should know, that ownership of another human being is morally repugnant. However, it will be beneficial to first consider that one part of Lincoln's moral objection to slavery was that he regarded it as being an unjust infringement on what one might call economic self-government. A republic properly so called is that in which people are free to eat the bread that they have earned by the sweat of their own brow. Lincoln believed that all know, or should know, that it is wrong to take food from another person's hand after that other person worked for it. He believed that one of the most damning parts of slavery is the denial of another person's freedom to work and to enjoy the fruits of that person's own labor. One of his favorite phrases to summarize this point was a play on Genesis 3:19: "In the sweat of thy face shalt thou eat bread, till thou return unto the ground, for out of it wast thou taken: for dust thou art, and unto dust shalt thou return." Lincoln wrote to a group of Baptists in 1864 that although the Bible teaches that "in the sweat of *thy* face shalt thou eat bread," defenders of slavery somehow manage to think that the Bible teaches that "in the sweat of *other mans* [*sic*] faces shalt thou eat bread."²⁹

Lincoln used the same metaphor in one of the great speeches in American history, his second inaugural. Stating clearly the injustice of slavery while also wanting to make national reconciliation possible, Lincoln said that "it may seem strange that any men should dare to ask a just God's assistance in wringing their bread from the sweat of other men's faces; but let us judge not that we be not judged."³⁰ Similar reasoning appeared earlier in his 1859 address to the Wisconsin State Agricultural Society. Whereas many throughout history believed that an educated elite should be free from manual labor and should be allowed to "eat their bread, leaving the toil of producing it to the uneducated," this was not compatible with a republican political order nor with the true moral reasoning that undergirds it. According to Lincoln, "The Author of man makes every individual with one head and one pair of hands," and as such, "it was probably intended that heads and hands should cooperate as friends; and that that particular head, should direct and control that particular pair of hands." Moreover, "as each man has one mouth to be fed, and one pair of hands to furnish food, it was probably intended that that particular pair of hands should feed that particular mouth[,] . . . and that being so, every head should be cultivated, and improved, by whatever will add to its capacity for performing this charge."³¹ In his speech in reply to Stephen Douglas, delivered at Chicago in 1858, Lincoln asserted his belief that "each individual is naturally entitled to do as he pleases with himself and the fruit of his labor, so far as it in no wise interferes with any other man's rights."³² To disagree was to do nothing less than to jettison republican government in favor of an oppressive kingship. If you were to look into history, Lincoln explained, you would find that "all the arguments in favor of kingcraft" treated human beings as animals to be ridden, not that the people wanted to be ridden "but because the people were better off for being ridden. That is their argument," and it is "the same old serpent that says, you work, and I eat, you toil, and I will enjoy the fruits of it."³³

In contrast with the perverse claim that some people should work so that other people may eat, Lincoln presented the moral basis of the American republic: the philosophic assertion of the equality of all people in their natural rights to life, liberty, and the pursuit of happiness. This was for Lincoln a truth incompatible with the belief that some should labor so that others may eat. He argued in his speech at

Cincinnati in 1859 that "the great principle for which this government was really formed" was the belief that "human nature is entitled" to an "improvement in condition" resulting from honesty, industry, and diligence.[34] He said much the same thing in his crucial "Message to Congress in Special Session" on July 4, 1861, when he described the Civil War as "a struggle for maintaining in the world, that form, and substance of government, whose leading object is, to elevate the condition of men—to lift artificial weights from all shoulders—to clear the paths of laudable pursuit for all—to afford all, an unfettered started, and a fair chance, in the race of life."[35] These metaphors—artificial weights and the race of life—appear throughout Lincoln's speeches and writings. In his 1860 speech at New Haven, Lincoln reflected on his own experience of growing up poor, one of his first jobs being work on a flatboat. From those humble beginnings, he did what was possible only in a free republic—namely, to improve his condition, even becoming president of the United States. Lincoln put it this way: "When one starts poor, as most do in the race of life, free society is such that he knows he can better his condition; he knows that there is no fixed condition of labor, for his whole life. I am not ashamed to confess that twenty five years ago I was a hired laborer, mauling rails, at work on a flatboat— just what might happen to any poor man's son!"[36] It was an opportunity to which he believed "a black man is entitled" by virtue of the natural rights endowed to humanity.[37]

It is important to observe also what Lincoln did *not* mean by his race of life and artificial weight metaphors. He meant that all people are somehow entitled not to a kind of material equality but rather to an equal opportunity. Much like James Madison, who said in Federalist No. 10 that the "first object of government" is protection of the "different and unequal faculties of acquiring property" from which "the possession of different degrees and kinds of property immediately results,"[38] Lincoln thought it "best for all to leave each man free to acquire property as fast as he can." He admitted that this would mean that "some will get wealthy," but he didn't "believe in a law to prevent a man from getting rich; it would do more harm than good."[39]

The point is not a material outcome but justice in an equal beginning as well as free pursuit of a better life—that is, freedom in the pursuit of happiness. As Jason Jividen has observed, "Lincoln's race of life metaphor implies a distinction between—and combination of—equality at the starting line, and liberty in the race. And this formulation assumes the justice of an unequal finish."[40] This means that later presidents, such as Franklin Delano Roosevelt and Lyndon Johnson, who appealed to the authority of Lincoln to achieve policy outcomes that were meant to approximate an equality of material outcomes, probably did not quite grasp the meaning of what Lincoln intended.[41] When he thought of a republic, Lincoln thought of a political order in which all are, or should be, afforded a fair chance in the race of life by having artificial weights lifted from their shoulders so that people would enjoy the protection of their natural rights of life, liberty, and the pursuit of happiness. The imposition of artificial weights to achieve more equal outcomes was not what Lincoln had in mind.

Race, Slavery, and the American Republic

Abraham Lincoln, Opponent of Slavery

Some scholars have advanced the thesis that Lincoln, so far from being a wise statesman who saved a country and restored it to its founding principles, actually derailed the country from its founding emphasis on liberty to an exorbitant emphasis on equality.[42] Some even suggest that Lincoln was a tyrant and a racist.[43] A complete review of the literature on this topic is well beyond the purpose of this book, but the opposition to Lincoln by some is so pronounced that it may be necessary to address it briefly. The simple fact is that Lincoln opposed slavery from a very early period in his political career. It must be granted that he became more forcefully antislavery as time went on, but at no point was he utterly indifferent to slavery. Quite the opposite.

A favorite quote of anti-Lincoln conservatives appears in Lincoln's 1862 letter to Horace Greeley in which he said that if he could "save the Union without freeing *any* slave I would do it, and if I could save it by freeing some and leaving others alone I would also do that."[44] Yet this does not demonstrate Lincoln's supposed indifference to slavery so much as it puts on display his statesmanship and his scrupulous regard for legal and constitutional limits on his own powers. Far from showing that Lincoln did not care about slavery, the letter in fact shows the opposite. It does so explicitly in the conclusion: "I have here stated my purpose according to my view of *official* duty; and I intend no modification of my oft-expressed *personal* wish that all men everywhere could be free."[45] What is more, unbeknownst to Greeley, Lincoln had already drafted a preliminary emancipation proclamation when he had penned this letter.[46] Indeed, Lincoln's opposition to slavery was often expressed throughout his public career. His first public opposition to it appeared in 1837, when he was twenty-eight years old, while he was serving as representative in the Illinois General Assembly. Lincoln's legislative colleagues had passed a resolution affirming that the US Constitution protected slavery (a point addressed in some detail in the next chapter). In opposition, Lincoln joined five other representatives in voting against the resolution, filing a protest stating that "the institution of slavery is founded on both injustice and bad policy."[47] This was a significant gesture, since Illinois public opinion was "notoriously hostile to both abolitionists and free blacks," suggesting that Lincoln had nothing to gain from the protest. Over twenty years later, in 1858, when slavery was the primary political issue of the day, Lincoln recalled that he had "always hated slavery . . . as much as any Abolitionist."[48] And in 1864, he remarked that "I am naturally anti-slavery. If slavery is not wrong, nothing is wrong. I can not remember when I did not so think, and feel."[49] This was not always obvious to his critics. It seemed to some that Lincoln failed to oppose slavery with sufficient zeal and urgency. This, of course, was the position of abolitionists who favored immediate, revolutionary action to end slavery; it was the position, for example, of John Brown, the (in)famous leader of the assault on the armory at Harper's Ferry.

What explains Lincoln's reticence to side with the radical abolitionists? One explanation appears in Lincoln's understanding of statesmanship, the chief virtue of which is prudence.[50] Prudential leadership means not always grasping at what is ideal but instead grasping at what is the best possible; grasping for an ideal outcome may at times squander a possible good future outcome because grasping for an ideal may involve an insistence on the immediate and perfect. In Lincoln's case, just because he "hate[d]" slavery because of "the monstrous injustice" of it (his words),[51] he could not simply abolish it by decree; raw expression or executive demands would not magically cause the end of slavery, even if that were within the constitutional power of the president. Insistence on immediate justice was for Lincoln less relevant than a reasoned calculation about the best means to achieve just results if and when that became a possibility. As Greg Weiner explains in his excellent study of Edmund Burke and Abraham Lincoln, the latter's approach to statesmanship consisted in opposition to rash decision even as he pushed on with "energy" and "vigilance" toward long-term goals.[52] What did this mean for slavery? Weiner explains, "Emancipation was right, but would not be wise" until the circumstances were right, since seeking emancipation before the right time "would be unenforceable."

CHAPTER 4

As Lincoln asked in 1862, "Would *my word* free the slaves, when I cannot even enforce the Constitution in the rebel states?"[53]

This point was suggested by Frederick Douglass's comments about Lincoln at the dedication speech of the Freedman's Memorial in Washington, DC, in 1876: "Viewed from the genuine abolition ground, Mr. Lincoln seemed tardy, cold, dull, and indifferent; but measuring him by the sentiment of his country, a sentiment he was bound as a statesman to consult, he was swift, zealous, radical, and determined." Although Lincoln "shared the prejudices of his white fellow countrymen against the negro," Douglass continued, "it is hardly necessary to say that in his heart of hearts he loathed and hated slavery." As "a statesman," Lincoln wished to accomplish two things: "first, to save his country from dismemberment and ruin; and second, to free his country from the great crime of slavery." Yet to "do one or the other, or both, he must have the earnest sympathy and the powerful cooperation of his loyal countrymen. Without this primary and essential condition to success his effort must have been vain and utterly fruitless."[54]

Lincoln's opposition to slavery grew more urgent and heated with the passing of the Kansas-Nebraska Act of 1854, which granted new states coming into the Union the right of popular sovereignty—that is, the ability to vote on the question of whether a new state would be free soil or would have slavery. Lincoln despised the policy. For one thing, using the phrase *popular sovereignty* to describe the ability to decide to have slavery was a demagogic perversion of language. Lincoln called the term *popular sovereignty* a "sugar-coated name" for a policy that has as its actual effect what everyone should be able to see is the exact opposite of true popular sovereignty and self-government.[55] In a self-governing republic, it is true, the people rule themselves through the decisions of the majority, but this does not grant the majority the moral right to withdraw the liberty of a minority. Weiner observes that authentic popular sovereignty includes "a personal right of consent that the slaveholder denied the enslaved person."[56] For Lincoln, the American republic stood for "the sacred right of self-government," and those who believed that new states should enjoy popular sovereignty violated that sacred right by insisting on an absolute, "*perfect* liberty"— a liberty of "making slaves of other people."[57] This perversion of the words *popular sovereignty* and *liberty* concealed a poison that was toxic to republican government and human liberty.

Lincoln believed that this pernicious wordplay also concealed the fact that popular sovereignty derailed the American republic from its inherent opposition to the institution of slavery. Lincoln had always hated slavery and was publicly opposed to it as early as 1837, but the chief reason why he was much more public in his denunciations of it after the Kansas-Nebraska Act in 1854 was that this law had not only repealed the Missouri Compromise but had also threatened to alter slavery's inherently unwelcome place in the American regime. The US Constitution created a system in which slavery "was in the course of ultimate extinction."[58] So-called popular sovereignty changed this trajectory. The reader suspicious of this view of the American republic and the US Constitution may wonder, Doesn't the existence of slavery show that the founders were either insincere when they said that all men are created equal or that they did not think that Black Americans were human beings? While it seems clear that the founders were people who often did not live up to their own principles, Lincoln was keen to show that human liberty and human equality were indeed principles that (almost) all the American founders affirmed. Consider Thomas Jefferson. While Lincoln's view of presidential statesmanship and of the American republic is most akin to that of Hamilton rather than Jefferson,[59] it was advantageous for Lincoln to show that Jefferson, far from being the southern Virginian who would have sided with the slavery cause, actually opposed it in principle, albeit in a way that contradicted his own practice. As a result, this southern star witness for the cause of popular sovereignty turned out to be someone who supported the cause of human liberty Jefferson was "a Virginian by birth and continued residence, and withal, a slave-holder," Lincoln explained at Peoria in 1854. Jefferson had tried in the 1780s to prevent the expansion of slavery from "ever going into the north-western territory" of Ohio, Indiana, Illinois, and Wisconsin. To that end, he "prevailed on the Virginia legislature to adopt his views, and to cede the territory" to the general government under the Articles of Confederation, but only on the condition that slavery would be prohibited in those territories. This effort being successful, the Confederation Congress passed the Northwest Ordinance of 1787, which, in Article VI resolved that "slavery should never be permitted therein."[60] (Article V, it should be added, required that any state formed out of the Northwest Territories would "be at liberty to form a permanent constitution and State government: provided the constitution and government so formed, shall be republican."[61])

Lincoln became much more openly antislavery after 1854, and he became a serious candidate for the office of president following his Cooper Union address in 1860, in which he explained in no uncertain terms that slavery was at odds with the moral principles of the American founding and with the actions of the founding fathers. The audience at the Cooper Union Institute in New York was packed with influential Republicans who wanted to hear from the man who battled Stephen Douglas in a series of Illinois debates in 1858 and who now was a candidate for the US presidency. Developing his themes first introduced in his speech at Peoria six years before, Lincoln explained that the Jefferson-inspired Northwest Ordinance was eventually passed by the First Congress, and sixteen of thirty-nine of the original framers of the Constitution were present and voted in favor of it, thereby showing their opposition to slavery. George Washington, the first president, signed the bill into law, making him the seventeenth Philadelphia framer to support the law prohibiting slavery in the Northwest Territories.[62] Subsequent to the Louisiana Purchase, additional constitutional framers had an opportunity to vote to prohibit slavery in new American territory, and many did so in the Missouri Compromise. Based on the Northwest Territories, the Missouri Compromise, and other votes in Congress, Lincoln told the audience at Cooper Union that twenty-one out of the thirty-nine framers of the Constitution showed their willingness to use the authority of the federal government to outlaw slavery. Only three of the original framers—one of whom was Charles Pinckney of South Carolina—voted against prohibiting slavery in new territories. The remaining sixteen framers of the Constitution never had a chance to vote in Congress, but, Lincoln suggested, there was good reason to suppose that most if not all would have agreed that slavery should be prohibited in any new territories.[63] Benjamin Franklin and Alexander Hamilton, for example, were well known for opposing slavery.[64]

Chapter 5 explains in more detail the structure and internal logic by which the Constitution was thought to lead slavery to extinction, so we will not take time here to explain this argument in full detail, but it is instructive to consider what the legislative implications of these framers' actions were. The view of people like Lincoln and Frederick Douglass, as well as the view of many of the framers of the Constitution, was that various clauses in the Constitution would have the effect of causing the United States to drift in a direction that would ultimately lead to an amendment to the Constitution that would abolish slavery, thereby making the Constitution complete in a way that it was not yet insofar as its toleration of slavery contradicted the moral principles of the Declaration of Independence. By slowly pushing slaveholding states into a smaller legislative minority, it was thought, or at least hoped by some, that slavery was on the road to ultimate extinction-by-amendment.

Lincoln's way with words allowed the new Republican Party to see that he was the man for a season when containment of slavery was a priority. It is interesting to observe from his first inaugural that even at that late hour, he was content to let slavery continue where it already existed, but this was not sufficient for some. Southern leaders like Jefferson Davis rightly saw Lincoln as an antislavery president who regarded slavery as being on the road to ultimate extinction, and they were not content to let slavery exist without the possibility of expansion. In 1860, South Carolina and then several additional states voted to secede, and when shots were fired on the US Navy at Fort Sumter, a peaceful solution was no longer a possibility. The American republic descended into its darkest hour as competing ideas of what it stood for became competing armies.

The Self-Evident Truth That Humans Are Humans

Lincoln, then, was always opposed to slavery, though his opposition to it became hotter, more focused, and more conspicuous as events developed. His was ultimately a moral opposition rooted in the belief in human equality. No human being has a moral right to own another human being. What is more, slavery is incompatible with republican government. Kings and tyrants may argue with some consistency that they may rule absolutely over another person, but in a republic, where people acknowledge the moral truth of human equality, slavery can have no place. Lincoln's idea of republican government was that people—*all people*—ought to govern themselves. The Declaration of Independence presents the claim that all men are created equal. One may not govern another human being without that person's consent. Slavery is the pinnacle of opposition to this belief. The only conceivable way to justify ownership of and arbitrary rule over another human being would be to deny that such a one was indeed a human being. Either explicitly or by implication, this was exactly what defenders of popular sovereignty were doing, and it was this that Lincoln emphasized again and again between the Peoria speech of 1854, the Lincoln-Douglas debates of 1858, and his great campaign speeches of 1860.

Lincoln laid out his case for opposing popular sovereignty and the Kansas-Nebraska Act in his great speech at Peoria in 1854. Popular sovereignty, Lincoln explained, was a moral indifference to a great moral wrong. How could one legitimately respond with indifference to a moral wrong? Lincoln, as we have seen, "hate[d]" this indifference, in part because of "the monstrous injustice of slavery itself."[65] He recognized that slavery was a monstrous injustice because he recognized that there was a distinction between human beings and animals. It may be true, said Lincoln, that one should "not object to my taking my hog to Nebraska." But some went further and said, "Therefore I must not object to you taking your slave. Now, I admit this is perfectly logical, if there is no difference between hogs and negroes."[66] Yet as Lincoln went on to explain, even defenders of popular sovereignty recognize that human beings are not to be equated with animals. In a kind of natural law argument that appears here and there in Lincoln's speeches and writings, all people recognize the truth that humans are humans and not animals. As such, all people recognize the injustice of slavery, even if at times some people have a robust financial interest in imagining that slavery is a positive good. In brief, all people recognize the fact that the words *human* and *animal* signify two very different realities. There is, Lincoln said, "in the bosoms of the southern people, manifest in many ways, their sense of the wrong of slavery and their consciousness that, after all, there is humanity in the negro." For example, all recognize that there is something disgusting and despicable about a slave-dealer—that is, a person who comes trying to purchase a slave only to resell the slave elsewhere at high profit. People allow their free children to play with slave children, but they do not let them near the slave-dealer, Lincoln pointed out. Virtually all people, including slave owners, have a "sense of justice, and human sympathy, continually telling you, that the poor negro has some natural right to himself."[67] If one is willing to admit to recognizing that a human being has a rational mind, the capacity for moral judgment, and intrinsic worth, then one should recognize that all human beings are equal in this fundamental sense, that no one may enslave another. Human beings are not animals. One might say that it is self-evident.

Lincoln continued this theme in what was perhaps his most philosophic public address, his speech at New Haven in 1860. In that speech, he grabbed low-hanging fruit from a Stephen Douglas address in 1858 in which Douglas said, "When the struggle is between the white man and the negro, I am for the white man; when it is between the negro and the crocodile, I am for the negro."[68] Here, Douglas claimed at once to be morally opposed to slavery and yet to be indifferent toward the policy question of slavery; in fact, he showed himself to affirm the moral desirability of slavery by providing a kind of moral ranking of white humans above Black slaves, which themselves were regarded as a small step above crocodiles and other animals. Whereas the Declaration of Independence included Blacks in declaring "all men" to be equal, the Democratic Party had, Lincoln said, "deliberately taken negroes from the class of men and put them in the class of brutes."[69] In the Peoria speech in 1854, Lincoln had pointed out that "there are in the United States and territories, including the District of Columbia, 433,643 free blacks. At $500 per head they are worth over two hundred millions of dollars. How comes this vast amount of property to be running about without owners? We do not see free horses or free cattle running at large. How is this?" Lincoln then explained that they would all "be slaves now, but for SOMETHING which has operated on their white owners, inducing them at vast pecuniary sacrifices, to liberate them. What is that SOMETHING?" Lincoln provided the answer: "Is there any mistaking it? In all these cases it is your sense of justice, and human sympathy, continually telling you, that the poor negro has some natural right to himself—that those who deny it, and make mere merchandise of him, deserve kickings, contempt and death."[70] As he said in 1865, "Whenever [I] hear any one, arguing for slavery I feel a strong impulse to see it tried on him personally."[71]

Again, besides being repugnant to the moral sense, a system of slavery based on race was, for Lincoln, arbitrary and incompatible with the principles of the American republic. As he explained in an 1858 speech in Chicago, the United States of America belongs to Americans because they are human beings, not because Americans are people of one race. As Lincoln observed, in the middle of nineteenth-century America, approximately half of all Americans were *not* descendants of the race to which the great majority of the founding generation belonged. Instead, "perhaps half our people" were "German, Irish, French and Scandinavian— men that have come from Europe themselves, or whose ancestors have come hither and settled here."[72] Why had they some right to claim the title American? It was not because of their race. It was because of their humanity. When those people "look through that old Declaration of Independence they find that those old men say that 'We hold these truths to be self-evident, that all men are created equal' and then they feel that that moral sentiment taught in that day evidences their relation to those men, that it is the father of all moral principle in them, and that they have a right to claim it as though they were blood of the blood, and flesh of the flesh of the men who wrote that Declaration, and so they are."[73] In the American republic in which people govern themselves as a matter of right because of the belief that "all men are equal upon principle," then if some insist on "making exceptions to it," it is only reasonable to ask whether "if one man says it does not mean a Negro, why may not another man say it does not mean another man?"[74] If Black Americans may be enslaved rather than live in freedom, then so too could people of German, Irish, French, and Scandinavian descent.

For Lincoln, then, the ability to live under only those laws to which you consent—only those laws that you have a hand in making even if indirectly—was incompatible with the exclusion of some portion of the community from the blessings of liberty. If Americans could exclude some from political liberty on account of race, Lincoln asked, "in all soberness, if all these things, indulged in, if ratified, if confirmed and endorsed, if taught to our children, and repeated to them, do not tend to rub out the sentiment of liberty in the country, and to transform this government into a government of some other form." Such arguments were those "that kings have made for enslaving the people in all ages of the world." All tyrants have always argued that they enslaved people, not because they wanted to be enslaved, "but because the people were better off" for it. "That is their argument, and this argument . . . is the same old serpent that says you work and I eat, you toil and I will enjoy the fruits of it."[75]

A republican government is a polity in which the people govern themselves through laws to which they give their consent. And the people ought to govern themselves because, Lincoln explained, no one person has any intrinsic authority to govern another person. What is more, the governed includes all the people, regardless of race, and a key part of self-government means a self-providence that leaves people free to enjoy the fruits of their labor without the obstacle of artificial weights. This certainly does not allow the possibility of slavery, which is incompatible with the American republic. So too is any suggestion that the American republic belongs only to people of one race.

This chapter brushed only the surface of the legal means by which the American people govern themselves through law. It is to this that we turn in the next chapter to make sense of the meaning of the Constitution of the United States of America. In a republic, the people govern themselves. In the American republic, the long term of the people is preserved in the US Constitution.

Chapter 5

The Federalist Papers and the US Constitution

> No legislative act . . . contrary to the constitution can be valid. To deny this would be to affirm that . . . the representatives of the people are superior to the people themselves.
>
> —Alexander Hamilton, Federalist No. 78

The Preamble to the US Constitution begins with "We the People." Why then does the Constitution seem to some to be so undemocratic? And why does it seem to be opposed to majority rule? Critics of the Constitution have raised such questions. A preliminary response appeared in the preceding chapter: Authentic republican government is one in which people govern themselves through majorities, yet they must also be free to govern themselves as individuals. In other words, majorities may not violate individual liberty. Yet this may seem too abstract. Are there not specific ways, critics have asked, in which the US Constitution wrongly thwarts the will of the majority of the American people?

Consider the Electoral College. Many Americans support it as a healthy limit on raw majoritarian power, while others see it as an unjust obfuscation of the will of the people. After all, Al Gore won the popular vote in 2000, as did Hillary Clinton in 2016. Others complain that it is simply too difficult to pass a law. (Bills must satisfy a bicameral legislature [Article I, Sections 2–3] and avoid an executive veto [Article I, Section 7] before becoming law.) Still others despise the Senate because of inequalities that it seems to support: A senator from California represents approximately eighty times the number of people as does a senator from Wyoming! This is not just a popular sentiment. It is a view held by a number of serious academics, including the legal scholar Sanford Levinson, author of *Our Undemocratic Constitution: Where the Constitution Goes Wrong*.[1] Besides the Electoral College, Levinson cites the disparity in popular representation in the Senate, by which citizens in Wyoming matter more, as it were, than do citizens in California.[2] Perhaps the basic idea of the Constitution is good, Levinson suggests, but Americans need once again to follow in the footsteps of the founding fathers by exercising "reflection and choice"—one of Levinson's favorite quotes from the Federalist Papers—by amending the Constitution to be more democratic.[3]

Why would anyone oppose such revisions? The simple answer is that the charge that the US Constitution is undemocratic is fundamentally misleading. The form of government that appears in the Constitution is a republic, not a direct democracy, but it is already essentially popular in the sense that it established a popular government and that it represents the true will of the American people. However, the *theory* of popular self-government must be protected in *practice* in the American republic by preventing the powerful from destroying the liberty of minorities. The only way to do this is to dilute the potency of the majority of the American people. As we will see, it does this by "slowing down" the majority to help make sure that the will of the majority at any particular moment is in fact truly the will of the majority. The Constitution is fundamentally a majoritarian document because it is fundamentally popular. One might even say that it is in spirit, though not in form, democratic, if what one means is that it derives its authority from the people. But unless there are limits to the power of the majority, it will trample over the first minority, and the best description for that is not democracy but tyranny. The theory behind the Constitution is popular self-government. In practice, the Constitution implements this theory through republican government. In America, the people are in charge of themselves, and they govern themselves through a supreme law to which they have given their consent.

We will see in this chapter that the US Constitution embodies the true, long-term will of the people. We know what the true will of the American people is because their stated will appears in this document. In examining the meaning of the Constitution, this chapter relies chiefly on the Federalist Papers—that is, *The Federalist*—at once a great work of political philosophy and a collection of essays written by Alexander Hamilton, James Madison, and John Jay. *The Federalist* sought first to explain and defend the newly drafted Constitution with the primary intention of seeing it ratified by the people of the several states, and in the process of drafting the papers, the authors produced the most original and profound work in political theory in the American political tradition. Thomas Jefferson called *The Federalist* "an authority to which appeal is habitually made by all," a book that one ought to study to understand the rights and duties of American citizenship.[4]

In this chapter, we consider why it can be said that the US Constitution embodies the true long-term will of the people. To understand this, one must also understand what students of history and politics call the distinction of theory and practice. *The Federalist* assumes and at times explicitly references this principle. It explains why the Constitution may at times appear *not* to affirm the will of the people and even seems to thwart it. Yet to preserve the theoretical principle of popular sovereignty in practice, it is necessary to deviate to some extent from that principle. This chapter considers several common objections to the idea that the US Constitution represents the will of the people. The Constitution *is* a popular and majoritarian document, but to ensure the long-term stability of the Constitution's popular character and authority, the document also divides power and limits popular influence to some extent. This chapter also considers perhaps the greatest criticism of the Constitution—namely, that it is a proslavery document. *The Federalist* and two of the greatest political thinkers in American history, Abraham Lincoln and Frederick Douglass, illustrate that this understanding is mistaken.

The American people, not the US Supreme Court, are the final arbiters of the Constitution's meaning. It is a common and dangerous misunderstanding to say that the Supreme Court is the ultimate interpreter of the meaning of the US Constitution. It is said that the Supreme Court *must* be the final judge of the meaning of the Constitution, for there is no way for the common person to understand the meaning of the words of the text insofar as they were written in a time and a culture different from our own. Yet if it were true that the Supreme Court determines the meaning of the Constitution, this would mean that the Supreme Court, not the American people, is sovereign. It is not. Rather, the Supreme Court is one of the penultimate interpreters of the Constitution, alongside other branches of government. The ultimate interpreter is the American people. The idea of the Supreme Court as the final determinant of the meaning of the Constitution is antidemocratic. It is an ironic claim insofar as those who condemn the Constitution as antidemocratic are also those who insist that the decisions of the Supreme Court and not popular amendments to the Constitution must be the last word on the meaning of the document's words.

The stakes are high. To continue to enjoy the benefits of liberty, we must do the hard work of learning what the Constitution really means. The costs of ignorance are too great. Through the medium of the words of the Constitution, the American people rule themselves. This fundamental law stands as a bulwark of liberty, embodying the will of the people and protecting the people against a perennial possibility of tyranny. The American people are not the obedient subjects of a king but are citizens of a republic. "We the People" rule here. In the United States of America, there is either the rule of law, the chief of which is the Constitution, or there is the rule of a man or group of men who are above the law and are free to rule as tyrants over the masses.

The True, Long-Term Will of the American People

According to the Declaration of Independence, governments derive their "powers from the consent of the governed," and the US Constitution is the practical realization of that claim. The Constitution is the "fundamental law of the land" (Article VI), but the powers of the government in this fundamental law have their source in the American people, who have delegated their sovereign power to the federal government. It is for this reason that the document begins with the Preamble's famous words "We the People." James Wilson, a member of the Constitutional Convention of 1787 who served on the Committee of Detail that composed the first draft of the Constitution, explained that the word *sovereignty* does not appear in the Constitution but that if it did, it would appear right there at the beginning of the Preamble.[5] Popular sovereignty also explains why the original document of 1787 concludes with the rules for ratification of the Constitution by *the people* of the several state ratifying conventions (Article VII). It explains why the Constitution spells out the process by which a supermajority of the American people can change the text of the Constitution to reflect a popular response to the changing conditions of history (Article V). It explains why "the Constitution nowhere speaks of the 'rights' of either states or of the federal government. Instead, it speaks of 'powers,' which are what masters delegate to servants."[6] The Constitution, in brief, is the blueprint of a political order called a republic in which the people rule over themselves, both in the federal government and in the state governments (Article IV).[7]

The authors of *The Federalist* explained that the "will of the people" exists not in any single law passed by Congress and certainly not in temporary public opinion but only in the fundamental law that is the US Constitution. Jay called the American people "the joint and equal sovereigns of this country," adding that these "fellow citizens and joint sovereigns cannot be degraded by appearing with each other in their own Courts to have their controversies determined."[8] Madison wrote in Federalist No. 37 that "republican liberty" means that "all power should be derived from the people,"[9] adding in Federalist No. 46 that the American people are the "common superior" and "ultimate authority" of both the federal and the state governments.[10] Similarly, Hamilton stated in Federalist No. 78 that the Constitution is "the intention of the people"—an intention that is superior to the intention of any of the representatives of the people if those ever contradict one another.[11] More emphatically, he asserted in Federalist No. 22 that "the streams of national power ought to flow immediately from that pure original fountain of all legitimate authority"—namely, "THE CONSENT OF THE PEOPLE."[12] A more well-known line from Hamilton appears in Federalist No. 1, where he wrote that "it seems to have been reserved to the people of this country, by their conduct and example, to decide the important question, whether societies of men are really capable or not, of establishing good government from reflection *and choice*."[13] The ratification of the Constitution was, according to Federalist No. 1 (and Article VII of the Constitution), the choice of the American people. As such, the foundational remedy for violations of the Constitution by the federal government is "the people whose creature it is." In the event of such violations, the people "must appeal to the standard [the Constitution] they have formed, and take such measures to redress the injury done to the constitution, as the exigency may suggest and prudence justify."[14] Prudence may suggest, for example, that a relatively minor violation may justify electing a new representative at the conclusion of a two-year term (Article I, Section 2), whereas a major violation may justify removal of a president (Article II, Section 4) or even a constitutional amendment, when a two-thirds majority of the (represented) American people propose an amendment and then three-quarters of the (represented) American people ratify it (Article V).[15]

A common misunderstanding is that the framers of the Constitution were not really establishing a popular government based on the consent of the people but were instead devising a system that would preserve their own wealth. While it is not our purpose here to provide an exhaustive consideration of this claim, it is still so widely held that a few comments are in order. First, this claim, advanced by the early progressive historian Charles Beard, has been shown to be weak; its continuation in high school history textbooks and popular histories, as in Beard's own work, is less the result of historical fact than of ideological commitment.[16] In his helpful commentary on the historiographical debates concerning the American founding, the political scientist Alan Gibson observes that early progressives' empirical claims about American society during the time of the Constitution's ratification "have never been proved."[17] Indeed, they have long been disproved. Beard believed that the Constitution's framers represented America's mercantilist and financial interest, who were allegedly in a class conflict with America's poor farmers. The historian Forrest McDonald has shown conclusively that this is empirically false. Most of the Constitution's framers were wealthy from agricultural property—property that was in no immediate danger and not in need of saving.[18]

Second, the claim that the framers designed the Constitution to protect their financial interests is couched in the broader claim held by some historians that the Constitution was an oligarchic reaction against the more democratic ideas of the Declaration of Independence. The fact is that both documents favor popular government. The Declaration asserts that the two criteria of good government are, procedurally, basing government on the consent of the people and, substantively, protecting certain rights. The Declaration is largely silent about the fact that there can be a conflict between these two, because it was not concerned with establishing a new government. It does say, however, that a people may organize its "powers in such form, as to them shall seem most likely to effect their Safety and Happiness." Similarly, the Constitution sought to "insure domestic tranquility" and "secure the blessings of liberty to ourselves and our posterity," and it did so by preserving the principle of popular government with the form of a republic rather than that of a democracy.[19]

Third, it is necessary to pause for a moment to consider some basic historiographical considerations. The Beardian interpretation depends on a prior philosophical assumption that denies the very possibility that the founders could have been motivated by anything other than material self-interest.[20] In this view, it is material self-interest that drives all human action, and any claim that one can understand the motivations of the founders from ideas stated in their writings is faulty, since any ideas stated by a historical actor are "projected rationalizations of underlying interests," the most fundamental of which are economic.[21] A careful reading of *The Federalist* yields a deeper understanding of the true meaning of the Constitution and of the political liberty that it was designed to protect.

The Distinction of Theory and Practice, and Why the Constitution Is Not Antidemocratic

The distinction between theory and practice helps us in understanding the misplaced indignation toward the disproportionate weight given to voters from different states. It will be helpful to recall the basic principle in Aristotle's thought that the study of politics is not the study of mathematics.[22] In mathematics, there is only one precisely correct number that goes to the right of the equals sign. By contrast, in politics, which is a practical science, the amount of precision that one can expect in any given situation is far less. Correct answers have less to do with precise calculation than with good judgment, which is why Madison warned in Federalist No. 55 that "nothing can be more fallacious than to found our political calculations on arithmetic principles."[23] There is no equation that one can apply to politics to produce a good society, and there is no pure theory that one can implement completely that yields perfect justice in practice. If the object of one's politics is to satisfy some rudimentary sense of justice, then arithmetical principles should guide political thinking. But if the authors of *The Federalist* were right in saying that "justice is the end of government," which means that governments should protect the "diversity in the faculties" of different human beings,[24] then one should be satisfied with an imperfect number or a partial deviation from perfect procedural equality as long as one finds a political community generally characterized by liberty, order, and justice. Madison, Hamilton, and Jay were concerned with a balancing of various interests in American politics so that we might enjoy a political community in which liberty would be as secure as possible to as many as possible. Legislators (ought to) serve their constituents by advocating for their political, economic, and social interests, an arrangement that assures that such interests receive representation and also that no interest can extinguish the liberties of others. In addressing a complaint that "the weight of a citizen's vote cannot be made to depend on where he lives," one might reply with Madison that the point is not the weight of a citizen's vote but the liberty of citizens.[25] *The Federalist* suggests that the theory of the American founders was the

Declaration of Independence's popular government (or government by the consent of the governed) and that the practical effort to secure that theoretical principle was the US Constitution's republican government, as a opposed to what might be regarded as a more theoretically pure version of self-government, what Madison in Federalist No. 10 called "pure democracy."[26] *The Federalist* explains that the US Constitution attempted to embody the principle of popular self-government. Yet in politics, often the preservation of a principle requires a wise, partial deviation from that principle lest the principle be swept away by practical realities. To the new student of the Constitution and *The Federalist*, this may seem suspicious. *The Federalist* makes plain that Madison and Hamilton thought about politics in exactly this way, and it explains why the founders, far from rejecting popular, republican self-government, were trying to preserve it. *The Federalist* also shows why it would be dangerous *not* to think about politics in this way.

The need to distinguish popular theory from republican practice explains *The Federalist*'s treatment of separation of powers. Since the beginning of the progressive movement, some Americans have criticized the separation of powers as being antithetical to democratic government. Woodrow Wilson did so, regarding it as an unacceptable obstacle to swift government action and popular will.[27] This also was the view of progressive scholar J. Allen Smith, who believed that "the system of checks and balances" could not be "reconciled with the theory of popular government."[28] Wilson's and Allen's criticisms may seem less persuasive if one understands *The Federalist*'s distinction between theory and practice. The theory of the separation of powers is easy enough: Because people are prone to abuse power, a combination of the legislative, executive, and judicial powers in the same hands was thought to be "the very definition of tyranny." But Madison did not conclude from this that the legislative, executive, and judicial powers be kept perfectly and entirely separate. He believed that in contrast to the state governments, which lacked "a competent provision ... for maintaining in practice the separation [of powers] delineated on paper," the proposed US Constitution sought to preserve the theory of separation of powers by deviation from that theory in the form of giving to each branch of government "the necessary constitutional means, and personal motives, to resist encroachments" of the other branches.[29] These necessary constitutional means included, among other things, a division of the legislature into two chambers, giving to the president the power to veto legislation, giving to Congress the ability to limit the executive power through impeachment and removal and through other, lesser means, and giving to the Supreme Court certain checks on the Congress and the presidency, even as the Supreme Court is checked by the joint appointment power of Congress and the presidency. J. Allen Smith may have thought that checks and balances are incompatible with the theory of popular government, but sound political thinking requires practical deviations from a theory in order that the principle may be preserved.

The US Constitution embodies the true, long-term will of the American people, but this does not mean that the framers of the Constitution were ignorant of the fact that sometimes majorities do harm to minorities. On the contrary, the founders were suspicious of political power in part because they were suspicious of human nature. They believed that absolute trust in any person or group of people should have no place in the American political system. Madison famously wrote in Federalist No. 51 that government is "the greatest of all reflections on human nature" and that because human beings are not "angels," serious limitations on power need to occur.[30] In fact, Madison believed that we can be sure that people who have power will abuse that power. It is one of the paradoxes of the modern political world that the loudest calls for democracy come from those most concerned with oppressed minorities. Who exactly does the oppressing of minorities? Do people change their nature, losing their capacity to do harm, when they find themselves members of the majority? The pages of history provide the answer.

Consider Madison's reasoning in the single most well-known part of his corpus: Federalist No. 10. Madison argued that the framers of the Constitution wanted "to preserve the spirit and the form of popular government" while also recognizing the historical fact that in all popular governments, the private rights of individuals and minorities suffer at the hands of more powerful majorities.[31] The tendency to form factions—groups with a shared interest at odds with the rights of others—is "sown in the nature of man."[32] So while there are "qualities in human nature, which justify a certain portion of esteem and confidence," it would be naive to rely on these qualities. Neither religion and morals nor "enlightened statesman,"[33] he claimed, can be trusted. In fact, "had every Athenian citizen been a Socrates," observed Madison in Federalist No. 55, "every Athenian assembly would still have been a mob."[34] The genius of the US Constitution is its combination of republican government, which is "a government in which the scheme of representation takes place" and which derives its authority from the people while at the same time mitigating the threat that a popular majority will violate the rights of minorities.[35] Because the framers of the Constitution were establishing a popular government that derived its powers from the consent of the governed, they understood that the best way to mitigate the dangers to individuals and minorities was to take their essentially popular and majoritarian principle and dilute the power of majorities to preserve a government of the people, by the people, and for the people in the long term.

The human tendency to abuse power means that one ought to be particularly vigilant in looking for abuses of power where that power exists in any given political order. This helps to explain why *The Federalist* sometimes paradoxically critiqued popular influence on government at the same time that it was defending a Constitution that embodied the will of the people. One should not be surprised to find the founders criticizing popular governments, because they were establishing popular government. As the political scientist Martin Diamond has explained, "*Of course*, the Founders criticized the defects and dangers of democracy and did not waste much breath on the defects and dangers of other forms of government. For a very good reason. They were not founding any other kind of government; they were establishing a democratic form, and it was the dangers peculiar to it against which all their efforts had to be bent."[36] According to Madison, in a hereditary monarchy, one should fear the monarch as the most likely source of tyranny. In a direct democracy, one should fear that tyranny may arise in the people themselves, because it is the people who hold power. But "in a representative republic, where the executive magistracy is carefully limited . . . and where the legislative power is exercised by an assembly, which is inspired, by a supposed influence over the people," it is in that same legislative assembly that one ought to fear that tyranny may arise.[37] Notice that Madison wants the reader to think about the kind of political order that exists as a heuristic by which to discover the most likely source of future threats to political liberty. Because the founders were attempting to establish a representative democracy in which the people were the source of the political authority, they looked for threats to liberty in that portion of the proposed government that was closest to the authority of the people—namely, the US Congress.

One should therefore expect to find the framers of the US Constitution erecting limits on the power of majorities, even though it is the majority that will rule. In a republican government, it was believed, "the legislative authority, necessarily, predominates."[38] We therefore find in the Constitution limits on the power of legislative majorities through things such as the president's veto.[39] There is also judicial review: If Congress passes a law and the president signs the law, it is still possible that a very small minority—namely, the Supreme Court—voids that law if it clearly contradicts the Constitution, thereby protecting individual rights.[40] Consider the Senate: According to Madison, a bicameral legislature in which the upper house derives its authority not immediately from the people but from the state legislatures (before the Seventeenth Amendment) and has six- instead of two-year terms can be a "defence to the people against their own temporary errors and delusions." The Senate therefore acts as a check on the House of Representatives "to suspend the blow meditated by the people against themselves, until reason, justice and truth, can regain their authority over the public mind."[41]

The framers of the US Constitution sought to implement a popular government—one exercised by the people and one that derives its authority from the people. The Constitution therefore not only derives its authority from the people but also dilutes the exercise of power by those representatives of the people. There can be little doubt that in the early twenty-first century, the federal government looks different from Madison's vision of a legislature that draws "all power into its impetuous vortex."[42] Too many public servants in the House of Representatives and Senate seem to be more interested in reelection than in the exercise of power, which is why some political scientists think that congressional term limits would attract a different kind of person to the legislative body that would check the power of the executive and judicial branches. The larger point here, however, is that Madison and other founders were critical of democracy not because they were secretly establishing an elitist system designed to protect their power and money but because they were designing a popular government.

The American people are the source of political authority in the United States. They govern themselves, and the US government is therefore a majoritarian one. Yet who can doubt that majorities err? To preserve the popular, majoritarian principle, it is necessary to mitigate its power in practice. The great achievement of the American political experiment is the realization of a popular government in which government of the people, by the people, and for the people can exist truly in practice rather than as a short-lived experiment that soon fails as a result of a dogmatic insistence on pure democratic doctrine. The political theory of the Federalist Papers explains how the theory and principle—popular government—can exist in practice. To achieve this, as in so many other things political, there must be some practical deviation from the theoretical principle in order to preserve the practical implementation of that principle in the long term.

The Long-Term Will of the American People

This chapter has thus far given attention to the claim that the US Constitution represents the will of the American people. To do this, the founders and the authors of *The Federalist* thought it necessary to distinguish popular theory from republican practice. We must also consider the claim that the Constitution represents the long-term will of the American people. Madison wrote that "in republican Government the majority however composed, ultimately give the law," but "ultimately" need not and must not mean "absolutely" and "immediately."[43] In fact, to understand Madison's political thought aright, one must see that to the extent that a determination of the people is immediate, it is unlikely to be the true will of the people. Stated more plainly, the institutional test by which Madison and the authors of *The Federalist* sought to examine the legitimacy of the will of the American majority was to place obstacles before the majority that would slow down the progress of legislation. To the degree that a majority survives the time-consuming institutional obstacles explained in this chapter, to that extent can it be said to constitute the true, long-term will of the majority.

Summarizing this feature of the political thought of *The Federalist* and of Madison's political thought generally, the political theorist Greg Weiner persuasively argues that central to Madison's political thought was his belief that "because time defuses the passions, majorities should prevail only after cohering for an interval sufficient to ensure that reason rather than impulse guides their will," a proposition that Weiner calls "temporal republicanism."[44] To be clear, Madison believed that majorities should govern. However, to do so justly, they should govern in a manner consistent with reason, which required that the US Constitution embody certain institutional features that slow down the decision-making of the majority. In Weiner's language, "one function of the Constitution was to serve as a metronome setting the tempo for republican politics." Through various checks—say, a bicameral legislature, a presidential veto, and so on—is born the idea of "temporal republicanism: majorities should prevail when they have cohered for a duration appropriate to a given set of circumstances."⁴⁵ We can return to Federalist No. 10 to see one example of how this temporal republicanism works. Because the Constitution established a republican government that would function by majority rule, it would be necessary to think of ways to limit the likelihood that a malicious majority of the American people would be able to form and to achieve its nefarious aims. Whereas "pure democracy" provides no protection of minorities, a republic, which Madison defined as a political system in which "all power should be derived from the people" but nevertheless has a "scheme of representation," was more promising because it makes possible a popular government in which people do not have to meet together at the same time and place, as was the case, say, in ancient Greece.⁴⁶ But what difference does that make? As the country gets larger, the representatives from those different parts of the country "take in a greater variety of parties and interests," and it therefore becomes "less probable that a majority of the whole will have a common motive to invade the rights of other citizens; or if such a common motive exists, it will be more difficult for all who feel it to discover their own strength, and to act in unison with each other."⁴⁷ In sum, a large republic, by increasing the different kinds of interests and needs that exist in a country, would make it less likely that a majority would form to oppress a minority, and if it were to form, it would be less likely to cohere across a sufficient span of time to codify its selfish desires into law. One could even say that if a majority *does* cohere for a sufficient span of time to codify its wishes into law, it is more likely to be just, and it is more likely to be democratic in an arithmetical sense of requiring not merely a quick vote in which 50 percent plus one is achieved.

It is certainly true that the founders in general and *The Federalist* in particular were critical of democracy, at least understood in the precise sense of a government in which a majority runs roughshod over minorities, but Madison's remedy for this was not to jettison popular influence but rather to provide checks on it to slow it down. He defended republican rather than democratic government. And as Greg Weiner argues persuasively in his work on Madison's political thought, the obstacles to majority rule in the Constitution and in *The Federalist* were not so much because Madison was antimajoritarian but because he was a majoritarian who wanted majorities to influence politics in a just manner. Having a "pure democracy," by which Madison meant direct, participatory democracy, may sound nice in theory, but in practice it "can admit of no cure for the mischiefs of faction," because an "overbearing majority" may wield their "superior force" over a minority.⁴⁸

The True, Long-Term Will of *All* the People?

Another common misunderstanding of the US Constitution is that it is undemocratic because it protected slavery. Far from being worthy of respect or veneration, it is said, the Constitution should perhaps even be abandoned as a relic of oppression and of white supremacy. Some charge that it did not even regard Blacks as human beings. In this view, the true beginning of America was 1619, when the first slaves were allegedly brought to Virginia. From 1619, according to this tale, to the twenty-first century, America has been a house built on the foundation of slavery and white supremacy, and the Constitution is the deed to the property. Given the repugnant stain of slavery on the pages of American history, this objection is at first glance quite plausible. But as with the objection that the Constitution is antidemocratic, this claim does not survive honest consideration of the evidence. The preceding chapter treated this topic as it relates to the American republic in general; while it also addressed the Constitution's handling of slavery, we do so now in greater detail.

Advocates of the position that the Constitution is a proslavery document and the view that the framers of the Constitution were all irredeemable white supremacists would do well to pay more attention to actual white supremacists. In his infamous Cornerstone speech, Vice President of the Confederacy Alexander Stephens explained that the inequality between the white and Black races was the "corner stone" on which the Confederate States of America was built, whereas the American founders erred in founding a political society on the principle of human equality spoken of in the Declaration of Independence.[49] The fact is that hundreds of thousands of Americans fought and died in a civil war to end slavery, and they ended it in fulfillment of American principles rather than in opposition to those principles. The years 1776 and 1787 were repudiations of whatever principles 1619 might have represented. The evidence is clear, when examined carefully, that the Constitution was not in its essence a proslavery document. Being a political document, the Constitution does show itself to be the result of compromise on matters that we may understandably feel should not be subjects of compromise, but although the Constitution did in some respects give a measure of protection to slavery, it was fundamentally a proliberty (and antislavery) document. In fact, we will see that the Constitution's antislavery nature depended on a temporary toleration of the evil of slavery.

But first we must further explore the case against the Constitution. Its critics point out that the Constitution did not abolish slavery. On the contrary, it explicitly provided protections of slavery, or at least acknowledged it. Article I, Section 9, states, "The Migration or Importation of such Persons as any of the States now existing shall think proper to admit, shall not be prohibited by the Congress prior to the Year one thousand eight hundred and eight, but a Tax or duty may be imposed on such Importation, not exceeding ten dollars for each Person." In other words, the Constitution stipulates that Congress would not ban the slave trade prior to 1808. Also repugnant to our moral sense is the hated fugitive slave clause in Article IV, Section 2: "No Person held to Service or Labour in one State, under the laws thereof, escaping into another, shall, in Consequence of any Law or Regulation therein, be discharged from such Service or Labour, but shall be delivered up on Claim of the Party to whom such Service or Labour may be due." The three-fifths clause in Article I, Section 2, is another allusion to slavery: "Representatives and direct Taxes shall be apportioned among the several States which may be included within this Union, according to their respective Numbers, which shall be determined by adding to the whole Numbers of free Persons, including those bound to Service for a Term of Years, and excluding Indians not taxed, three fifths of all other persons."

To understand these clauses aright, we must revisit the distinction of theory and practice in *The Federalist*. The foregoing clauses existed in practice. This does not mean that they represented the underlying theoretical principle of the majority of American founders. The principle was human liberty. In practice, however, immediate abolition was impossible. The only morally appropriate option at the time was to limit slavery insofar as possible in hopes of its future destruction. Publius hints at such logic in *The Federalist*.[50] Yet, "the great principles of the Constitution" were not, strictly speaking, new but instead were meant to embody the "fundamental principles of the revolution"—namely, the "rights of humanity."[51] One difficulty in securing these rights was the possibility that the southern states would form a distinct confederacy if they did not join the northern states in ratifying the Constitution. In this event, it would become much more difficult to imagine the possibility of abolition occurring at any point in the proximate future. In brief, the Union would make abolition conceivable, but the slave states left to themselves would be able to preserve slavery in perpetuity.

It would therefore be necessary to preserve the principles underlying the Constitution (viz., liberty) by practical, temporary deviations from those principles, and those deviations were legal acknowledgments of slavery in the Constitution. Accordingly, concerning the clause granting Congress the power to abolish the slave trade, Madison wrote in Federalist No. 42 that "it were doubtless to be wished that the power of prohibiting the importation of slaves, had not been postponed until the year 1808," but he asked his readers to consider, "as a great point gained in favor of humanity, that a period of twenty years may terminate" the slave trade "for ever." Although attempts were made by some people "to pervert" the clause concerning the abolition of the slave trade "into an objection against the Constitution, by representing it . . . as a criminal toleration of an illicit practice," it is clear that Madison viewed it as an antislavery clause.[52] The same is true of the three-fifths clause. In Federalist No. 54, Madison observed that some people say that slaves are mere property and should not be considered for purposes of congressional representation, but "we must deny the fact that slaves are considered merely as property, and in no respect whatever as persons." Madison conceded that American law sometimes treated slaves as property for purposes of taxation; but contrary to the wishes of some in the southern states, the Constitution regards slaves as persons for purposes of representation in Congress. Although in practice some laws of the time treated slaves as property, the truth was that considering "human brethren" as property was, said Madison, a "barbarous policy."[53] This is all consistent with his words on the floor of the Constitutional Convention, where he said that he "thought it wrong to admit in the Constitution the idea that there could be property in man."[54]

This understanding of the Constitution was the understanding also of two of its greatest defenders—Frederick Douglass and Abraham Lincoln—during that period of American history when the question of the Constitution's handling of slavery was most contested. In 1849, Douglass shared the abolitionist William Lloyd Garrison's errant view of the Constitution as a proslavery document.[55] In Douglass's words, the Constitution was "a most cunningly-devised and wicked compact, demanding the most constant and earnest efforts of the friends of righteous freedom for its complete overthrow,"[56] but by the 1860s, he had a very different view, saying that "the Federal Government was never, in its essence, anything but an anti-slavery government. Abolish slavery tomorrow, and not a sentence or syllable of the Constitution need be altered. It was purposely so framed as to give no claim, no sanction to the claim, of property in man." Indeed, for the Frederick Douglass of the 1860s, the Constitution was a "glorious liberty document." As evidence, Douglass relied partly on a reading of the plain meaning of the Constitution, which he said does not countenance slavery by not speaking of it directly: "It so happens that no such words as 'African slave trade,' no such words as 'slave insurrections,' are anywhere used in that instrument." As a result, the Constitution could be (as it later was) amended to abolish slavery in the United States without changing or contradicting any of the language of the original document. In fact, although the Constitution did to some extent provide temporary protections for slavery, the Constitution nowhere refers to slaves as slaves but only as persons. The result was that Frederick Douglas could say that the language of the Constitution "is 'we the people;' not we the white people, not even we the citizens, not we the privileged class, not we the high, not we the low, but we the people; not we the horses, sheep, and swine, and wheel-barrows, but we the people, we the human inhabitants; and, if Negroes are people, they are included in the benefits for which the Constitution of America was ordained and established. But how dare any man who pretends to be a friend to the Negro thus gratuitously concede away what the Negro has a right to claim under the Constitution?" Douglass's conclusion was that "the constitutionality of slavery can be made out only by disregarding the plain and common-sense reading of the Constitution itself." Slavery was connected intimately to the Union in Douglass's mind: "My argument against the dissolution of the American Union is this: it would place the slave system more exclusively under the control of the slaveholding States, and withdraw it from the power in the Northern States which is opposed to slavery."[57]

Douglass's understanding of the Constitution was in all these respects quite similar to Lincoln's. In his 1854 speech at Peoria, Lincoln explained that slavery, like a "cancer," was "hid away, in the constitution." This cancer the founders did not dare "cut out at once," lest the new country "bleed to death." Yet the founders made a "promise, nevertheless, that the cutting may begin at the end of a given time"—after 1808. In the meantime, between 1808 and 1854, the US Congress had confined slavery within "the narrowest limits."[58] In his famous 1860 Cooper Union address, Lincoln not only carefully showed that the federal government could limit slavery (which the Supreme Court denied in *Dred Scott v. Sandford* [1857]) but in addition painstakingly illustrated that almost all the delegates to the Constitutional Convention of 1787 had, at some point in their careers, indicated their support for the abolition of slavery. Among them, for example, was George Washington, who signed into law an act of the First Congress that renewed the Northwest Ordinance, which was a law of the Confederation Congress that abolished slavery in the frontier territories west of the Ohio River.[59]

The US Constitution provided legal protections for slavery. Yet these were temporary protections, and indeed, without these temporary protections, it would have been nearly impossible to abolish slavery where it existed. Such legal protections should therefore not be understood so much as an endorsement of slavery as a practical toleration of the evil of it until such a time as slavery could be abolished in a manner consistent with the true principles of the Constitution. As one political scientist puts it, "The compromises they agreed to . . . were designed to tolerate or limit slavery where it currently existed, not to endorse or advance the institution, let alone grant that slavery was acceptable under or consistent with the foundational principles of the American Founders."[60]

The Will of the People, or the Words of the Supreme Court?

According to one common theory, the US Constitution's alleged unintelligibility derives from its age and origin. It is old, written in a different time and culture than our own, so how could we really know what it means? While there are some questions about the meaning of ambiguous clauses here and there, most of the Constitution is sufficiently clear to allow self-governing citizens to understand it. In his famous *Commentaries on the Constitution of the United States*, US Supreme Court Justice Joseph Story wrote that "every word employed in the constitution is to be expounded in its plain, obvious, and common sense, unless the context furnishes some ground to control, qualify or enlarge it" and that constitutions are "instruments of a practical nature sounded on the common business of human life, adapted to common wants, designed for common use, and fitted for common understandings."[61]

Either the words of the Constitution have meaning, determined by the American people and capable of being understood by them, or else politicians give it the meaning that *they* want, and they rule over Americans not as citizens but as subjects. How could it be otherwise? If the words of the Constitution have no meaning that citizens can understand apart from a decree from the Supreme Court, why not jettison the Constitution and stop the charade of self-government? Let the Supreme Court issue decrees and be done with interpretation of a law that has all the constancy of an unstable gas. Common assumptions about the possibility of knowing the meaning of the words in the Constitution favor the forfeiture of liberty more than they favor self-government. While it is true that the "interpretation of laws is the proper and peculiar province of the courts" (Federalist No. 78), this does not require that the meaning of the Constitution is forever settled by the Supreme Court. How could the United States of America be a republic that derives its authority from the consent of the governed if the meaning of its fundamental law is not determined by the people? If a country has a written constitution that serves as its fundamental law, then that person or entity with the authority to say what the law means is the ultimate authority. If the Constitution claims to represent "We the People" but the people do not have ultimate authority to say what the Constitution means, then it does not truly represent "We the People" but rather represents whoever it is that has that authority to fix its meaning.

A classic illustration of the connection between power and language appears in Lewis Carroll's *Through the Looking-Glass*:

> "When *I* use a word," Humpty Dumpty said in rather a scornful tone, "it means just what I choose it to mean—neither more nor less."
>
> "The question is," said Alice, "whether you *can* make words mean so many different things."
>
> "The question is," said Humpty Dumpty, "which is to be master—that's all."[62]

The Supreme Court, like Humpty Dumpty, has at times claimed for itself power to be master of the meaning of words.[63] What is so concerning about this is that a sizable portion of the American people seem happy to play along. Why else are US presidential elections and Senate confirmation hearings for Supreme Court appointees so contentious? Is it not because more power in American politics increasingly rests in condensed, centralized form in the chambers of the Supreme Court? If the American people still retained all the authority that truly is theirs alone, then one would expect that some of the most contentious of all moments in American politics would occur in moments of debate over whether and how to amend the US Constitution. Instead, constitutional amendments have become rarer than in early American history precisely because the functional meaning, if not the words, of the Constitution changes by means of the decisions of the Supreme

Court. Rather than see attempts at constitutional amendments, one more commonly sees attempts to change law by ensuring that Supreme Court justices share one's own ideology.

This also explains why the same kinds of people who clamor for more and more democracy—indeed, the very same people who attack the Constitution for being undemocratic—see the Supreme Court as a kind of liberator and vanguard, overturning the opinions of majorities as it blazes trails on the frontier of historical development.[64] In such a view, the court is understood as being a defender of individual rights. The truth is that one cannot understand judicial review aright apart from a correct understanding of the US Constitution as the true will of the people. In fact, judicial review *is* undemocratic without this fact. However, as long as the Supreme Court justices exercise the power of judicial review correctly, even if they void a law of Congress or of the states, then they are not acting contrary to the will of the American people but are in fact upholding the true, long-term will of the American people.

Hamilton argued in Federalist No. 78 that if Congress passes an unconstitutional law, that law cannot in any true sense represent the will of the people, especially if it were to represent only some temporary spasm of political desire by the majority of the country. According to Hamilton, when Congress passes a law that it had no authority to pass, it effectively "enable[s] the representatives of the people to substitute their will to that of their constituents." When this happens, the Supreme Court may lawfully act as "an intermediate body between the people and the legislature, in order, among other things, to keep the latter within the limits assigned to their authority." This explains the essentially popular nature of the practice of judicial review. According to Hamilton, "If there should happen to be an irreconcilable variance" between the Constitution and a law of Congress, "that which has the superior obligation and validity ought of course to be preferred; or in other words, the constitution ought to be preferred to the statute, the intention of the people to the intention of their agents."[65]

Rather than being undemocratic, judicial review defends the long-term will of the American people. It is an essential part of the checks and balances of the separation of powers in the US Constitution. However, abuse of judicial review constitutes a dangerous deviation from democratic principles. Hamilton explained that judicial review does not "suppose a superiority of the judicial to the legislative power. It only supposes that the power of the people is superior to both."[66] When the

US Supreme Court strikes down laws of Congress that are not in "irreconcilable variance" with the Constitution, then the Supreme Court effectively substitutes its own will for the long-term will of the people as embodied in the Constitution as the final measure according to which all laws should be judged. As Lincoln argued, this renders the American polity an oligarchy instead of a democratic republic, and it is no better than Congress passing laws that it has no authority to pass. Both actions constitute an attempt by public servants to substitute their own will in place of the long-term will of the people as embodied in the Constitution. In fact, Madison and Hamilton were clear in the Federalist Papers that although all three departments of government play a role in the interpretation of the Constitution (interpretations that receive institutional force in powers such as the legislative power of Congress and the executive power of the president), the "people themselves . . . can alone declare its true meaning and enforce its observance" through such measures as elections and more fundamentally through constitutional amendments.[67] The point is that the Supreme Court does not, any more than the president or the Congress, provide a final interpretation of the Constitution for which there can be no appeal. Rightly understood, judicial review is an essential bulwark of American liberty, but wrongly understood, it is an abuse of court power, an abuse made more dangerous by the increasing ignorance of the fact that the American people alone have the power to determine the true meaning of the US Constitution.

While a fully developed consideration of competing views of constitutional interpretation is beyond the purpose of this chapter, it is necessary to comment on one common misunderstanding. We already referred to the claim that historical progress requires that the Supreme Court interpret the Constitution anew for each new period of American history to keep the Constitution up with the times. We also suggested that the primary way of constitutional change is through constitutional amendment and not through having an unelected panel of judges inject meaning into words that do not have that meaning. To this we must add a related misunderstanding of the role of the Supreme Court—namely, to give the Constitution meaning because it is impossible to know the meaning of words written long ago in a culture far away, since "all constitutional meanings [are thought] to be *nothing more than* interpretations that exist only in History."[68] The political thought and jurisprudence of the twentieth-century US Supreme Court Justice William Brennan was an exemplar of this view; according to Brennan, "It is arrogant to pretend that from our vantage we can gauge accurately" the true meaning of the Constitution as it was understood when it was drafted and ratified. This also "turn[s] a blind eye to social progress," of which the Supreme Court justice is the ostensible vanguard. In this view, the interpreter of the Constitution must ask, "What do the words of the text mean in our time?," since the task of the Supreme Court justice is the "adaptation of overarching principles to changes of social circumstances."[69]

The popularity of the view that it is impossible to know the meaning of words that were written long ago, a view that has made its way into college classes on constitutional law, English literature, and comparative religion, may make Justice Brennan's views plausible.[70] His assertion that it is hubristic to think that one can understand the meaning of words written in 1787 may sound humble, but consider that in the same law review article in which Brennan humbly asserted that it was arrogant to claim knowledge of the American founders' understanding of the Constitution, he also asserted that "our Constitution was not intended to preserve a preexisting society but to make a new one, to put in place new principles that the prior political community had not sufficiently recognized."[71] How, one might wonder, does Brennan know such a thing? Is he, too, an arrogant man? One is tempted to answer in the affirmative when one considers his view of the role of the Supreme Court as adapting principles that "will never cease to evolve" to new historical moments.[72] Rather than seeking to change the Constitution through means that seem to be more consistent with popular self-government—namely, constitutional amendments, which Brennan points out "require an immense effort by the People as a whole"[73]—the Supreme Court should serve as the sole expositor of ever-evolving principles that should lie "beyond the reach of temporary political majorities."[74] Rather than rejecting arrogance and embracing judicial humility, Brennan's position, which is today quite common, seems to enshrine the Supreme Court as the sole interpreter of the Constitution.

The assertion that the Constitution's language is too difficult for most Americans to understand ultimately strikes at the very heart of law itself. As Madison wrote in 1791, "Where a meaning [of a legal text] is clear, the consequences, whatever they may be, are to be admitted." This is not to say that all the Constitution is altogether clear, in which cases, said Madison, "the meaning of the parties to the instrument, if to be collected by reasonable evidence, is a proper guide."[75] In other words, clauses whose meanings are unclear may be made clearer by a consideration of what the understanding of the clause was by the people who had a hand in the creation of the document. If the American people as a whole cannot come to an agreement about the meaning of the Constitution after giving it an honest reading, then this is a sad situation indeed; but Americans have recourse, including through the use of constitutional amendments.

Preserving the Constitution

Although the founders regarded the US Constitution as the long-term will of the American people, it would be misleading to suggest that the authors of *The Federalist* relied only on the Constitution itself to preserve that reality. The people must know that the Constitution embodies the true, long-term will of the people, and what is more, they must feel it. To ensure this, Madison believed, the Constitution must not live only on paper and in the minds of Americans. It must also settle in American customs and habits. It must have a home in American hearts. To achieve this, two things were necessary. First, Madison argued, it would be necessary to lock in the gains of the Constitution, a political achievement greater perhaps than any in recorded history. America had the Constitutional Convention, a gathering of flawed human beings, though we should note, human beings of uncommon learning, who deliberated, correcting one another's errors and biases in the summer of 1787. Madison draws our attention in Federalist No. 37 to the "real wonder," which is "that so many difficulties should have been surmounted; and surmounted with a unanimity almost as unprecedented as it must have been unexpected."[76] Indeed, the delegates were humans subject to the "depravities of the human character," yet they were at that moment seemingly exempt from "the pestilential influence of party animosities; the diseases most incident to deliberative bodies, and most apt to contaminate their proceedings." Moreover, the delegates had a "deep conviction of the necessity of sacrificing private opinions and partial interests to the public good," or if they lacked such a conviction, they held their private opinions in check out of the caution that comes from undertaking such a "new experiment."[77] In brief, the Constitutional Convention was one of those rare moments in history in which a deliberative body could truly deliberate about what would be best for their political community, not because these men were gods but because the historical moment gave them this opportunity. They recognized their own limitations; thus they sought mainly "to avoid the errors suggested by the past experience of other countries, as well as of our own," and they made it possible to rectify their own errors through constitutional amendments as seen fit by future generations.[78]

It would be the height of folly to squander such fortune—fortune so great that "the man of pious reflection" may "perceive in it, a finger of that Almighty hand which has been so frequently and signally extended to our relief in the critical stages of the revolution."[79] And while the delegates to the Constitutional Convention were but men, the "leaders" of the American Revolution "pursued a new and more noble course" and in so doing won "a revolution which has no parallel in the annals of human society."[80] It is worth observing that *The Federalist* does not employ the word *leader* except in reference to the leaders of the Revolution.[81]

Second, Madison believed that the ultimate viability of the American republic depends on some threshold of civic virtue in the American people. Although *The Federalist* presents a rather low view of human nature, other aspects of its political theory illustrate a trust in the judgment of the American people. One should hardly expect anything else if the US Constitution does in fact establish a popular government: If the people govern themselves and put their will into a law, they must be up to the task. This is perhaps not the most obvious or most distinctive feature of *The Federalist*. The Anti-Federalists charged that there was too little provision for education and inculcation of virtue under the new Constitution, but Madison was clear in Federalist No. 55: "Republican government presupposes the existence of" qualities in human nature that merit respect and trust "in a higher degree than any other form."[82] Similarly, in the Virginia Ratifying Convention, Madison asserted the "great republican principle" that "the people will have virtue and intelligence to select men of virtue and wisdom. Is there no virtue among us? If there be not, we are in a wretched situation. No theoretical checks—no form of government can render us secure." Instead of relying on the ability of political rulers, the US Constitution presupposes the "virtue and intelligence" of the people.[83] Madison understood the people to be the linchpin that holds the system together, which follows rather naturally from the fact that the people themselves were the spring of political authority under the Constitution. If future developments would reveal the Constitution to be flawed, and Madison was sure that they would, the "prudence" of the American people would decide what might be the necessary constitutional change.[84]

This raises the uncomfortable question of whether the people themselves are to blame for the apparent decline of constitutional norms in twenty-first-century America. If, for example, a sitting US president can claim with impunity that he has total authority, then whatever problems that such a president may cause are merely superficial rather than fundamental. If the American people elect to Congress individuals who pass laws they have no authority to pass, then the problem is more fundamental than politicians and is a problem that no constitutional amendment can fix. Even more fundamentally, if the American people do not realize that it is their will embodied in the US Constitution and they are the ones, not the Supreme Court, who ultimately get to say what the Constitution means, then the fault is with the American people. They must do the work of learning anew who they are and what their Constitution means.

Chapter 6

George Washington and Religious Liberty

> The establishment of Civil and Religious Liberty was the Motive which induced me to the Field [of battle].
>
> —George Washington,
> "To the German Congregation of New York"

Most treatments of the life of George Washington appropriately give greatest attention to his willingness to lay down arms and to give up political power, not once but twice, for the sake of a new republic where people could live freely and safely under their "own vine and fig tree" (to quote one of Washington's favorite biblical phrases).[1] Washington hoped that America would be a place where people could live without the fear that kings would plunder their purses or that bloody contests for political power would disturb the order and liberty that is a precondition for enjoying so much that is good about life. After the American Revolution, he laid down his sword and returned his military commission to the Continental Congress, an act that according to King George III made him the "greatest character of the age."[2] And in his second term as president of the new United States, Washington, fearing that he may not survive a third term in office, declined to seek reelection so that the country would live out the republican truth that presidents are not kings who enjoy political power for the full duration of their lives.

Compared with James Madison, Alexander Hamilton, John Adams, or Thomas Jefferson, George Washington may seem an unimpressive intellect. Yet while he never received a college education (a fact that haunted him throughout his life) and never visited Europe (he was at times self-conscious about appearing too provincial), Washington was a statesman whose thoughtfulness, self-restraint, and carefulness in speech grew out of a deep sense that America would be shaped by his actions and words. As he said in a letter to the author Catherine Macaulay Graham in 1790, "I walk on untrodden ground. There is scarcely any part of my conduct wch. may not hereafter be drawn into precedent."[3] With this in mind, Washington was keen to use actions and appearances to stabilize the country on a republican foundation. Even his manner of dress reveals this concern. At his inauguration, he wore a simple brown woolen suit coat, rather than, say, the ostentatious ermine of a monarch. By this, he meant to suggest that presidents will be public servants rather than kings and queens who rule over subjects.

But we must not overlook the degree to which Washington shaped America not only with his actions and appearances but also with his words, whether in written or in spoken form. A few of the greatest instances illustrate his deliberate way with language. With his words, he penned (albeit with Hamilton's help) his Farewell Address, one of the most important political statements in American history. With his words, he stabilized the revolutionary cause when it threatened to veer off the path of republican law and constitutional self-government into the ditch of force and monarchy. In 1782, he wrote to a disgruntled officer, Lewis Nicola, who had communicated his opinion—and the opinion of others—that the bumbling errors of the Continental Congress, not to mention its horrible neglect of the needs of the army, showed the desirability of monarchy over republican government and the need for Washington to be a king. Washington replied that he hoped to see justice done to the army in a "constitutional" manner. As for the idea of Washington being king? He wrote plainly that "if you have any regard for your Country, concern for yourself or posterity, or respect for me, to banish these thoughts from your Mind, and never communicate, as from yourself, or any one else, a sentiment of the like Nature."[4] Similarly, in 1783, he had defused the so-called Newburgh Conspiracy, again a response to congressional neglect of the army's needs. The would-be coup d'état ended when Washington discovered their murmurings and delivered an address skillfully designed to win (again) their affections and turn them back to the republican course. As one political theorist describes the event, "Washington entered unannounced and read prepared remarks after fumbling for his glasses and begging the pardon of the officers, saying 'for I have not only grown gray, but almost blind, in the service of my country.' According to an eyewitness, many of the officers were in tears by the time Washington finished."[5]

Washington's great error was his lifelong toleration of slavery. As Ron Chernow explains in his biography of Washington, George and Martha often overlooked the actual plight of slaves at Mount Vernon. Yet however imperfectly, Washington had begun to lay the groundwork for slavery's eventual abolition. Through the process of the American Revolution, in which numerous Black Americans fought alongside whites for the cause of American independence, Washington came by force of circumstances to see how slavery was incompatible with the principles of human liberty for which they were fighting. This is why he wrote down in his Last Will and Testament a plan to free his slaves and to ensure that they would be provided with a means of education and of learning a useful trade. He was providing a blueprint for America to follow, should it choose to do so.

One of Washington's contributions to the American republic that is not as well known as those outlined above is his contribution to religious liberty. Like his insistence on republican government and deference to law and representative government, Washington hoped that a policy of religious liberty would save America from the violence and discord that had plagued Europe through the ages. After the Treaty of Paris in 1783, Washington retired to private life at Mount Vernon, bidding farewell to his officers at an emotional gathering at Fraunces Tavern in Manhattan. Often compared with the ancient Roman Cincinnatus, who was called from his plow and given dictatorial powers to defend the republic against her enemies only to return promptly to a private life of agriculture when the threat ended, Washington was more than happy to be left alone after serving his country. Of course, he did not stay long in the quiet of his farmland. Eventually, he was pulled back into public service yet again, first by giving an air of legitimacy to the Constitutional Convention of 1787 in Philadelphia and then as the first president of the United States of America.

It was at that final post of his public career as president from 1789 to 1796 that Washington penned his words on the meaning of religious liberty. Soon after becoming president, he received inquiries from representatives of all manner of religious denominations wishing to know what their place would be in the new republic. Before the Revolution, a small number of groups, most notably Anglicans and Presbyterians, along with some other groups, enjoyed official recognition as legitimate religious denominations in colonial America and in the British

Empire at large.[6] What would happen now that the Americans no longer answered to the king of England and to Parliament? Were Baptists permitted to worship freely, although they often were second-class citizens in colonial America? Would they be protected by the new government or be able to serve in it? What about Methodists, who were a relatively new scion of the Church of England? What about Roman Catholics? What of Jews, so long hassled and persecuted throughout European history? Washington's responses to the inquiries of these various groups serve as a civil catechism for understanding the meaning of religious liberty in the American republic.

Just as he knew that posterity would be watching when he laid down his sword and returned to Mount Vernon and when he penned his last will and testament, he knew that future generations would read his letters and speeches on religious liberty. This chapter suggests that a careful consideration of Washington's political thought regarding religion's place in American political life helps us better to understand both what religious liberty means and why it was so important to Washington and to the other founders.

What this study of Washington's political thought shows is that religious liberty or "freedom of religion" means the freedom to believe and the freedom to live one's life according to those beliefs. This definition has two parts. First, religious liberty means the freedom to believe—and to believe not what government or society says must be believed but to believe according to the dictates of one's own conscience. This view partly rests on the idea that the right to believe something about the ultimate questions of life does not depend on the granting of that right by the government; the founding generation believed, as do many Americans today, that questions of religious belief are more important than political considerations. To suggest that a president or a legislature or a court would compel belief or to prevent people from living their lives according to their religious beliefs would have struck Washington and the founding generation as being a pernicious tyranny utterly incompatible with free government. This leads to the second aspect of religious liberty. To suggest that religion is something that happens chiefly inside one's own mind or, at most, inside of the walls of a church is to suggest something foreign to the way in which nearly all the founding generation conceived of religion. To protect the freedom to believe something means, to use the language of the First Amendment, the protection of the "free exercise" of that religion. A religion that does not alter the decisions that one makes in life is no religion at all. Nevertheless, this freedom of exercise has in the early years of the twenty-first century become more precarious than perhaps at any point in the history of the American republic.

At the conclusion of the American Revolution, Washington recalled that "the establishment of Civil and Religious Liberty was the Motive which induced me to the Field [of battle]."[7] What did Washington understand religious liberty to entail? As Vincent Muñoz explains in a careful study of Washington's conception of the place of religion in American politics, "Although not the 'Father of the Constitution,' the father of our country stands ready to inform our deliberations on the meaning of religious freedom should we choose to enlist him."[8] Washington thought deeply about religious liberty. Madison and Jefferson, although they were no advocates of a secular society as is sometimes suggested, were less interested in general government support of religious sects than was Washington, who believed that the social utility of religion made it natural to conclude that a government should give broad support to various religious sects (even as Washington agreed with the founding generation that there must not be a nationally established church). Washington wanted America to be a place in which people were free to believe and to live their lives on the basis of those beliefs, but he did not think that this required a society that was secular and devoid of religion.

Washington and the Natural Right of Religious Liberty

Washington's conception of religious liberty in the new country is clear in his May 1789 letter "To the General Assembly of the Presbyterian Churches." This correspondence was not Washington's first experience with that sect; he was well acquainted with Presbyterians as a result of their the undaunted commitment to the revolutionary cause. Originating in Scotland and then spreading to England, Ireland, and beyond, Presbyterianism is a Calvinistic branch of the Protestant Reformation. No religious group was uniform in its commitment or opposition to the American Revolution.[9] However, Presbyterians were sufficiently patriotic that King George III reportedly called the American Revolution "a Presbyterian war."[10] One historian writes that the Scotch-Irish, most of whom were Presbyterians, "constituted the very back-bone of Washington's army. At Valley Forge, when many deserted him, they remained despite cold and hunger, to keep alive the waning cause."[11] And it must be remembered that John Witherspoon, the president of

Princeton (then a Presbyterian seminary known as The College of New Jersey) and the only clergyman to sign the Declaration of Independence, was a Scotch Presbyterian immigrant who was rock solid in his support for the cause of liberty; under his watch during the years leading up to the Revolution, Princeton was excoriated by one commentator as the "seminary of sedition" for its success in churning out clergy supportive of American independence.[12]

This same spirit of liberty that made Presbyterians reliable patriots in the cause of American independence also, one suspects, made Washington leery of a doctrinaire, sectarian spirit that could threaten to undermine his plan to set the country on a stable and long-lasting foundation. Muñoz notes that "Presbyterians were the first religious group to write to Washington after his election to the presidency," and their letter was packed with praise for Washington, whom they lauded as "a steady, uniform, avowed friend of the Christian religion" whose "private conduct adorns the doctrines of the Gospel of Christ."[13] But as Muñoz observes, Washington's response declined to repeat any explicit acknowledgment of the truth of the Christian religion or of the Gospel of Christ; instead, he took the opportunity to instruct them on the meaning of religious liberty in the new American republic. "At the very point that the Presbyterians become sectarian," Muñoz explains, "Washington becomes ecumenical."[14] Rather than drawing attention to the particulars of Christian doctrine, Washington instead instructed that "piety, philanthropy, industry, and oeconomy [sic] seems, in the ordinary course of human affairs, particularly necessary for advancing and conforming the happiness of our country." The most politically relevant characteristic of a good citizen of the United States would not be doctrinal commitment but civic virtue; to this end, Washington thanked the Presbyterian ministers for their role in making their Americans "sober, honest, and good Citizens, and the obedient subjects of a lawful government."[15]

Washington handled a different group of Presbyterians in similar fashion later that year in November 1789. Although this group from Massachusetts and New Hampshire approved of the religious test ban in the new US Constitution, they would have preferred, they told Washington, "to have seen some Explicit acknowledgment of the *only true God and Jesus Christ, whom he hath sent* inserted some where in the *Magna Charta* of our country."[16] Washington replied that he believed "the path of true piety is so plain as to require but little political direction. To this consideration we ought to ascribe the absence of any regulation, respecting religion, from the Magna-Charta of our country." Again eschewing any explicit reference to Jesus Christ, Washington in this missive preferred more general language such as "the munificent Rewarder of virtue."[17]

In this correspondence, Washington responded to Presbyterians not only as president but as a preceptor of civic virtues, and the theme of these epistolary lectures on the topic of religion was that good citizenship should be unhitched from religious identity. This was, at the time, revolutionary; as Muñoz explains, "For the first time in human history political citizenship would no longer be based upon religious affiliation."[18] It was the same sort of thinking that drove him to make decisions about hiring farmhands at Mount Vernon, at one point explaining that as long as someone were a good worker, it mattered not whether "they be Mahometans, Jews or Christians of an[y] Sect, or they may be Athiests [sic]."[19]

But Washington's greatest concern was not for the political utility of getting good citizens (or help on the farm) from all possible sources. The ultimate basis for such thinking appears in greatest clarity in Washington's most well-known treatment of the topic—his letter "To the Hebrew Congregation in Newport." As in all his explanations of religious liberty, Washington here repeats the point that America requires only of her citizens "that they who live under its protection should demean themselves as good citizens in giving it on all occasions their effectual support." What is most significant about this letter is Washington's explanation that religious liberty is a "natural right." In this, he agreed with virtually all the founders who wrote about the topic. It was their view that as with life, liberty, and the pursuit of happiness, religious liberty was a birthright of all human beings. This did *not* mean, of course, that religious liberty means that people ought to have the freedom to use religious belief to conduct themselves in a manner at odds with the liberty of others. (If our religion compels us to unprovoked violence against other people, for example, there is no freedom of exercise for such religious belief, for that is not liberty properly so called, as we saw in chapter 1.)

It is necessary to add as well that such a conception of religious liberty is not necessarily at odds with the pursuit of truth in matters of religion.[20] It may seem that speaking of a natural right to religious liberty could never be something that a person of faith could affirm.[21] Does a person have a natural right to believe what is false? The short answer is no—no more than someone has the liberty to murder or steal. Washington's view of religious liberty was not based on a modern religious skepticism that would ask, Why should we compel religious belief when no one knows who is right anyway? Instead, it was rooted chiefly in a particular anthropology. Of importance to readers with religious convictions, this anthropology is not that which has its roots in secular Enlightenment ideas. As he explained in his letter "To the United Baptist Churches of Virginia," it was his view that "every man, conducting himself as a good citizen, and *being accountable to God alone for his religious opinions*, ought to be protected in worshipping the Deity according to the dictates of his own conscience."[22] Indeed, how could it be otherwise? It is not our purpose here to provide an exhaustive history of the development of the idea of religious liberty, which has a long pedigree going back centuries in the history of the Christian tradition. The historian Robert Louis Wilken explains that the philosophical basis of religious liberty as we know it today has its roots in the early Christian church during periods in which apologists sought to defend Christian belief and practice against persecution. The first recorded use of the phrase *religious freedom* was by the second-century Christian thinker Tertullian, who argued in his *Apology* that authentic religious belief cannot be coerced and that attempts to force religious piety actually produce irreligion and bad morals.[23] Justin Martyr, Athenagoras, and Lactantius were three other Christian thinkers of the second and third centuries who developed similar arguments.[24] Religious persecution that emerged during the first two centuries following the Protestant Reformation also proved a period of intellectual fertility on this topic. Martin Luther wrote that since "belief or unbelief is a matter of every one's conscience, and since this is no lessening of the secular power, the latter should be content and attend to its own affairs and permit men to believe one thing or another, as they are able and willing, and constrain no one by force. For faith is a free work, to which no one can be forced."[25] The seventeenth-century English theologian John Owen, Wilken explains, believed that power over matters of religious truth is "God's prerogative," whereas "the magistrates, like wise husbandmen, should allow the tares to grow among the wheat until the harvest."[26] Owen reasoned that God left the domain of conscience free from intrusion from other men. At about the same time, Roger Williams, founder of Providence, Rhode Island, cited Tertullian and Martin Luther in defense of the same preposition.[27] Albeit this is a small list of names, these thinkers illustrate that before the emergence of the authors of political modernity typically associated with the origins of religious freedom—people like John Locke or Voltaire—orthodox Christians had been advocating religious liberty for well over a thousand years. In our own time, the Christian theologian David VanDrunen summarizes the matter well: While people do not have "an absolute or ultimate right of religious liberty before God," a proper understanding of the Bible "indicates the importance of a qualified right of religious liberty *before fellow human beings* as a matter of civil justice."[28]

Religious Liberty, Religious Toleration, and Freedom of Worship

By insisting that religious liberty was a natural right, Washington rejected one historical approach to answering the perennial question of how to manage differences of religious opinion residing in the same political community: religious toleration. A policy of toleration entails the granting of a measure of civil liberty to adherents of a nonpreferred religious sect. This means that not everyone will practically enjoy freedom of religion. It also presumes that it is the prerogative of government to determine whether a religious sect should be free to believe a religious doctrine and to exercise that religion freely. As Jeffry Morrison explains, "Toleration often assumes an established church and is always a revocable grant of the state rather than a natural inalienable right."[29]

In contrast to the policy of toleration that governed the British colonies in America, the United States of America would have a policy of religious liberty: There would be no established church, and religious liberty would be understood to be a natural right. Washington assured the Hebrew Congregation in Newport that "all possess alike liberty of conscience and immunities of citizenship," adding that "it is now no more that toleration is spoken of as if it were the indulgence of one class of people that another enjoyed the exercise of their inherent natural rights." No, "the Government of the United States, which gives to bigotry no sanction, to persecution no assistance, requires only that they who live under its protection should demean themselves as good citizens."[30] By contrast, toleration was, by and large, the policy of the American colonies, with the result that equal free exercise and equal enjoyment of political and civil liberty were often out of reach. For example, Jews in the New World were assured the same "civil and political rights," but they were allowed "free religious exercises [only] in their homes."[31] In 1783, the Philadelphia Synagogue appealed to the state government of Pennsylvania, pointing out that the religious test in the state's constitution that required belief in the divine inspiration of the Old and New Testaments deprived Pennsylvania of the good public service of Jews in that state. They also argued that it would lead to Jews moving to other states rather than to Pennsylvania. Most important to them, it was unjust: They were being denied political rights even though Judaism was consistent with the safety and happiness of the people of Pennsylvania and even though many Jews had served honorably in the American Revolution.[32] Washington would agree with this reasoning, though he would have to wait until 1790 when he wrote letters to Jews, Catholics, and others to assure them of their place in the American republic. The fact that Jews and other religious minorities in many of the colonies had a right of meeting for worship privately only in their own homes illustrates one important weakness of a policy of toleration: It may allow you to believe whatsoever you wish, but you may not live out your religious beliefs freely if you are not part of a favored sect. In contrast to a policy of toleration, a policy of religious liberty allows people to have a synagogue, for example, and to live their lives more generally in accordance with those beliefs.

Religious liberty does *not* mean that people have a right *not* to interact with people who have different beliefs. Paradoxically, while a policy of religious liberty is very different from a policy of religious toleration, the former does demand that members of society exercise a kind of virtue of toleration—and more so than in a society with a policy of toleration. It means giving the appropriate respect to those in a society with whom one shares fundamental disagreements, not because deep down we think that those disagreements do not matter but because we *know* that they are of paramount importance and that we need a political order in which people maintain the distinction between the most important things (religious beliefs) and those that are only of penultimate importance. In other words, the most important matters of human existence should be protected from intrusion from a political order that is itself of secondary importance.

Washington and the founding generation understood this. In our time, it has become more common to hear people speak of freedom of worship as if this is what the founders meant by freedom of religion. President Obama, for example, spoke in 2014 of the need to protect "freedom of worship and access to holy sites for all faiths" so that people could worship without being afraid that they would be subject to a terrorist attack or other violence while at a place of worship.[33] The phrase *freedom of worship* has been used more broadly by other progressives, ranging from US Senator Bernie Sanders to Vice President Kamala Harris.

What, then, is meant by the phrase? It is best understood as a nefarious species of the broader genus of religious toleration: It suggests that one is free to believe whatsoever one wishes but that one may not let those beliefs affect how one lives. Yet it is distinct from the religious toleration of the American colonies precisely because its purpose appears to be the same thing that the First Amendment speaks of while in fact meaning something totally different. As one political theorist has explained, "Freedom of worship, at least in idea, seems to be designed to distinguish or separate religious freedom from freedom to worship." That is, the phrase has the purpose of making it seem as if First Amendment rights are being protected even when US government actions may involve "forcing religious believers to support government programs contrary to their faith."[34] To take one prominent example, those who believe that bakers should be compelled to bake wedding cakes for gay couples even if doing this violates their conscience because of their religious convictions, or as another high-profile example, those who believe that an organization that employs nuns to care for elderly people in poverty should be forced nuns against their conscience to provide contraception as part of health care coverage—these people favor the words *freedom of worship* for the very simple reason that they do not want people to have religious liberty. In the view of Supreme Court Justice Samuel Alito, "'Freedom of worship' means freedom to do these things that you like to do in the privacy of your home or in your church or synagogue or your mosque or your temple. . . . But when you step outside into the public square in the light of day, you had better behave yourself like a good secular citizen."[35] To summarize the matter, freedom of worship is a deceptive policy that pretends to respect people's traditional religious convictions while demanding conformity to a prevailing social orthodoxy that is inconsistent with those religious convictions.

Washington understood religious liberty to be something beyond a freedom of belief or a freedom to go to a place of worship. His letters and speeches imply, and at times state explicitly, that religious liberty entails the freedom to worship and to live one's life in accordance with those beliefs—both in places of worship and beyond. By explaining to Catholics, Jews, Baptists, and others that they enjoyed the rights of conscience provided that they conducted themselves as good citizens, Washington was departing from the practice of religious toleration, as well as from a perversion of religious liberty that restricts the domain of religion to the conscience alone, as if the rights of conscience do not come with an implied freedom of action based on those beliefs. Religious liberty means the freedom not only to believe; it means the freedom to worship in accordance with that belief and the freedom to live one's life based on that belief. Perhaps nothing better illustrates that fact in Washington's writings and speeches than the ubiquitous use of the Old Testament phrase *vine and fig tree*. To the Hebrew Congregation in Newport, he wrote that he hoped that "the children of the stock of Abraham who dwell in this land continue to merit and enjoy the good will of the other inhabitants—while every one shall sit in safety under his own vine and fig tree and there shall be none to make him afraid."[36] The allusion was to the fourth chapter of the Old Testament Prophet Micah: "But they shall sit every man under his vine and under his fig tree; and none shall make them afraid, for the mouth of the LORD of hosts hath spoken it."[37] Daniel Dreisbach has observed that Washington cited this passage nearly fifty times in his writings.[38] Clearly, it was a personal favorite and was used in various settings and for different purposes, but various use need not imply incoherence. Washington used the vine and fig tree metaphor to capture the various aspects of individual liberty that he hoped that Americans would enjoy. In his letter "To the Hebrew Congregation in Newport," the phrase signified the security of free exercise of religion that Americans could expect to enjoy, but the metaphor referred also to security for property. In a letter written to a friend during his final retirement, Washington expressed his satisfaction that he could finally retreat to Mount Vernon—"my Vine and Fig tree," he called it—where he could enjoy liberty and security in his personal property, although he regretted that he saw signs that the French, who were allies in the Revolution, were now in the late 1790s "endeavouring, if not to make us afraid, yet to despoil us of our property; and are provoking us to Acts of self-defence."[39] It was a similar concern that drove him to write in the Fairfax County Resolves of 1774 that "Taxation and Representation are in their Nature inseparable" and that "the Right of withholding, or of giving and granting" of one's own money "is the only effectual Security to a free people against the Incroachments of Despotism and Tyranny."[40] Washington was a defender of religious liberty, but he was also determined in his support for the rights of property. The vine and fig tree metaphor served to capture both of those aspects of liberty, as well as the interrelatedness of those aspects. In effect, Washington knew what some scholars today show indisputably—that there is a positive correlation between economic liberty, on the one hand, and religious liberty, on the other. By contrast, when a state seeks to suppress religious liberty, it historically does so through contractions of economic liberties or outright violation of property rights for unapproved minority sects.⁴¹ If religious liberty is a natural right, and if that means free exercise of religion, then religious liberty must enjoy a concomitant commitment to free enterprise. A policy of religious liberty means that people have the freedom to believe what they wish to believe and to live their lives without fear that their economic and political liberties will be violated because of the convictions of their consciences.

Washington most certainly did not conceive of religious liberty as a kind of right never to be exposed in any degree to another citizen's belief, expression, or practice of their religion. He not only thought that America would be a place where people would be free to make public expressions of their religion. He thought that such public expressions of religion were a necessary means of preserving political liberty in the American republic.

Although Washington regarded religious liberty as a natural right, and although he rejected the idea that there should be a single, established religion of the United States of America, he did opine in his Farewell Address that "of all the dispositions and habits which lead to political prosperity, Religion and morality are indispensable supports." What is more, he thought that no one could "claim the tribute of Patriotism, who should labour to subvert" the "great Pillars of human happiness"—that is, the pillars of religion and morality.⁴² To be clear, Washington said nothing here about what was conducive to an individual's happiness, whether temporal or eternal. However, he was unwavering throughout his life in affirming that a general commitment to religion and morality was a necessary condition for the well-being of a political community. So while he was willing to hire "Mahometans" to work at Mount Vernon, he did not understand religious liberty to mean some kind of minority right to be free from hearing about public expressions of the religion professed by a majority of the political community as if non-Christians have a right *not* to live in country that had a president who issued Thanksgiving Proclamations that spoke of "true religion." It is also relevant that Washington issued his famous Thanksgiving Proclamation the very day after the US Congress passed the First Amendment of the US Constitution. Neither he nor Congress thought that the First Amendment's protection of religious liberty somehow meant that a president was somehow prohibited from any sort of public expression of religion.

Washington took actions throughout his military and political careers to encourage religion, even as he defended the rights of conscience and the free exercise of religion. This is particularly evident in how Washington's conception of religious liberty differed from that of James Madison. Where Madison as president was lukewarm about the issuance of public declarations of thanksgiving or prayer, Washington was happy to respond to Congress's request, in 1789, that the first president proclaim a day of public thanksgiving to God.[43] Where Madison's famous "Memorial and Remonstrance Against Religious Assessments" thought that tax dollars used to support religion would do violence to religious liberty, Washington was comfortable with such measures, unless for some reason they disturbed public tranquility.[44] Jeffry Morrison explains that "though he was just as liberal as [George] Mason, Madison, Jefferson, and other antiassessment Virginians regarding the free exercise of religion, Washington was more conservative regarding public support for religion, financial or otherwise. To Washington, Christianity was a crucial support of republican government in Virginia, and it was to be supported monetarily."[45] Because of the suspicion that some may have that this was some sort of conspiracy to support Christianity through the disguise of religious liberty, it is worth noting here that Washington stated in a 1785 letter to George Mason that if the people of a political community consisted not of Christians but of "Jews, Mahometans or otherwise," he would similarly be supportive of public support of religion because of the salutary effect that he believed it has on the majority of people.

Most American school children should know that the Stamp Act of 1765 alarmed Americans who insisted that as British citizens, they ought not to be taxed without appropriate representation. Fewer may know that concern for proper limitation on the parliamentary authority to tax the American colonies was only part of the story—and maybe not even the most important part. In 1766, Parliament both repealed the Stamp Act and passed the hated Declaratory Act, which asserted that Parliament "had, hath, and of right ought to have, full power and authority to make laws and statutes of sufficient force and validity to bind the colonies and people of *America*, subjects of the crown of *Great Britain*, in all cases whatsoever."[46] This language of "in all cases whatsoever" alarmed the Americans and echoed in speeches, pamphlets, broadsides, and sermons throughout the revolutionary period. The Declaratory Act suggested two things. First, in spite of the Stamp Act's repeal, Parliament made clear that it had the right to do what it had done in the Stamp Act—and more. Second, "in all cases whatsoever" seemed to suggest that Parliament could even make religious determinations for the American colonies. While no account of the years leading up to the American Revolution can do without the Stamp Act crisis, the Boston Massacre, and cries of "no taxation without representation," religion was just as important to the patriots of 1776. Years after the Revolution, John Adams recalled that part of the "universal alarm" of those years was that a Parliament that could tax the Americans without their consent would by implication possess the power to "establish the Church of England," not to mention "prohibit all other churches."[47] There was even concern, albeit concern that was not well justified, that the authorities in London would turn back the clock to the days when Protestants were burned by the hundreds in London streets in the 1550s. Thankfully, Washington and the American founders were determined to protect religious liberty, not merely toleration. That which pushed Washington and many others to the field of battle would not be a cause of violence in the new republic. A policy of religious liberty not only protected freedom of religion in America but encouraged peace as well. Americans would do well to remember this today.

CHAPTER 7

Friedrich Hayek and the Free Market

> It is often said that political freedom is meaningless without economic freedom. This is true enough, but in a sense almost opposite from that in which the phrase is used by our planners. The economic freedom which is the prerequisite of any other freedom cannot be the freedom from economic care which the socialists promise us and which can be obtained only by relieving the individual at the same time of the necessity and of the power of choice; it must be the freedom of our economic activity which, with the right of choice, inevitably also carries the risk and the responsibility of that right.
>
> —Friedrich Hayek, *The Road to Serfdom*

In the years immediately following the Cold War, free markets and capitalism seemed destined to be the new economic orthodoxy among politicians and economists. But with the passage of time, free markets lost their appeal among conservatives, progressives, and socialists.[1] To understand the free market and to defend it against this growing antipathy, there is no better thinker to whom to turn than Friedrich Hayek, whose writings on economics and politics made him one of the most important—and most controversial—economists of the twentieth century. He is arguably the greatest defender of the free market in the history of economic thought. Hayek's brilliance as an economist led him on an academic career during which he taught at leading universities in the United Kingdom and in the United States.[2] His books influenced not only economists and social scientists but also state leaders ranging from Winston Churchill to Margaret Thatcher and Ronald Reagan.[3] Although Hayek wrote voluminously in various matters of economics, his most widely read book is *The Road to Serfdom*, a daring work that argues that "the rise of fascism and naziism [sic] was not a reaction against the socialist trends of the preceding period but a necessary outcome of those tendencies."[4] In other words, the primary cause of the rise of German Nazism was socialism, and political commentators mislead their audiences when they speak of Nazism simply as a right-wing movement. Hayek also warned, in 1944 no less, that the United States and Great Britain were in danger of following the destructive path trod by Germany if it did not change course.[5] But what was that course exactly? During the war, those in the United States and in Britain had seen significant governmental direction of the economy as part of the war effort, and it seems to have worked quiet well. With the end of the war now a real possibility (the Allies had successfully executed the D-Day invasion of Europe by the time that Hayek wrote *The Road to Serfdom*), economists were beginning to ask why at least *some* measure of government direction of the economy ought not to continue after the conclusion of the war.

Beyond the apparent effectiveness of government direction of the economy during the war, another reason for growing support for government intervention into the economy resulted from changes in the language that people used to think about economics and politics. While economists previously emphasized "liberty" and "the free market," many in the 1940s spoke of the importance of "economic freedom," "material security," and "freedom from want." Hayek's response to these phenomena was bold and jarring. Having lived through increasing central direction of the economy in Germany and Austria, he explained that he was well positioned to see similar patterns that he believed were emerging in the United States and in Great Britain. What is more, he believed that it was governmental direction of an economy that made possible if not the type then at least the severity of the Nazi tyranny. While the threat was still not immediate, he believed that it was "necessary now to state the unpalatable truth that it is Germany whose fate we are in some danger of repeating."[6]

Even if this shocking claim were true, however, would it not be possible to avoid the danger of tyranny by finding a middle way between a totally free market and a directed, socialist economy, enjoying the productive capacity of the market system while also achieving more just and equal distributions of wealth? Would it not likewise be possible to have a partially free market by using government steering of the economy to avoid the danger of another Great Depression? During the Depression, as now, many economists and politicians regarded this as being an appropriate and necessary means by which to harness the unparalleled productive capacity of a free market while preventing it from collapsing into depression or sliding into unjust social inequality. Hayek regarded any combination of a truly free market with piecemeal government intervention into the economy to be a dysfunctional and in fact a dangerous scenario that could lead into the more complete government direction of the economy that was a necessary condition of the Nazi tyranny. A middle way between the free market and government control of the economy was for Hayek not an option because, as he explained in *The Road to Serfdom*, "the close interdependence of all economic phenomena makes it difficult to stop planning just where we wish," and "once the free working of the market is impeded beyond a certain degree, the planner will be forced to extend his controls until they become all-comprehensive."[7]

To understand these bold claims and to understand what Friedrich Hayek meant by "free working of the market" is the purpose of this chapter. Unless Americans understand what the free market is, we can have no reasoned debate about whether we should pursue the freedom of the market, the social justice of democratic socialism, or something in between. What is more, we can have no confidence that American citizens can continue to live in a free society unless we can defend liberty and the free market against demagogic or ignorant attacks.

The best way to grasp Hayek's conception of the free market is to think about it as a set of structural conditions that maintain individual freedom. Each of these structural conditions shows that Hayek understood the free market to be an economic arrangement that protects individual freedom by maintaining a healthy suspicion of human nature.[8] This is critical. One of the most fundamental questions in the study of political ideas is, What is human nature? This question arises because human nature necessarily affects how we should structure the government and society. In his study of human nature past and present, Hayek developed a healthy suspicion of political power, and this influenced his understanding of how we should protect the free market by protecting three major structural conditions of the free market. This suspicion led him to conceive of a free market as an economic system in which certain structural conditions—including (1) private property, (2) the rule of law, and (3) free prices—make liberty possible.

Private Property

Private Property and the Connection Between Political and Economic Power

Hayek was a defender of private property. This was in part because of his suspicion of any perspective on human nature that would purport that people are inherently good. Flawed people abuse power, and because the holding of private property disperses social power, he thought it a necessary part of a free society. If the means of production were held by the state, it would have infinitely greater power not only over the means of production but also over much else about society. He was therefore similar to the nineteenth-century liberal and English parliamentarian Lord Acton, who said famously that "power tends to corrupt, and absolute power corrupts absolutely."[9] This contrasts with the eighteenth-century French philosopher Jean-Jacques Rousseau, who believed that man is inherently good and that it is only society, especially the "invention" of private property, that corrupted people and caused inequality and violence.[10] Hayek believed that the free market society was one that protected an individual's private property, which in turn protected individual freedom and economic flourishing.

It is difficult to overstate the importance of private property to liberty, and Hayek spoke about it in superlative form, saying, "The system of private property is the most important guaranty of freedom."[11] Hayek stands in a long line, not only of classical liberals, but of all serious defenders of liberty in recognizing the importance of private property and the perennial interconnectedness of political power and economic freedom. Hayek's famous argument in *The Road to Serfdom* was that a middle way between the free market and a socialist economy was not possible. That argument rests on the premise that one cannot have political freedom on the one hand without economic freedom on the other. The power of a government to have a hand in one's property is tantamount to its having power in one's life in general. For some thinkers in the history of political philosophy, most famously John Locke, private property is a natural right. Locke was so concerned to show the necessary reliance of one's life and liberty on property that at some point in his *Second Treatise on Government*, he simply summarized "life, liberty, and property" with one word—"property."[12]

Hayek would not necessarily have disagreed, for his primary concern with property lay elsewhere. He liked private property because it tended to decentralize social power. Any infringement on the freedom of individuals to do as they please with their property must necessarily lead to greater power by those who do the limiting. He explained that it is only because of the dispersal of property in society "that nobody has complete power over us, that we as individuals can decide what to do with ourselves."[13] By contrast, if the society as a whole or a single dictator were to have power over property and the means of production, then "whoever exercises control has complete power over us."[14] He therefore believed that one of government's most important tasks in a free society is its responsibility to protect private property from any infringement.[15] Hayek was not the only thinker to have understood the necessity of private property for preventing the concentration of governmental power. His contemporary, the free market economist Milton Friedman, wrote that "the preservation of freedom requires the elimination of such concentration of power to the fullest possible extent.... By removing the organization of economic activity from the control of political authority, the market eliminates this source of coercive power. It enables economic strength to be a check to political power rather than a reinforcement."[16] The journalist Tom Bethell eloquently captured the spirit of Hayek's and Friedman's thinking about property when he wrote in *The Noblest Triumph: Property and Prosperity Through the Ages* that "it would be nice if we were perfect beings who could get along without the rules, boundaries and sanctions of ownership." But, he explained, until that time comes, property will be "indispensable." The problem for liberty, Bethell observed, was that some modern thinkers imagined that man was not limited by flaws in his nature, suggesting that man and society could be transformed by the appropriate economic arrangements: "For over a thousand years, in the Western world, the institution of property had been upheld by the doctrine of the Fall of Man, which was thought to have embedded a flaw deep within human nature."[17] Hayek was in a long line of defenders of private property going back to the High Middle Ages or even earlier.

What Hayek and Friedman wrote appears to be borne out by the empirical data. The Heritage Foundation's annual Index of Economic Freedom ranks every country in the world according to the degree of economic freedom, as ranked by things such as property rights and financial freedom.[18] The index reveals what ought to be an obvious fact: There exists a clear relationship between the degree of economic liberty that a country has and the degree of political freedom that a country enjoys. While countries that annually rank in the top ten include Switzerland and Taiwan, countries that rank near the bottom include Venezuela and North Korea.

The tragic human laboratory of twentieth-century communism in which as many as one hundred million people died also testifies to the horrible truth of Hayek's and Friedman's claims.[19] Great is the power of any government that controls what people own. As Bethell writes, those who lived under Communist regimes "understood that without property rights, all other rights mean little or nothing."[20] Bethell notes that the idea that societies can do without private property "would have seemed absurd and childish, not to say impious and heretical," to thinkers prior to Rousseau, Karl Marx, and the socialist tradition of economics.[21]

Marx, and his collaborator, Friedrich Engels, famously wrote in *The Communist Manifesto* that there would be no equality, freedom, or peace until private property were abolished throughout the world and the system of "capitalism," as he called it, were overthrown. As John Lennon put it in "Imagine," we should reach for a world in which there were no religion, no countries, and no possessions. All this appears in part 2 of *The Communist Manifesto*, which includes an itemization of policy proposals to enact in the interim between the current age of suffering and the future, stateless, and classless age of bliss. Among the proposals that Marx listed were abolition of private ownership of lands and centralization of the means of production in the hands of the state. Marx believed that human nature was radically malleable such that what we can expect of human behavior would be radically different as people lived in different class systems. He also claimed that class structure alone accounted for human conflict: If we abolish all classes, we thereby abolish all conflict.[22]

The study of history renders absurd the notion that people can be fundamentally fixed by a change of social structure. The structural conditions of twentieth-century socialist and fascist regimes were both conducive to tyranny as a result of a concentration of economic—and therefore of political—power. Hayek opposed significant contraction of the freedom of private property as inconsistent with a free society and conducive to totalitarianism. Any shift in the United States toward socialism constitutes a shift of the United States toward conditions favorable to tyranny. One does not give over control of a significant amount of one's possessions without also giving over control over one's life.

Economic Freedom and Freedom from Want

In the 1930s and 1940s, some economists and politicians began advocating a kind of liberty they variously called "economic freedom," "material security," and "freedom from want."[23] Such concepts continue to hold a prominent place in political debate, and while they sound pleasant enough, all of them mean in fact the opposite of freedom. They constitute threats to private property. When we speak of the free market, we do not mean that people are, or ought to be, free to enjoy material security as a result of having a legal claim to certain goods and services.

This false notion of freedom is sometimes summarized as "economic freedom" or simply "security." It is also not necessary to true freedom to enjoy an alleged "right" to various things such as education, housing, and so on. Political debate about economic matters is often reduced to an assertion of one's right to such things on the grounds that "true freedom does not occur without economic security,' but as we saw in chapter 1, claiming that one has a right to something does not make it so.[24]

Franklin Delano Roosevelt in his famous Four Freedoms speech in 1941 stated his intention to build a world founded on four essential freedoms, one of which was freedom from want. By this he meant "economic understandings which will secure to every nation a healthy peacetime life for its inhabitants—everywhere in the world."[25] Similarly, in his 1944 State of the Union address, Roosevelt advocated an economic bill of rights, among which were the right to a job, to a home, and to a good education, as well as "protection from the economic fears of old age, sickness, accident, and unemployment." He declared, "All of these rights spell security."[26] Roosevelt explained in his 1944 State of the Union that "true individual freedom cannot exist without economic security."[27] People therefore have a right to security, since they have a right to freedom. After all, the president argued, it was lack of economic and material security that fostered the social unrest preceding World War II, and preserving the liberty of the democracies of the world must now mean protecting people against such economic insecurity.

In response to this plausible argument, we may consider Hayek's reasoning. First, Hayek thought the terms *economic freedom* and *economic security* were ambiguous, These words are "often represented as an indispensable condition of real liberty," he wrote.[28] Citing the 1944 State of the Union, Senator Bernie Sanders argued in 2015 that "true freedom does not occur without economic security."[29] The problem with such reasoning, Hayek would suggest, is that economic security is neither the same thing as liberty nor a precondition of it. "It is often said that political freedom is meaningless without economic freedom," Hayek observed.[30] This is true only if one defines economic freedom correctly and not in the way it is used by socialists and others advocating for significant government intervention into the economy. Hayek continues, "The economic freedom which is the prerequisite of any other freedom cannot be the freedom from economic care which the socialists promise us and which can be obtained only by relieving the individual at the same time of the necessity and of the power of choice; it must be the freedom of our economic activity which, with the right of choice, inevitably also carries the risk and the responsibility of that right."[31] More generally, Hayek argues that promises of security have the demagogic effect of drawing well-intentioned people to support conditions that may lead to the loss of liberty, not to mention that they also fail to deliver security.[32] Another defender of the free market (and the subject of the next chapter), the German economist Wilhelm Röpke, agreed, explaining that the notion of freedom from want is a demagogic perversion of the word *freedom*; true freedom from want can be found in prison, but no one wants to become an inmate. In other words, talk about economic liberty can be misleading and can obfuscate the truth, tantamount to a kind of coercion incompatible with actual liberty. Hayek illustrates this point in *The Road to Serfdom* when he takes issue with the progressive intellectual and erstwhile science fiction author H. G. Wells and his "Declaration of the Rights of Man," a document that went on to influence the United Nations Universal Declaration of Human Rights. Hayek applauded Wells's claim that everyone "shall have the right to buy and sell without any discriminatory restrictions."[33] Still, he departed from Wells's claim that people may buy and sell only "in such quantities and with such reservations as are compatible with the common welfare," which qualified the apparent right to buy and sell without restriction.[34] Like Röpke, Hayek was making the point that one cannot consistently or practically claim that one has the liberty to enjoy one's property and the fruits of one's labor if one also claims that one has the liberty to enjoy something that is effectively contingent on governmental force being used to take another's property and the fruits of another's labor. This point will be clearer if we consider examples from the United Nations Declaration of Human Rights. Article 17 of this document asserts that "everyone has the right to own property" and that "no one shall be arbitrarily deprived of his property," but this is misleading. The document begins in Article 1 with the demand that human beings "should act towards one another in a spirit of brotherhood"—and we all know what happens to our property when siblings are involved. Later in the document, we find, for example, that everyone has the "right to social security" (Article 22), to fair wages (Article 23), to "rest and leisure, including reasonable limitation of working hours and periodic holidays with pay" (Article 24), to education (Article 26), and so on. In other words, what in Article 17 appears to be a protection of economic liberty and of one's property turns out to be a protection of property with a long list of exceptions tantamount to a freedom that other people have that involves the taking of your property. It is perhaps for this reason that Article 3 of the Universal Declaration of Human Rights replaces John Locke's famous triad of life, liberty, and property with the declaration that "everyone has the right to life, liberty and *security of person*."[35]

Hayek had more respect for opponents of the free market who avoided the language of freedom entirely, because such people were more honest and more consistent.[36] He argued that socialists were originally quite open about the incompatibility of central direction of the economy with liberty; they readily acknowledged that their ideas could be put into practice only by "a strong dictatorial government."[37] In order to have success, socialists realized, they needed to frame their efforts as economic freedom, which eventually became more popular among the European intelligentsia than was a more traditional conception of liberty.[38]

A Freely Operating Price System

Hayek's suspicion of human nature also led him to support the free operation of prices in the marketplace. He recognized that humanity does not have a godlike knowledge of a society adequate either for wholesale economic planning or for piecemeal engineering of particular aspects of the economy. So while he defended individual freedom throughout his career and in all his writing, Hayek was suspicious of any conception of humanity that viewed individual people as having a great bank of reason or knowledge from which to draw insights on how a government can direct an economy to particular outcomes. As a result of this skepticism of the powers of individual reason, he advocated for a freely operating price system and opposed not only wholesale engineering of the economy but also piecemeal tweaking of the economy that would artificially change prices.

Manipulation of prices is regularly proposed as a solution for market outcomes that appear to be unsatisfactory or that may offend an untutored sense of justice. What too often happens is that well-intentioned efforts to achieve a more just outcome tend to worsen the problem by worsening scarcity of resources. For example, in the event of a catastrophic hurricane, it may appear just for a state governor to prohibit sudden increases in prices for gasoline, generators, or chain saws. However, without the higher prices, there would be little incentive for producers and merchants to make the extra effort to make such items available in the midst of such scarcity. Similarly, without higher prices, consumers would have little reason to purchase only what they would need and could afford, thereby exacerbating the scarcity of those sorely needed products. One might also consider the perennial debate regarding the minimum wage. It may appear that if some people make a small and apparently unjust wage that legislatures should increase the minimum wage at which someone may lawfully be employed. But one must understand that minimum wage laws are simply controls on the price of labor that an employer is able to offer to a laborer. When it becomes illegal to pay a laborer less than some specified amount, what too often happens is that people whose labor is not worth more than the minimum wage end up unemployed. Hayek concluded that "wage fixing is quite as effective a means as any other of keeping out those who could be employed only at a lower wage."[39]

Hayek provides the theoretical foundation for understanding why *all* governmental interference with prices is destined to be problematic at best. Hayek maintained that no one, and no group of people, ever has access to all the economic information that is necessary for helping people at a social level. At the level of the family or household, we have enough information for knowing whether we should buy an electric generator in the aftermath of a natural disaster, but we often lack adequate information for deciding this for other people at the aggregate level of public policy.[40] To understand this idea, we must step aside from *The Road to Serfdom* to a less well-known but no less important portion of Hayek's writing.

Hayek argued in 1945 in his seminal essay "The Use of Knowledge in Society" that the knowledge that is necessary to make an economy work well is never united together in one person, in one legislature, or in one group of regulators. Hayek explained that part of the reason for an assumption that the knowledge or decisions of government regulators is better than the knowledge of individuals in the marketplace is attributable to a bias in favor of "scientific" knowledge, both in economics and in other areas of study.[41] Negative consequences follow from a lack of respect for the problem of what Hayek called "divided knowledge." In "The Use of Knowledge in Society," Hayek made a basic but crucial observation: All knowledge in an economy that is necessary for the production and distribution of goods throughout that economy never exists in any one mind (hence divided knowledge). How should societies respond to that fact? Should no central planner, no bureaucrat, or no well-intentioned politician do the planning in an economy necessary to bring about economic growth and stability? Should a central planner or regulator take the lead in preventing the economic recessions and depressions that not only bring about human suffering but also bring about the political radicalism of the sort that plagued Europe in the 1930s and 1940s? No, Hayek answered, we must avoid at all costs the central direction of an economy. Why? Most importantly, he argued that the economic knowledge that is divided among so many individuals in an economy at no point ceases to be divided and can never be conveyed to a single mind or a single board of economic planners. To believe otherwise is to believe that people can, like God, know all things.

Hayek consistently advocated a modest anthropology basically consistent with that which we have already seen in Edmund Burke. He identified himself more broadly with what he called the "Anglican" tradition of liberty, which sees individuals as having a limited amount of knowledge that thereby requires that society be bound by tradition as a kind of teacher, since only through tradition does humankind truly find out what helps an economy to flourish. In addition to Burke, Hayek regarded Charles de Montesquieu, Alexis de Tocqueville, and Benjamin Constant as representative of the thought of the so-called Anglican tradition.[42] He rejected what he called the Gallican tradition, the greatest exponent of which was Rousseau, who drew inspiration from ancient Sparta and who advocated a centrally planned society in contrast to Burke's emphasis on organic, unplanned growth.[43] What this suggests is that a modest anthropology and a limited view of human reason lay at the root of Hayek's opposition to central direction of an economy.

However, even though knowledge is always divided throughout a society, it nevertheless *is* true that it can be made useful at the collective level. But how? The answer is the price system. Freely operating prices connect the individual decisions of people in business to the larger economic system by acting as a signal to individuals in the market.[44] As Hayek put it in "The Use of Knowledge in Society," the "price system is just one of those formations which man has learned to use . . . after he had stumbled upon it without understanding it. Through it not only a division of labor but also a co-ordinated utilization of resources based on an equally *divided knowledge* has become possible."[45]

In other words, no government official actually has the ability to determine what price is fair or just. Many people seem to believe that prices are reflective of nothing more than the greed of a producer or a merchant. While undoubtedly this is sometimes true, one must realize that when someone attempts to sell a smartphone, for example, at a high price, no consumer is under any compulsion to purchase it.

What tends to happen is that the seller, to make any profit, will lower the price to a point at which someone is willing to make the purchase. (Another possibility is that people do wish to purchase the smartphone at a higher price, at which point other sellers take notice and slightly lower their prices, thus lowering the price for all through competition.) This simple example illustrates something basic but also important and often not realized: Prices, when left to operate freely in the marketplace, do not so much indicate the greed of the businessperson as represent the underlying reality of the amount of demand for a product and the amount of supply of that product. This underlying reality, moreover, is not something that anyone can actually know in the absence of prices, which serve as a signal to indicate to consumers whether to purchase the product and to indicate to producers how much to produce. The purpose here is not to attempt a complete introduction to the role of prices in the free market; superb introductory explanations of prices already exist.[46] Rather, the purpose is to explain that although the knowledge in society about what and how much to produce becomes useful, it never becomes united in any one mind. And when governments attempt to manipulate prices to achieve more just outcomes, they give misleading indicators to consumers and producers about the underlying reality of supply and demand, and this leads to significant economic problems.

The housing crisis of 2007–2008 is an example. While the causes of the Great Recession of 2008 are varied and complex, a basic reason for the housing bubble and bust of those years is clearer than many vote-seeking politicians want to accept. The economist Thomas Sowell explains that the primary cause of the decline of the housing market was not a free market but government regulation.[47] In particular, regulations and government mortgage agencies lowered mortgage interest rates as well as down payment requirements such that, in effect, the price of borrowing a home loan went down, with the result that demand increased.[48] In other words, in the years preceding the crash of the housing market, politicians from both major American political parties advocated for home ownership for more Americans, including those with poor credit or no available down payment. The result was the mortgaging of homes by many people who could not have obtained a home loan if banks were free to lend only to those who would confidently be able to pay back the loans. As a result, prices for homes in the US skyrocketed in the years preceding 2008 as more and more people purchased homes and the supply of homes went down. In response to high prices and low supply, home builders went on a building spree.

Unfortunately, when investment into an industry (in this case real estate) is not driven by actual savings and wealth, but by artificially high prices that reflect the government's illusion of savings and wealth, the result is collapse of that sector of the market as prices return to levels reflective of the actual level of wealth supporting the investment. As one journalist put it, "In 2007, the house of cards fell. Home prices that had been bid up too high began collapsing. The bubble popped, taking down huge numbers of jobs in the housing industry, erasing billions in paper wealth, and costing many individuals homes that they should never have borrowed to purchase."[49] In 1946, the economist Henry Hazlitt explained the phenomenon so well it reads like it could have been written as real-time coverage of the 2008 housing crisis: "Government-guaranteed home mortgages," Hazlitt wrote, "especially when a negligible down payment or no down payment whatever is required, inevitably mean more bad loans than otherwise. They force the general taxpayer to subsidize the bad risks and to defray the losses. . . . In brief, in the long run they do not increase overall national production but encourage malinvestment."[50] Hayek regarded freely operating prices as a necessary part of the free market, because without them, knowledge of supply and demand could not be made useful, and the market would cease to function properly.

The Rule of Law

The Rule of Law as a Structural Condition of the Free Market

This leads us to a third and final structural condition of the free market. Inherent in Hayek's conception of the free market is the rule of law. To understand what this means, we return to *The Road to Serfdom*, where Hayek explains that the rule of law means that the government must be bound by fixed rules known beforehand. To enjoy freedom, predictable laws must be in place so that people can plan their own lives and can predict with some certainty the actions of others, whether those in the government or in the marketplace.[51] In this respect, good laws share a kinship with the laws of nature that we encounter in everyday life; we can safely and freely move because the law of gravity does not (significantly) change, because it is known to all, and because it applies to all equally.[52] Whether in the laws of the state or in the laws of mechanical physics, people need to be able to rely on their general application and consistency in order to proceed safely and freely throughout their lives. A state whose laws benefit some and harm others, or whose laws change frequently, treats its citizens not unlike vertigo treats a swimmer. If people cannot predict what the consequences of their economic behavior will be, then they cannot effectively make use of the knowledge that only they have access to in their particular circumstances, and they therefore cannot make that knowledge useful to others in the marketplace.[53]

All this means that government officials must not have the power to direct people to individual outcomes; such an exercise of power must necessarily be arbitrary and would mean that there would be no limit to what tyrannical ends a government official may choose for people.[54] Notice the anthropological assumptions here. First, this line of reasoning suggests that if people in some government agency have the power to use their power for nefarious ends, then they will do just that. Second, even if we assume for a moment that people will commonly exercise good will in positions of power (and Hayek does not assume that), they simply lack the knowledge of circumstances of time and place necessary to allot individual outcomes appropriately.[55]

The rule of law is a necessary structural condition of the free market. But what does this look like? First, and most fundamentally, the rule of law in the free market means that people must have equal access to market exchanges. In *The Road to Serfdom*, Hayek explains that the rule of law requires that the law must apply equally to all and that all therefore must be permitted access to the market and, furthermore, that entry into different trades must be "open to all on equal terms." Unlike some classical liberals, Hayek was comfortable with some kinds of business regulation such as limitation of working hours, laws protecting the environment, and the prohibition of certain kinds of products in a society. The critical point for Hayek was that the law must apply equally to all.[56] One of government's most important tasks is to protect the liberty of all citizens equally to enter the market place, to enter into contracts, and to enjoy private property—the fruits of one's labor. No more repugnant—and, sadly, no more common—way in which governments jettison the free market is by allowing some to engage in market interaction while preventing others from doing so. Governments treat people unequally—and deny them the equal protection of the laws— when they allow some to access the market while denying that access to others. Governments treat people unequally, for example, when they permit employment in a particular trade only to those who are licensed by the state to do so. This practice, sometimes called occupational licensure, enjoys the benefit of having the public's safety in mind. Who would object, for example, to the requirement that doctors receive state approval before being allowed to practice medicine? Some would, in fact, argue just that.[57] In some states, braiding hair without a license is illegal. What possible reason for this could there be? Government revenue provides one reason; a standard result of regulation and licensure requirements is more tax revenue for governments. But more important is that licensure has the effect of providing economic security (meaning economic freedom) for some people (those who already braid hair) while preventing a means of income for others (those who do not already braid hair). Occupational licensure serves to do little more than to provide the imprimatur of law to the stifling of competition, and it serves as a means by which to undermine the rule of law by having a law that allows some people but not others to enjoy the fruits of their labor. While some types of licensing has a plausible connection to public safety, as appears to be true of medical licensing and driver's licenses, some kinds of licensing requirements plainly have no such basis.

Governments also depart from the rule of law when they benefit large businesses without doing anything for others—as, for example, when they bail out particular companies facing bankruptcy.[58] When the federal government provides $1.5 trillion in tax exemptions to particular industries and special interests, it departs from the rule of law.[59] Corporate welfare is at odds with the free market.

The Rule of Law and the Pursuit of Fairness and Social Justice

Hayek explains in *The Road to Serfdom* that the rule of law is "in conflict, and in fact incompatible, with any activity of the government deliberately aiming at material or substantive equality of different people," adding that "any policy aiming directly at a substantive ideal of distributive justice must lead to the destruction of the Rule of Law. To produce the same result for different people, it is necessary to treat them differently."[60] Hayek wrote elsewhere that "there is all the difference in the world between treating people equally and attempting to make them equal."[61] In other words, since people are different and provide different kinds of services to society, they may be governed by a law to which all are subordinated and from which all enjoy protection. By contrast, the effort to ensure equal material outcomes for all members of society requires treating them unequally, which is to say, abandoning the rule of law. Someone may reply that even if you preserve the rule of law, the outcomes of the marketplace simply are not fair. Even Hayek himself admitted that "the Rule of Law produces economic inequality" and that the free market phenomenon of people who suffer job or income loss through no fault of their own offends our sense of justice.[62] But he did not conclude from the harsh realities of free market society that government steering of market outcomes provides the way forward. Instead, he argued, it steers society on the road to serfdom. To understand why, we must return to the concept of divided knowledge, which when applied to Hayek's version of price theory reveals two reasons why no one ought to attempt to determine the fair price of something apart from the workings of the market.

First, economic regulators ought not attempt to determine the fair price of a thing partly because there is no means available by which the government can know what constitutes a fair outcome in any particular case. This, in turn, is partly because government officials must produce fair outcomes by allotting outcomes according to the relative merit of the needs of different people, but no one has such knowledge. Second, because governments lack the ability to assign to everyone their appropriate remuneration, then the idea that they would do so is merely an arbitrary decision on the part of the one in authority.[63] In the case of minimum wage laws, for example, why set the minimum wage at $15 per hour? Why not $25 per hour? Why not $15,000? The market alone, Hayek argued, should determine prices, not only of commodities but also of labor—that is to say, a worker's wages. Someone is paid for their labor not because of their subjective ability or effort, which no one can actually measure, but with the objective benefit to society. Otherwise, remuneration for labor ceases to have "any relation to actual usefulness."[64] If wages do not correspond to social benefit, then the market ceases to be a reliable guide to production, and people "would have no basis for deciding whether the pursuit of a given object is worth the effort and risk."[65] Since no one actually knows what a fair price should be in any given case, governmental regulation of prices means that the government official now has the arbitrary power of determining the price. This, to be clear, constitutes significant power in the hands of the government official. In the case of policies in which prices themselves are directly kept artificially low (as in rent controls in major cities, for example) or artificially high (as in the case of government subsidies for agricultural products[66]), the government effectively makes an arbitrary determination of how much a thing ought to cost. The result is that the consequent prices surrounding rent for an apartment or cost of an agricultural product lead to scarcity of available housing or an overproduction of agricultural product, respectively. In these cases, the government violates the rule of law by benefiting some people at the expense of others. In the case of price controls, the government protects those who already have an apartment to rent at the expense of those who do not and who cannot find affordable housing as a result of the increased demand for apartments being let at a lower price. In the case of agricultural subsidies, the government provides greater material security for farmers and less for those whose tax money was taken from them and given to farmers in the form of agricultural subsidies.

Hayek argued that such unjust treatment risks turning societies into places where people are not only given differing degrees of security but also into tyrannies of the kind that existed in Nazi Germany. This extreme claim rests on the idea that economic phenomena are so dependent on the free market that once the free market is impeded beyond a certain point, production declines so much that the government takes on itself the determining of individual incomes and of who gets what job.[67] In the early twenty-first century, perhaps nothing illustrates this as well and as tragically as the case of Venezuela, which went from being the wealthiest country in Latin America to suffering from extreme poverty and autocratic dictatorship in just a few decades. After all, if the prices of goods no longer have any connection to supply and demand, and if wages no longer have any connection to the objective social benefit of that labor, then what else is there to determine them except the arbitrary will of government officials? And if government officials have such power, it seems unlikely that they will use it well.

More than anything else, what Hayek wanted readers of *The Road to Serfdom* to understand was that either one's income and material well-being are determined by the free market or else they are governed by the arbitrary power of the government. In Hayek's own day, what this meant was that there really is no middle ground between the free market on the one hand and economic planning on the other. Today, we might say that there is no middle ground between the free market on the one hand and socialism on the other. There is no "democratic socialism," no matter how often peddlers of that chimera claim that they want neither the free market nor pure socialism. There is no "common good capitalism" that is truly conducive to the common good if one does violence to the structural conditions of the free market as part of promoting the common good.

The free market, when understood properly, may rightly be said to be an essential bulwark of liberty, the most effective means of wealth creation for all, and a necessary part of the free society. As we have seen, the free market, when rightly defined and rightly understood, has little to do with the economic injustices. Yet despite its great strengths, and despite its necessary role in supporting liberty, we cannot look solely to structural conditions for the creation and perpetuation of the free market, because its success in producing wealth leads some people to demand prosperity without the freedom that produces it. Hayek himself remarked in *The Road to Serfdom* that as a result of the "material improvements" consequent to the free market, many people have forgotten the importance of liberty itself, focusing on material well-being instead of on the conditions that made their material well-being possible.[68] Commitment to liberty and to a free market requires a free price system, the rule of law, and limited government, but it requires more than that. What is necessary is a moral and cultural commitment to the goodness of freedom. It is to this that we turn in the next chapter.

CHAPTER 8

Wilhelm Röpke and the Cultural Conditions of the Free Market

> The vital things are those beyond supply and demand and the world of property. It is they which give meaning, dignity, and inner richness to life.
>
> —Wilhelm Röpke, *A Humane Economy*

In February 1933, a German professor of economics named Wilhelm Röpke delivered a public address that drew the malicious eye of the new Nazi leadership. He lamented that Germany's new leadership was "proceeding to turn the garden of civilization into fallow land and to allow it to revert to the primeval jungle."[1] For this public criticism of the nascent Third Reich, the economist lost his professorship at Marburg University.[2] He fled to Amsterdam, and later to Istanbul, before completing his career at a university in Geneva, where he died in 1966.[3] A master of the science of economics, Röpke was at the time of his hiring at Marburg the youngest university professor in Germany. After the World War II, his economic thought provided the groundwork of the *Wirtschaftswunder*, the German economic miracle that saw West Germany move rapidly out of the destruction of total war to being the most robust economy in Europe in only a few decades.

Looking back in 1946 on the rise of Nazism, Röpke joined many others in wondering how such an obvious evil with its international aggression and racial genocide could have emerged in a historically great culture. What is more, he wondered how the broader non-German world could have allowed Nazism to consume a once great nation. Röpke argued that the main reason for the rise of Nazism "lay in the weakening of the moral reflexes," by which he meant that it was a symptom of a mass cultural failure.[4] In his book *The Solution of the German Problem*, he explained the various cultural, political, and intellectual forces that led to this "weakening of the moral reflexes" both in Germany and throughout the world.

Röpke's view that a failure of culture and morality accounted for the rise of Nazism reflects the distinctive feature of his broader economic and political thought. Just as he argued for the centrality of a robust moral culture in *The Solution of the German Problem*, he argued for the centrality of a robust moral culture as an essential buttress of the free market in his most important book, *A Humane Economy*, to which this chapter devotes most of its attention. In this work, he explained that although a healthy structural framework of free prices, property rights, and the rule of law—all the things that Friedrich Hayek defended so ably—were indispensable supports of a free economy, a healthy moral and cultural support was even more fundamental. A prominent theme of *A Humane Economy* is that the "vital things" in any society are those that are "beyond supply and demand and the world of property."[5] Any complete defense of the free market—and to be sure, *A Human Economy* was a sophisticated defense of the free market—must give careful consideration to those vital things. Although Röpke was first and foremost an economist, or perhaps *because* he was a well-rounded economist, he understood morality and culture to be the key to understanding what makes the free market possible in the long term.

The writings of Wilhelm Röpke invite readers to consider that a mature and robust defense of the free market requires moving beyond an "all good" perspective to one that views the free market as a positive but imperfect good. Röpke's thought shows that the necessary structural conditions of the free market depend on equally necessary cultural conditions, without which the free market cannot survive. This chapter explains in two main sections this understanding of a free market. First, it explains why Röpke thought a healthy culture so important for supporting the structural conditions of the free market. Second, it gives particular attention to specific threats to the endurance of the free market that robust culture can mitigate; these threats include materialism, the welfare state, and something that Röpke called the "asymmetry of the market."

The Free Market and Economic Culture

Röpke was unwavering in his defense of the free market. As he explained in *A Humane Economy*, the free market alone is the economic system that "adapt[s] economic policy to man" rather than "man to economic policy."6 The free market alone, then, is what Röpke called "a humane economy." Never forgetting the necessary relationship between one's anthropology and one's economic policy, he explained through *A Humane Economy* that the free market, among all economic systems, does no violence to how people naturally operate for it alone respects the importance of incentives and recognizes that all free human actions follow from one's own perceived self-interest. Moreover, the free market alone makes possible adequate material well-being and social flourishing. For Röpke, those who in the name of some higher morality criticize the free market for not exhibiting the kind of love they would expect of members of a biological family attack the possible and the good in the name of the ideal and the perfect.

Yet Röpke thought it not enough merely to affirm the goodness of the free market. After all, no social arrangement outside of heaven is perfect; it is the error of Marxists, Jacobins, and utopians of all types to deny this. For Röpke, it is not enough to say that the free market is not perfect. Instead, he thought that a robust defense of the free market required identifying particular weaknesses unique to that system. He argued that the free market system's particular weakness was that left to itself, it tends to foster the very conditions, especially materialism, that could undermine its perpetuation. This understanding of the free market therefore presents us with a paradox. It is a positive and necessary good at the same time that it can create the social conditions that can undermine itself. Defenders of the free society must ask not only what structural conditions are necessary parts of a free society but also what conditions are needed to prevent the free market from cannibalizing itself. Those conditions, in brief, are robust institutions of civil society that teach citizens to remember that life is more than material production and consumption.

In other words, Röpke's economic thought encourages readers to consider that a true definition of the free market includes a consideration of the importance of culture. A free market depends necessarily on certain cultural conditions without which it will not flourish and endure. According to this view, an accurate definition of the free market combines an element of structural conditions of the market, such as free prices and private property protection, with an element of culture that sustains those structural conditions. Röpke viewed a free market as an economic system in which people may act freely in the market place because they have the moral habits necessary to sustain free activity in the marketplace. In brief, Röpke's understanding is one that recognizes that the free market cannot remain free unless those higher things of life such as religion, family, tradition, and community inform the culture in which that free market flourishes.

Socialists sometimes argue that their ideal system is more moral than the selfish greed of market life, but some of the best defenses of the free market argue that it in fact encourages virtuous behavior.[7] It is in everyone's interest to be honest and hardworking, for example, since news of one's not being so can easily spread throughout the marketplace and harm one's ability to make money.[8] Röpke shared this reasoning with other defenders of the free market, which he thought encourages morality: "In 'capitalism' we have a freedom of moral choice, and no one is forced to be a scoundrel. But this is precisely what we are forced to be in a collectivist social and economic system" because people there are forced "to act against their own nature."[9] Why? He explained that "if the collectivist economy is to function, it needs heroes or saints, and since there are none, it leads straight to the police state." In all socialist economies or modern welfare states, moreover, the allegedly higher morality behind social programs is propped up by "police and penalties [that] enforce compliance with economic commands."[10] As a result, heavy tax burdens paid under threat of force make people unable to care for those closest to them as much as they may like, therefore effectively legislating what people in many cases would judge to be immoral. By contrast, only under political and economic freedom do people have the ability to be good, for to be good, an action must be committed freely.

Nevertheless, unlike some defenders of the free market, Röpke argued that the free market's ability to foster virtue had its limits, for he thought that virtue must come primarily from outside the marketplace. The free market, after all, does *not* have as its primary purpose the development of virtue, but other social phenomena, such as parental care and religious practices, do. In an argument reminiscent of what we saw in Edmund Burke in the first chapter, various local institutions provide an irreplaceable source of virtue in free market societies.

In other words, while the free market depends on a culture of virtue, it *cannot* provide the sole foundation for that culture. Instead, virtue must come primarily from outside the marketplace, from institutions whose main purpose lies beyond economic productivity. Röpke argued that a free market order could not grow and flourish without the fertile soil of a sound morality. Social features such as family, religion, and tradition provide the economy with an indispensable "bourgeois foundation" in which people exercise virtues such as individual effort and responsibility, absolute norms and values, independence based on ownership, prudence and daring, calculating and saving, responsibility for planning one's own life . . . firm moral discipline, respect for the value of money, the courage to grapple on one's own with life and its uncertainties, a sense of the natural order of things, and a firm scale of values."[11] Such local institutions have as part of their primary purpose the inculcation of virtue and the enjoyment of higher-order goods, and they teach people "a firm scale of values"[12] that reminds us that the creation of wealth and the spending of money are lower-order goods. In other words, the free market is a positive good that can nevertheless do little to show us the meaning of life. When people living in a market society forget this, they expose themselves to the danger of losing the free market and a free society altogether. Röpke's explanation of that fact receives careful attention in the next section.

Culture and Perennial Problems of the Free Market

Röpke thought that any robust defense of the free market required accurate perception of its weaknesses, not to mention honest admission of them, and the free market is not without its weaknesses. To deny this, he believed, was to commit the error of "social gnosticism," or "immanentism," an idea that he borrowed from the great twentieth-century political theorist Eric Voegelin.[13] The social gnostic believes, among other things, that the perfect society is attainable on earth and that the poor arrangement of society prevents the realization of social perfection. Indeed, the appropriate rearrangement of social structures into the ideal social structure could solve social problems. By contrast, Röpke and Voegelin believed that one of the fundamental barriers to the realization of the ideal was not sociological so much as anthropological. Röpke and Voegelin shared a suspicion of the possibility of social perfection that resulted largely from their shared Augustinian anthropology that regards humankind as inherently prone to sin. While some social arrangements clearly may surpass others, a ceiling above which society may not ascend prevents the realization of perfection before the end of history.

Röpke feared that inadequate attention to the dangers of the free market suggested that some classical liberals effectively exhibit social gnosticism in their economic thought, thereby placing too much faith in the idea that the right social arrangement can realize the good society. Röpke was more suspicious than were classical liberals of the possibility of any social arrangement to achieve a good society, and he was more expectant of any social arrangement—even good ones like free market societies—to exhibit some pathology that could destroy itself. Röpke looked for—and found—problems native to the free market that must be recognized and counteracted. What were some of those problems?

The Free Market and the Problem of Materialism

Like the great free market economist Adam Smith, Röpke believed that a free market is a moral good that can bring about great wealth and material well-being.[14] But at the same time, he agreed with Smith that it is not a perfect economic system, and it even has the capacity to stultify those virtues that are necessary for its own perpetuation. Röpke reasoned that the market, dealing as it does primarily with trade in goods and services, tends to train people to be concerned solely with material improvement. He therefore expressed concern that repetitive pursuit of material well-being, along with "the habit of constantly thinking about money and what it can buy," tends to suffocate concern for higher things such as freedom, justice, love, beauty, and truth. Far from making people virtuous, then, the free market in the absence of a robust social and moral order can habituate people to a stunted view of life that appeals only to our necessary, but lower-order, need for material well-being. In brief, the free market is a positive good that also has a corresponding danger: the tendency to teach people that material well-being is the point of their existence. To nip materialism in the bud, Röpke believed, societies must be mindful of sustaining the necessary cultural conditions that undergird the free market and moderate materialist excess.

As bad as materialism is for the individual, the consequences at the social level are just as grave. Röpke argued that habitual pursuit of material well-being could well produce the loss of the free market and of political liberty. He prophesied that people concerned chiefly with material well-being were part of a "cult of the standard of living" and would suffer from "a misjudgment of the true scale of vital values, a degradation of man not tolerable for long" because it would soon end in the loss of liberty.[15] Indeed, one might ask how people could desire liberty if by their own description they are desiring not liberty but material comfort. Such a morally degraded free market society in which people concern themselves chiefly with making (and spending) money is not, after all, particularly different from a socialist or advanced welfare state economy in which achieving a certain standard of living ostensibly becomes the sole purpose of life.

At this point, no doubt, some of my fellow free market-defending readers will be not just a little skeptical. It may therefore be worth reminding the reader that Röpke was known in his own time as a fierce defender of the free market. His promarket writings were smuggled into Nazi Germany and read by Ludwig Erhard and others who led the German economic recovery after World War II.[16] Friedrich Hayek praised his writings, even though the two economists had significant differences. In spite of his critiques of the free market, Röpke was no socialist, and he despised Keynesian thought, referring to Keynes in *A Humane Economy* as one of the great intellectual "ruiners of history—like Rousseau or Marx."[17]

Röpke's position may appear more plausible if one considers a similar argument made by another defender of the free society whose thought receives attention previously in this book, Alexis de Tocqueville. Tocqueville was no friend of socialism, having scornfully critiqued its emergence in the Revolution of 1848, but he did observe with concern the persistent commercial activity of Americans in *Democracy in America*.[18] Tocqueville feared that this habitual pursuit of material improvement would train people to love material comfort so much that they could be willing to trade large portions of their political liberty and civil rights to a state strong enough to plausibly promise material comfort. This was arguably realized to some extent in the next century in what Tocqueville called "soft despotism." He therefore believed it necessary that the great benefits of modern commerce be maintained not only through free legal institutions but especially through a robust moral culture that helps a people to maintain moderation and restraint in the midst of material pursuits. Tocqueville, in other words, conceived of the benefits and dangers of the free market in a manner similar to that which appears in the more developed economic thought of Wilhelm Röpke.

Röpke's economic thought in general and concerns about the free market's risk of degenerating into materialism in particular cannot be understood fully apart from a grasp of Röpke's anthropology. A "humane economy," we have seen, respects the human person. It "adapt[s] economy policy to man, not man to economic policy."[19] But what is man, really? To adapt economic policy to man means, in part, that it recognizes man as *homo religiosus*, which is to say that man is a worshipping being.[20] Man will always worship something, and the atheist, far from worshipping nothing, will by his nature find idols as substitutes for God. A humane economy recognizes this and recognizes that the prevailing religious beliefs of a society provide a salutary hummus, or a caustic herbicide, for the health or deterioration of the economic and political life of a people. For this reason, Röpke identified the historic Christian religion as one of the sources of the virtues that provide the necessary sources of cultural morality that augments the functioning of the market.[21]

Those who deny that man rightly understood is *homo religiosus* tend to commit one of two errors of economic thinking. On the one hand, they tend to endorse social rationalism, which is the tendency to think that a carefully devised social system (in this case the free market) can be transplanted onto any cultural soil whatsoever and expect it to work well. Röpke had in mind the kind of economists we today would identify as libertarians, who arguably display an exorbitant confidence in what Hayek and others called "spontaneous order" to emerge out of a system that allows people to pursue their own self-interest apart from a robust cultural foundation. Röpke regarded his friend Hayek to be overly sanguine about the possibility of freedom without the kind of serious sociological attention that needs to be given to cultural factors. One might say that one errantly employs the phrase *free market* if attention is not given to such cultural factors, for a free market will not long be free in the absence of a healthy moral culture.

Yet, those who deny that man rightly understood is *homo religiosus* tend to forget that one does not stop worshipping something—not even the atheist does. What is more, although people who do not worship God "cling to surrogate religions of all kinds, to political passions, [and] ideologies," a common default "religion" for an irreligious person in market society is what Röpke called "the cult of the standard of living"—which is to say, materialism—and "the sheer mechanics of producing and consuming."[22] This cult constitutes "a disorder of spiritual perception of almost pathological nature." It "misleads us into directing the full weight of our thought, endeavor, and action towards the satisfaction of sensual wants," as if their satisfaction can truly satisfy humankind. Röpke employed the term *homo sapiens consumens* as the anthropological paradigm of the cult of the standard of living.[23] It is a cult whose devotees forget that people who live for the acquisition and the consumption of material things "cannot live at all for any length of time, in spite of television and speedways and holiday trips and comfortable apartments."[24] Economists and citizens in general must remember that humanity "does not live by cheaper vacuum cleaners alone."[25] A free market society in which citizens think only in terms of material production and consumption sooner or later will not live in a free market society.

But maybe that is the critical point. It may be that people do not care about the future. Röpke believed that the implied anthropology of materialism and of much of modern economics—*homo sapiens consumens*—suffered from a contracted or imminent time horizon that led people to pursue immediate gratification, and such a cultural outlook is incompatible with the long-term perpetuation of a free society.[26] Too many people in free market societies are "living for today," to quote John Lennon. Too many say with John Maynard Keynes that "in the long run, we are all dead." The corollary to this is demand for immediate material gratification, whether through the marketplace or through socialism. It is therefore not optional that the free market be supported by religion and by other features of civil society that teach us that there is something beyond this life and something to live for besides iPhones, macchiatos, and new cars.

A people who demand material comfort above all else tend to realize, after all, that voting for candidates who promise to reallocate material benefits is an easier and less risky means of short-term material security than is daily diligence, hard work, self-reliance, and long-term planning. This leads us to a second threat to the free market that one finds in Röpke's economic thought.

The Free Market and the Problem of the Welfare State

If the free market depends on cultural morality and on bourgeois virtues that must come from outside the marketplace, then economists, lawmakers, and citizens ought to do what is necessary to prevent conditions antithetical to the thriving of those bourgeois virtues. Unfortunately, one of the most common features of modern democratic life tends to be an acid that dissolves those virtues. I refer to the modern welfare state. While arguably rooted in good intentions, sympathy, and a (rudimentary) sense of justice, the modern welfare state, Röpke feared, like materialism, tended to undermine the cultural conditions and bourgeois virtues necessary to support the functioning of the free market.

How does the welfare state undermine social morality? Is it not obviously good to care for the poor among you? Is it not social morality itself to care for the helpless? Röpke agreed that it is right to care for those who need help and that societies have a moral obligation to provide a minimum of some kind of social security for their citizens.[27] However, he feared that the growth of the welfare state, with its tendency to level society, takes away the individual's sense of responsibility, because it takes away the risks of failures and the rewards of performing well, thereby undermining the virtues of self-reliance, morality, and responsibility for planning one's own life.[28] In addition, as the welfare state grows in size, decision-making shifts from impersonal, centralized authority and away from the genuine, local communities that are the cultivators of bourgeois morality.[29] Not only does the welfare state shift social decision-making away from local communities, it also tends to harm those local communities, especially the family, because the ability of people to care voluntarily for others decreases as a result of the tax burdens in modern welfare states.[30] In his *Memoirs on Pauperism*, Tocqueville made similar observations about early welfare policies: When acts of charity were local and personal, there emerged a moral bond between the needy and the benefactor in which the latter had a financial interest in seeing improvement of conditions for the recipient of assistance. They also often developed affection for the recipient. By contrast, when assistance for the poor became depersonalized by funneling it through a third party such as the state, opposite results occurred: The taxed citizen became suspicious and resentful. Furthermore, because the state has less tangible incentive to see improvement, recipients of assistance often became recipients in perpetuity, and in cases in which poverty was the result of the actions of the penurious person, those actions often continued.[31] Evidence from the various New Deal and Great Society social programs suggests that twentieth-century welfare state programs in the United States have had similar effects.[32]

A full appreciation of Röpke's thought on this matter once again requires an understanding of his anthropology. His conception of man as *homo religiosus* involves a recognition that people have an inherent dignity and worth that is part of their nature that has a transcendent source. The human being is no mere animal. To study humankind is not, therefore, some kind of advanced zoology or husbandry, for humankind is ontologically of a different order than the animals.[33] Any public policy that treats humans as livestock to be fed and to be provided for materially is not part of a humane economics. Röpke put it this way: "It is also too often forgotten that anyone who is serious about human dignity should measure progress less by what the State does for the masses than by the degree to which the masses can themselves solve the problem of their rainy days out of their own resources and on their own responsibility."[34] Defenders of a free society must therefore be aware of the "overriding danger of degrading man into an obedient domestic animal in the state's giant stables, into which we are being herded and more or less well fed."[35]

Röpke argued that politicians, academics, and the influential in all levels of society must do what they can to encourage individual and local responsibility and to contract the welfare state whenever possible. Unfortunately, he also argued that certain features of the welfare state made it recalcitrant to change or repeal.[36] There are several reasons for this. First, and most important, if the foregoing analysis is correct that the welfare state dissolves bourgeois virtue, then the remaining lacuna tends to be filled in with more welfare state programs. Second, as the welfare state expands, the taxation necessary to support it erodes the resources necessary for individuals and small groups to provide for themselves voluntarily; this means that it is difficult to prevent the welfare state from expanding in order to provide more and more for people, and it is arguably impossible to stop once a society advances past a certain point.[37]

A third reason for the difficulty of repealing the welfare state requires greater explanation. The process of contraction and repeal may be difficult because the welfare state tends to obscure the fact that welfare state benefits do not come from some impersonal bank of resources called the state but instead come from other taxpayers.[38] Those who describe the welfare state as embodying "social justice," "economic justice," or "a truly free market" use misleading language that conceals the truth that politicians and government bureaucrats are often the real beneficiaries of welfare programs, which consist of taking from one citizen and giving to another such that tax money is taken from all, which pays the bureaucrats, and then gives back to the people but with losses proportionate to the salary and operating costs of the bureaucrats.[39] In *Welfare, Freedom, and Inflation*, Röpke spoke bluntly of this scam: "The morality of the policy of robbing Peter to pay Paul is very far from obvious, especially when almost everybody is giving and taking at the same time, so that it becomes harder and harder to know, on balance, whether one is giving or receiving." He goes on to say that "the continual staking of claims for assistance and insurance which can only be satisfied at the expense of somebody else is made easier for both individuals and groups by a mental short-circuit, namely, the habit of seeing the State as an economic fourth dimension and forgetting that in the long run—or indeed, the short-run—it is the taxpayers who must fill its coffers."[40] Not realizing this, too many voters fail also to realize that politicians effectively purchase their votes by promising new social programs or the continuation of existing social programs with the use of voters' own money.

The Free Market from the Problem of Asymmetry

Röpke used "asymmetry of the market" to describe a slow drift in market economies in which market forces move into areas of society where they do not belong, with the result that they effectively snuff out the higher things of life and the virtues that emerge from them. This occurs because the market, he believed, favors those quantifiable and monetizable things that offer financial gain. By contrast, market societies tend to neglect those things that offer no monetary gain, with the result that they atrophy.[41]

Röpke offered several examples to illustrate his concern. We will consider just a few. First, consider the beauty of the landscape. Because of the near impossibility of quantitative measurement of beauty, market societies tend to sacrifice the beauty of the natural world for the benefits of advertising, which scars vistas, landscapes, and even areas of human habitation. In this way, the beauty of one's surroundings, which "give to all a sense of well-being that cannot be measured by the market," suffers for the sake of efficiency and financial gain.[42] Second, Röpke feared that the bleeding of competition into numerous noneconomic areas of life had socially disintegrating consequences that would make life "unbearably ugly, undignified and dull." The same ubiquity of advertising and the spirit of marketing that scars landscapes also affects human relationships more and more "until every gesture of courtesy, kindness, and neighborliness is degraded into a move behind which we suspect ulterior motives."[43] Before the reader suspects Röpke of having some kind of curmudgeonly paranoia, consider whether you, like me, have ever had an awkward conversation with an insurance agent or had an encounter with some businessperson whose social skills were pockmarked from many years of sales and marketing "best practices." With such people, it becomes difficult to enjoy a kind word or a kind action without noticing the artificial concerns, phrases, and tones that one usually hears only from a car salesman. Third, consider Röpke's suspicion that the mission creep of the market does not spare even the most traditional sources of the inculcation of good morals—namely, religion.[44] Surely here, if anywhere, one may find truth, goodness, and beauty unstained by financial motives. Surely here is true human community and respite from concerns of this hectic life! Anyone paying attention knows that this is not the case, however. Like Charlie Brown lamenting the commercialization of Christmas, Röpke mourned the way in which this-worldly forces of the market do not spare even places of worship. Churches in Western society too often seem less concerned with pondering the next life than with the concerns of this one. Smith argued in *The Wealth of Nations* that one of the benefits of avoiding an established church is that churches would be less likely to cause political turmoil, since their concerns would shift to keeping patrons and parishioners in the pews for adequate financial provision. Röpke might have said that Smith's plan to keep religion docile may have worked too well. Some Americans go to places of worship and other dispensaries of religion in a manner akin to going to their preferred department store for their shopping needs: If one store does not provide preferred goods and services, they simply move on to another vendor. The clear benefit of all this is that the government is (mostly) absent from this picture; furthermore, there is no religious warfare in modern America, and after all, there of course are benefits to religion. But Röpke explains that "such extreme commercialization" is not merely harmful to the essence of religion (and to the landscape and to human relationships) but also "an infallible way of destroying the free economy by morally blind exaggeration of its principle."[45]

We are brought back to a primary theme of Röpke's definition of the free market. It is not just that the asymmetry of the market might put a billboard on a mountainside or result in competition between two churches for more members. (And for those with a taste for the beauty of creation or with a concern for orthodox religious belief and practice, this is no small thing.) For the purposes of the free economy, the asymmetry of the market goes further by undermining the free market itself, for the true economic and political danger of the asymmetry of the market consists in its erosion of the noneconomic sources of economic freedom.

Röpke's Solutions

At this point, Röpke's thought presents a difficulty. If the free market needs healthy culture as much as it needs free market public policy, then what can people do to protect, encourage, or restore culture? Put simply, he prescribed cultural solutions to cultural problems. The institutions of civil society must remain focused on doing their jobs. Families must do the work of families—instilling virtues and habits of morality in children. Parents must raise up their children to be adults and not beneficiaries of the state. Churches, too, must teach morality, but not primarily as a tool of social utility but instead as part of a religion that raises up the eyes of devotees to the next life, drawing away the minds to something beyond the pursuit of material well-being. Religious establishments, like other institutions such as schools and universities, must teach universal truths and not merely specialized skills, thereby protecting the values on which a free society depends but that the market cannot produce.[46] The wealthy must serve as patrons for the arts, for environmental conservation, and for other things that do not commonly become ugly and vulgar if left to the workings of the market alone.[47] In brief, the institutions of civil society must counteract the problems of materialism, the welfare state, and the asymmetry of the market.

In all this, Röpke called on the good people in every city, town, and village to lead the way in preserving communities wherein the virtues take root and mature. Every community needs a group of leaders from all walks of life who make up what he called the *nobilitas naturalis*—natural leaders who show from a good moral life and good judgment what is good for the community. While perhaps an unpalatable label in this democratic age, this natural nobility must realize their duty to serve their community even if—and maybe because—those around them do not share their good judgment. These people must lead by example, they must persuade, and they must come to the aid of those aspects of society that are, or should be, beyond the reach of market forces.[48] This may mean something very local: preservation of local business and the local environment. Or it may mean something global: refusal to do business with China or at least refusal to comply with Chinese demands to comply with regulations designed to oppress its own people.

Of course, the idea of good people persuading and leading communities has one significant problem: It is really hard to do. But, as Röpke explained in *A Humane Economy*, either the natural nobility and the various institutions of civil society can strap down and do the work they need to do, or the coercive hand of the state will do it in their stead.[49]

Röpke's economic thought helps us to steer away from a simple black-and-white picture of the free market. The free market is a positive good, but it is not purely good. It must be buttressed by a healthy culture and sound morals. Röpke therefore fills in gaps left by Hayek's otherwise excellent defense of private property, free prices, and the rule of law. Whereas Friedrich Hayek focused his economic thought on the indispensable structural supports of the free market that would help it to avoid dangerous recessions and depressions, Röpke wanted more work to be done to encourage the cultural habits and morals necessary to help a people to survive a depression and to commit to a free society in spite of a depression.[50] Whereas Hayek explicitly stated that no complete code of ethics exists that could guide society, Röpke denied that any society could exist without belief in and guidance from such a code. Whereas Hayek admitted that the economic productivity of the free market brought about so much material well-being that people could become lazy, take liberty for granted, or even develop an openness to socialism, Röpke actually explained what can be done to counteract that problem. If Hayek teaches us that the free market must have certain structural conditions, Röpke teaches us that the true definition of the free market also acknowledges that a free market cannot be free for long in the absence of essential cultural conditions.

Röpke helps us to think and to speak more carefully about the free market. For socialist, progressive, and conservative critics of the free market, Röpke's work suggests that it is misleading to use the term *free market* to refer to that caricatured laissez-faire economy that has no concern with morality or with its cultural foundations. The moral pedants who disdain free market society because it appeals to self-interest rather than operating according to the self-denying code of a monastic order are, in a sense, prescribing an inhumane economy, for they demand more selflessness of most humans than what is realistic. In addition, such selflessness would, paradoxically, soon lead to more greed, for in the absent of self-interest, the incentive to produce would vanish. If we rely on charity and selflessness in everyday market interactions to get our services and commodities, we will soon all be hungry and homeless. Were we all mendicants, we would soon perish for want of almsgivers. The phrase *free market* refers not to an unrestrained agora but to an economic arrangement rooted in a healthy culture that produces absolutely essential virtues like justice, thrift, and honesty.

All this has implications not only for the opponents of the free market but also for those who seek to defend it without adequate attention to those virtues. For those such as some libertarian defenders of free enterprise, Röpke seems to suggest that it is a kind of caricature of the free market to think about it without the greatest attention to the moral foundations of that culture. If the market should not be condemned because it is not a monastery, neither should we shrug when people speak of putting all parts of life up for sale as if prices rather than a transcendent moral order is what determines justice and injustice. People who wish to have a free market but who do not consider the moral ecosystem of that market will soon find that they have not even a modicum of freedom.

Conclusion
Anglo-American Principles and the US Constitution

The future of the American republic depends on a recovery of rational discourse, and great thinkers and leaders of the past such as the ones examined in this book are excellent guides. Each of these thinkers teaches us principles that are foundational to the Anglo-American political tradition, which values individual liberty, limited government, the rule of law, free markets, and religious liberty. In a time when people of various political views wonder whether those principles are worth preserving, the thinkers discussed in this book can help them to understand what they risk losing.

Edmund Burke

If the Anglo-American political tradition cherishes individual liberty, then Edmund Burke reminds us that liberty is a freedom to do what is right and good rather than an absolute freedom to realize all our desires. Were liberty the freedom to do whatsoever you please, then others who have that same liberty may well use their freedom to take away yours. Burke therefore observed that "there is an extreme in liberty, which may be infinitely noxious to those who are to receive it, and which in the end will leave them no liberty at all."[1] In consequence, self-regulation is a necessary condition of real political freedom, because for people who are utterly lacking in virtue, Burke thought, "a state of strong constraint is a sort of necessary substitute."[2] But whence comes this ability to self-regulate? Burke rejected the now-common notion that people emerge from the womb with more-or-less complete moral aptitude. Instead, people become fit for social life with others through a kind of moral training that happens in their local community—in "little platoons"—in groups like family, friends, villages, and churches. Just as he rejected an absolute and unqualified understanding of political liberty, he also disdained simplistic assertions of rights as a substitute for serious political discourse—not because he did not think that natural rights exist but because he thought that such language was of limited utility in the real, political world. "What is the use," Burke asked, "of discussing a man's abstract right to food or medicine? The question is upon the method of procuring and administering them."[3]

Alexis de Tocqueville

Alexis de Tocqueville teaches us that equality means equality before the law because of equal human dignity. By contrast, democratic culture tends to foster an insatiable passion for equality that is conducive not to equality before the law but to equality in all respects. That can be a problem insofar as social equality does not always coincide with liberty but does at times with tyranny. He believed that democratic societies should be vigilant not only against tyranny as a despotic power of rulers over the ruled but also against two additional kinds of tyranny: majority tyranny, which he conceived as an oppressive moral power of the majority over thought; and "soft despotism," which he said was the type of tyranny that democratic nations should most fear. This latter type, he said, was a tutelary power that does not harm bodies so much as it enervates souls, always keeping people in a condition of chronic underdevelopment, as if they were children or even animals. Although he was a Frenchman, Tocqueville was a political thinker whose ideas are nearer to what Friedrich Hayek called the "Anglican" tradition of liberty that values individual liberty and limited government than to the "Gallican" tradition that prioritizes central direction of political and economic activity.[4] Hayek classified Tocqueville as belonging to a group of thinkers whom he named "true individualists," which included Edmund Burke, Adam Smith, and Lord Acton. Hayek contrasted these thinkers who valued individual liberty to the "false individualists"—thinkers like Jean-Jacques Rousseau and René Descartes—who valued individual liberty less than wise legislators who wield great political power.[5]

Abraham Lincoln

As we have seen from Abraham Lincoln, republican government means a political order in which people govern themselves. This idea has three major implications: No person may enslave another; people must have the freedom to work and to enjoy the fruits of their labor; and they must be the source of the laws, since they are the ultimate political authority. To fulfill this role, republican citizens must have the capacity to reason and to deliberate. Lincoln's political thought is important for our time, and for every generation, for it reminds Americans that the United States of America is "dedicated to the proposition that all men are created equal." Although the American republic is in one sense a congeries of disparate peoples, it is most fundamentally a single people, a nation bound together by its commitment to the idea that American citizens should govern themselves. As none is born with the right to rule another, so slavery ought to have no place here, and neither citizenship itself nor voting rights should be limited to people of particular races. These ideas were codified in the Thirteenth, Fourteenth, and Fifteenth Amendments to the US Constitution, ratified shortly after the Civil War. Against twenty-first-century conservative critics of the principles discussed in this volume who suggest the time has come to cast off republican self-government in favor of some kind of caesarism, Lincoln's political thinking and his rhetoric stand as robust bulwarks, reminding those who are willing to study his thought why Americans have argued for—and if necessary fought for—republican self-government.[6]

The Federalist Papers and the US Constitution

We learned from *The Federalist* that the US Constitution illustrates a practical implementation of the principle of republican self-government in the American context. The US Constitution represents the true, long-term will of the American people. Instead of a number of possible substitutes such as public opinion polls, recent elections, the laws of Congress, or the decisions of the US Supreme Court, Alexander Hamilton, James Madison, and John Jay explain in *The Federalist* that the Constitution is the ultimate will of the American people, for it is they who are sovereign. Jay called the American people "the joint and equal sovereigns of this country."[7] Madison wrote in Federalist No. 46 that they are the "common superior" and "ultimate authority" of both the federal and the state governments.[8] And Hamilton said in Federalist No. 22 that the consent of the people is "that pure original fountain of all legitimate authority,"[9] later explaining in Federalist No. 78 that the people give their consent particularly through the words of the Constitution. However, because the theory of the Constitution is democratic and popular, while the practical workings of government that the Constitution lays out are more republican, it might appear that the Constitution is antidemocratic. *The Federalist* teaches us of the constitutional means by which individual liberties may be secured in the American context, and it also teaches us the means by which appreciation for the Constitution can be kept alive. Madison believed that the Constitution must not live only on paper but must thrive in American hearts; in Federalist No. 37, he urged Americans to appreciate the "real wonder," that in the Constitutional Convention of 1787, "so many difficulties should have been surmounted; and surmounted with a unanimity almost as unprecedented as it must have been unexpected."[10] That assembly was one of those rare moments in history in which a deliberative body could fully consider what was good for their country. They recognized their own limitations, and they therefore sought "to avoid the errors suggested by the past experience of other countries, as well as of our own," and they made it possible to rectify their own errors through constitutional amendments as seen fit by future generations.[11] It would be foolish to cast off such an advantageous system of government.

George Washington

Another major contribution to the Anglo-American political tradition by America's founders was the commitment to religious liberty in the new American regime. George Washington, the "father" of his country, was certainly a statesman, but he was also a political thinker in his own right. In addition to his serious reflections on politics in his public addresses and documents like his Farewell Address or his 1783 "Circular to the States," Washington's correspondence with different religious sects show his acuity about human affairs and, in particular, about government's relationship to religion. We saw from Washington that religious liberty, or "freedom of religion," means the freedom to believe and the freedom to live one's life according to those beliefs. Washington insisted that people have a natural right to religious liberty, which he differentiated from religious toleration in his famous letter "To the Hebrew Congregation in Newport" and related missives. Toleration implies that a state's grant of freedom could be revoked in the future: "It is now no more that toleration is spoken of as if it were the indulgence of one class of people that another enjoyed the exercise of their inherent natural rights." Instead, "the Government of the United States . . . requires only that they who live under its protection should demean themselves as good citizens."[12]

The Free Market

The last two chapters of this book explored the meaning of the free market. As we have seen from Friedrich Hayek, the free market is an economic system that preserves individual economic liberty through certain structural conditions—namely, private property, the rule of law, and free prices. All these, Hayek argued, are key features of the "Anglican" tradition of liberty. One of the most important features of Hayek's thought is his notion of divided knowledge, which suggests that the knowledge on which social cooperation depends can never be united in only one person or group of persons. Consequently, Hayek insisted that in economics, the state ought to have limited authority, with social coordinating occurring as a result of freely operating prices.

Wilhelm Röpke complements Hayek's political thought in helpful ways; according to Röpke, the free market depends not only on structural conditions but also on necessary cultural conditions, without which the free market will not survive. Even as he agreed with Hayek in the main, insisting that free prices and property rights were a necessary condition of a "humane economy," his political thought was in important respects more sociological, more cultural, and more holistic. Hayek did not utterly neglect these matters, but where he mentioned them in passing, Röpke wrote whole books. In his most important volume, *A Humane Economy*, he explained how the vital things of life—things like family, art, friendship, community, religion, and the environment—make it possible to preserve the free market and a free society.

Both Hayek and Röpke influenced the politics of the twentieth century. The first was associated with the free market thought of the Austrian school of economics, the second with the "ordoliberal" tradition of the Freiburg school. Together, their writing shaped postwar politics in the United States, Great Britain, (West) Germany, and elsewhere. It is worth observing that conservatives who are skeptical of the principles described in this book often speak disparagingly of what they call the "post-war consensus" or "dead consensus" of the twentieth century, which among other things included free markets that lead to a "soulless society of individual affluence."[13] By contrast, Hayek and Röpke show that free markets are a necessary part of a free society and need not lead to "soulless" commercialism.

Some regard liberty, equal protection of the law, republican self-government, religious liberty, and free markets as remnants of a liberal world order that is passing away. The great political thinkers of the Anglo-American political tradition discussed in this book show that there is a reason why these principles are still with us. We should understand and preserve them in the years to come.

Acknowledgments

In various ways large and small, friends in the academy assisted through their willingness to help or to make suggestions during the writing of this book. A complete list of the names of those who listened to me talk about this book would be far too long, but a few people deserve mention here. Mark Hall read a draft of a portion of the manuscript and provided feedback. Jacob Wolf was a sounding board, helping me to think and to write more clearly. Matt Franck, Nick Higgins, Jason Jividen, Joshua McMullen, and David VanDrunen provided helpful suggestions or other support along the way. Eric Kasper reviewed the manuscript and provided expert suggestions and critique. Thanks also to a second anonymous reviewer, who provided thoughtful feedback that improved the manuscript. My editor Amy Farranto made me a better writer and provided warm support and incisive critique through the editorial process. Thanks to my teachers, Larry Arnhart, Michael Coulter, and Gary Glenn, who first introduced me to some of the names in the table of contents.

A small grant from the Acton Institute made it possible to write the two chapters in the book related to the free market, and Regent University kindly gave me a semester-length sabbatical in which I could finish the manuscript.

Most of all, thanks to my loving family. Joyce, Elias, and Simeon were understanding and supportive when I spent nights and weekends in the study finishing up this book.

Notes

Introduction

1. George Washington, "To the Ministers, Elders, Deacons, and Members of the Reformed German Congregation of New York," in *George Washington: A Collection*, ed. W. B. Allen (Indianapolis: Liberty Classics, 1988), 271.

2. George Washington, "To the Hebrew Congregation in Newport," in *George Washington: A Collection*, 548. For more on this motif in Washington's speeches, letters, and public writing, see Daniel L. Dreisbach, *Reading the Bible with the Founding Fathers* (New York: Oxford University Press, 2016).

3. Samuel Gregg, *Reason, Faith, and the Struggle for Western Civilization* (New York: Gateway Editions, 2019).

4. Friedrich Hayek, *The Constitution of Liberty* (Chicago: University of Chicago Press, 1960).

5. Russell Kirk, *The Conservative Mind: From Burke to Eliot*, 7th rev. ed. (New York: Gateway Editions, 2014).

6. See, e.g., Josh Abbotoy, "Is a Protestant Franco Inevitable?," *First Things*, October 2023, accessed March 21, 2025, https://www.firstthings.com/web-exclusives/2023/10/is-a-protestant-franco-inevitable; Michael Anton, *The Stakes: America at the Point of No Return* (Washington, DC: Regnery, 2020); and Patrick Deneen, *Regime Change: Toward a Postliberal Future* (New York: Sentinel 2023), and *Why Liberalism Failed* (New Haven, CT: Yale University Press, 2018).

7. Russell Kirk, *The American Cause* (Wilmington, DE: ISI Books, 2002), chap. 1.

8. Alexis de Tocqueville, *Democracy in America*, trans. Harvey C. Mansfield and Delba Winthrop (Chicago: University of Chicago Press, 2000), 15 ["Introduction"].

9. Harvey C. Mansfield and Delba Winthrop, introduction to *Democracy in America*, trans. Harvey C. Mansfield and Delba Winthrop (Chicago: University of Chicago Press, 2000), xvii.

10. A helpful explanation of this point appears in Peter J. Stanlis, *Edmund Burke and the Natural Law* (Shreveport, LA: Huntington House, 1986), 14–28.

11. Thomas Hobbes, *Leviathan* (New York: Penguin Books, 1985), II.17.

12. Aristotle, *Aristotle's "Politics,"* trans. Carnes Lord (Chicago: University of Chicago Press, 2013), 1253a.

13. Thucydides, *The Landmark Thucydides: A Comprehensive Guide to the Peloponnesian War*, ed. Robert B. Strassler (Washington, DC: Free Press, 1998), 3.82.4.

14. Paul Johnson, *Modern Times: The World from the Twenties to the Nineties* (New York: Harper Perennial, 2001), 110–111; Mark Lilla, *The Reckless Mind*

(New York: New York Review of Books, 2001), 49-58; and William L. Shirer, *The Rise and Fall of the Third Reich* (New York: Simon & Schuster, 1960), 150-187.

15. Aristotle, *Nicomachean Ethics*, trans. Robert C. Bartlett and Susan D. Collins (Chicago: University of Chicago Press, 2011), 1.3 [1094b20-1095a4].

16. J. S. Mill, *On Liberty* (Indianapolis, IN: Hackett, 1978), 16.

17. See Greg Lukianoff and Jonathan Haidt, *The Coddling of the American Mind: How Good Intentions and Bad Ideas Are Setting Up a Generation for Failure* (New York: Penguin, 2019), 114-121. For thoughtful treatments of the ideological sources of this phenomenon, see Roger Scruton, "The Threat of Free Speech in the University," *Modern Age: A Conservative Review* 59, no. 3 (Summer 2017): 7-15; and Carl Trueman, *The Rise and Triumph of the Modern Self: Cultural Amnesia, Expressive Individualism, and the Road to Sexual Revolution* (Wheaton, IL: Crossway, 2020).

18. An influential leading example of this thinking appears in Herbert Marcuse, "Repressive Tolerance," in *A Critique of Pure Tolerance*, ed. Robert Paul Wolff, Barrington Moore Jr., and Herbert Marcuse (Boston: Beacon Press, 1965), 81-117.

19. George Washington, "Speech to the Officers of the Army," in *George Washington: A Collection*, 219.

1. Brief Biographies

1. The treatment of Edmund Burke in his chapter is indebted to, among other sources: W. J. Bate, introduction to *Selected Writings of Edmund Burke*, ed. W. J. Bate (New York: Modern Library, 1960): 3-39; F. P. Lock, "Burke's Life," chap. 1 in *The Cambridge Companion to Edmund Burke*, ed. David Dwan and Christopher J. Insole (New York: Cambridge University Press, 2012): 15-26; and Peter Stanlis, "Burke, Edmund (1729-97)," in *American Conservatism: An Encyclopedia*, ed. Bruce Frohnen, Jeremy Beer, and Jeffrey O. Nelson (Wilmington, DE: ISI Books, 2006): 103-107.

2. My overview of Alexis de Tocqueville's thought in this chapter is indebted to Hugh Brogan, *Alexis de Tocqueville: A Life* (New Haven, CT: Yale University Press, 2008); Joseph Epstein, *Alexis de Tocqueville: Democracy's Guide* (New York: Eminent Lives, 2006); Harvey C. Mansfield and Delba Winthrop, editors' introduction to Alexis de Tocqueville, *Democracy in America*, trans. Harvey C. Mansfield and Delba Winthrop (Chicago: University of Chicago Press, 2000), xvii-lxxxix; and Daniel J. Mahoney, *The Statesman as Thinker: Portraits of Greatness, Courage, and Moderation* (New York: Encounter Books, 2022). For the "world altogether new" quote, see Tocqueville, *Democracy in America*, 7.

3. Richard Reeves, *American Journey: Traveling with Tocqueville in Search of Democracy in America* (New York: Simon & Schuster, 1983), 317.

4. Mahoney, *Statesman as Thinker*, 80.

5. Tocqueville, *Democracy in America*, 395-396.

6. Alexis de Tocqueville, *The Recollections of Alexis de Tocqueville* (London: Harvill Press, 1948), 10-14, 33.

7. Tocqueville, *Recollections*, 10.

8. Epstein, *Alexis de Tocqueville: Democracy's Guide*, 125.

9. Tocqueville, *Recollections*, 199-200.

10. Tocqueville, *Democracy in America*, 15.

11. Abraham Lincoln, "Letter to J. W. Fell, Inclosing Autobiography," in Abraham Lincoln, *The Language of Liberty: The Political Speeches and Writings of Abraham Lincoln*, ed. Joseph R. Fornieri (Washington, DC: Regnery, 2003), 543.

12. Allen C. Guelzo, *Abraham Lincoln: Redeemer President* (Grand Rapids, MI: Eerdmans, 1999), 35.

13. Abraham Lincoln, "Speech at New Haven," in Abraham Lincoln, *The Language of Liberty: The Political Speeches and Writings of Abraham Lincoln*, ed. Joseph R. Fornieri (Washington, DC: Regnery, 2003), 770.

14. Abraham Lincoln, "To the People of Sangamo County: Political Announcement," in Abraham Lincoln, *The Language of Liberty: The Political Speeches and Writings of Abraham Lincoln*, ed. Joseph R. Fornieri (Washington, DC: Regnery, 2003), 13.

15. Abraham Lincoln, "The Perpetuation of Our Political Institutes: Address Before the Young Men's Lyceum of Springfield, Illinois," in Abraham Lincoln, *The Language of Liberty: The Political Speeches and Writings of Abraham Lincoln*, ed. Joseph R. Fornieri (Washington, DC: Regnery, 2003), 31. Italics in original.

16. Lincoln, "To the People of Sangamo County," 13.

17. Abraham Lincoln, "Protest in Illinois Legislature on Slavery," in Abraham Lincoln, *The Language of Liberty: The Political Speeches and Writings of Abraham Lincoln*, ed. Joseph R. Fornieri (Washington, DC: Regnery, 2003), 22.

18. Abraham Lincoln, "Second Inaugural Address," in Abraham Lincoln, *The Language of Liberty: The Political Speeches and Writings of Abraham Lincoln*, ed. Joseph R. Fornieri (Washington, DC: Regnery, 2003), 795.

19. Abraham Lincoln, "Second Inaugural Address," 795.

20. Abraham Lincoln, "First Inaugural Address," in Abraham Lincoln, *The Language of Liberty: The Political Speeches and Writings of Abraham Lincoln*, ed. Joseph R. Fornieri (Washington, DC: Regnery, 2003), 574.

21. Forrest McDonald, *Novus Ordo Seclorum: The Intellectual Origins of the Constitution* (Lawrence: University Press of Kansas, 1985), 68.

22. Tony Williams, *Hamilton: An American Biography* (Lanham, MD: Rowman & Littlefield, 2018), 71–77.

23. Ron Chernow, *Alexander Hamilton* (New York: Penguin Books, 2004).

24. Williams, *Hamilton*, 1–7.

25. Williams, *Hamilton*, 13–14.

26. Chernow, *Alexander Hamilton*, 110–111.

27. Williams, *Hamilton*, 40–41.

28. Gordon S. Wood, *Revolutionary Characters: What Made the Founders Different* (New York: Penguin Books, 2006), 133.

29. Chernow, *Alexander Hamilton*, 708.

30. Douglass Adair, *Fame and the Founding Fathers: Essays by Douglass Adair*, ed., Trevor Colbourn (Indianapolis: Liberty Fund Press, 1998), 177.

31. Adair, *Fame and the Founding Fathers*, 179–181.

32. Wood, *Revolutionary Characters*, 144–145.

33. Adair, *Fame and the Founding Fathers*, 192.

34. Adair, *Fame and the Founding Fathers*, 193.

35. Alexander Hamilton and James Madison, *The Pacificus-Helvidius Debates of 1793–1794*, ed. Morton J. Frisch (Indianapolis: Liberty Fund Press, 2007).

36. Wood, *Revolutionary Characters*, 165.

37. Chernow, *Alexander Hamilton*, 424–427.

38. Jonathan Den Hartog, *Patriotism & Piety: Federalist Politics and Religious Struggle in the New American Nation* (Charlottesville: University of Virginia Press, 2015), 22–40.

39. John Jay, "Federalist No. 2," in *The Federalist*, ed. George W. Carey and James McClellan (Indianapolis: Liberty Fund Press, 2001), 6.

40. "Jay, John," in *The Oxford Companion to the Supreme Court of the United States*, ed. Kermit L. Hall (New York: Oxford University Press, 1992), 446–447.

41. Jeffry H. Morrison, *The Political Philosophy of George Washington* (Baltimore, MD: Johns Hopkins University Press, 2009), 3–17.

42. Morrison, *Political Philosophy*, 21–32.

43. Richard Brookhiser, *Founding Father: Rediscovering George Washington* (New York: Free Press, 1996), 103.

44. Many of the details about Washington's life in this section are taken variously from Brookhiser, *Founding Father*; Morrison, *Political Philosophy*; and Ron Chernow, *Washington: A Life* (New York: Penguin Books, 2011).

45. Many of the details about Hayek's life in what follows are taken from Bruce Caldwell, *Hayek's Challenge: An Intellectual Biography of F. A. Hayek* (Chicago: University of Chicago Press, 2004); and Nicholas Wapshott, *Keynes Hayek: The Clash That Defined Modern Economics* (New York: Norton, 2011).

46. Wilhelm Röpke, *The Solution to the German Problem* (New York: Putnam's, 1947), 48-49.

47. Röpke, *The Solution to the German Problem*, 6.

48. Samuel Gregg, *Wilhelm Röpke's Political Economy* (Cheltenham, England: Edward Elgar, 2010).

2. Edmund Burke and the Meaning of Liberty

1. Of relevance for this volume, George Washington was not one of those people. Washington wrote to Lafayette in 1788: "I like not much the situation of affairs in France. The bold demands of the parliaments, and the decisive tone of the King, shew that but little more irritation would be necessary to blow up the spark of discontent into a flame, that might not easily be quenched." Quoted in Jeffry H. Morrison, *The Political Philosophy of George Washington* (Baltimore: Johns Hopkins University Press, 2009), 44.

2. Edmund Burke, *Burke's Politics: Selected Writings and Speeches of Edmund Burke on Reform, Revolution, and War*, ed. Ross J. S. Hoffman and Paul Levack (New York: Knopf, 1959), 279.

3. Burke, *Burke's Politics*, 279.

4. Russell Kirk, *The American Cause* (Wilmington, DE: ISI Books, 2009), 52.

5. Edmund Burke, *Reflections on the Revolution in France*, vol. 1 of *Select Works of Edmund Burke*, ed. with foreword and introduction by E. J. Payne (Indianapolis: Liberty Fund, 1999), 172.

6. Burke, *Burke's Politics*, 279.

7. Patrick J. Deneen, *Why Liberalism Failed* (New Haven, CT: Yale University Press, 2018), 34–38.
8. Burke, *Reflections on the Revolution in France*, 92–93.
9. Samuel Gregg, *Reason, Faith, and the Struggle for Western Civilization* (Washington, DC: Regnery Gateway, 2019), 42–43.
10. Burke, *Reflections on the Revolution in France*, 171.
11. Burke, *Reflections on the Revolution in France*, 151–152.
12. Burke, *Reflections on the Revolution in France*, 93.
13. Burke, *Reflections on the Revolution in France*, 93–94. Emphasis in original.
14. Burke, *Reflections on the Revolution in France*, 93.
15. Burke, *Reflections on the Revolution in France*, 94.
16. Burke, *Reflections on the Revolution in France*, 94.
17. Burke, *Burke's Politics*, 279.
18. Burke, *Reflections on the Revolution in France*, 92–93.
19. Edmund Burke, *Letters on a Regicide Peace*, vol. 3 of *Select Works of Edmund Burke*, ed. with foreword and introduction by E. J. Payne (Indianapolis: Liberty Fund, 1999), 135.
20. Edmund Burke, "Letter to a Member of the National Assembly," quoted in Yuval Levin, "Edmund Burke's Economics of Flourishing," in *Economic Freedom and Human Flourishing: Perspectives from Political Philosophy*, ed. Michael R. Strain and Stan A. Veuger (Washington, DC: American Enterprise Institute, 2016), 87.
21. J. S. Mill, *On Liberty* (Indianapolis: Hackett, 1978).
22. As David Boaz writes, "The right of self-ownership certainly implies the right to decide for ourselves what food, drink, or drugs we will put into our own bodies; with whom we will make love (assuming our chosen partner agrees); and what kind of medical treatment we want (assuming a doctor agrees to provide it). These decisions are surely as personal and intimate as the choice of what to believe.... The role of government is to protect our rights, not to poke its nose into our personal lives." The basis of Mill's political ethics was not abstract right but utility, but his view of liberty appears, for example, in libertarian thought. See David Boaz, *Libertarianism: A Primer* (New York, Free Press, 1998), 79.
23. Barry Alan Shain, *The Myth of American Individualism: The Protestant Origins of American Political Thought* (Princeton, NJ: Princeton University Press, 1994), 3–47; Matthew Spalding, *We Still Hold These Truths: Rediscovering Our Principles, Reclaiming Our Future* (Wilmington, DE: ISI Books, 2009), 136–139.
24. George Washington, "Farewell Address," in *George Washington: A Collection*, ed. W. B. Allen (Indianapolis: Liberty Classics, 1998), 537.
25. John Adams, "From John Adams to Massachusetts Militia, 11 October, 1798," *Founders Online*, National Archives, accessed February 28, 2025, https://founders.archives.gov/documents/Adams/99-02-02-3102.
26. Mercy Otis Warren, *History of the Rise, Progress, and Termination of the American Revolution, interspersed with Biographical, Political and Moral Observations*, 2 vols., foreword by Lester H. Cohen (Indianapolis: Liberty Fund, 1994), chap. 30. Some decades later, Frederick Douglass would say something similar, saying in the 1880s that despite the discrimination they faced, southern Blacks must

"live industrious and virtuous lives, establish a character for sobriety, punctuality, and general uprightness," for "if we are vicious and lawless, the virtues and good behavior of others will not save us from our vices and our crimes." These things were necessary for the full enjoyment of liberty and, sounding a Lincolnian theme, "for an equal chance in the race of life." Quoted in Herbert J. Storing, "Frederick Douglass," in *American Political Thought: The Philosophic Dimension of American Statesmanship*, ed. Morton J. Frisch and Richard Stevens (New York: Scribner's, 1971), 162–163.

27. Plato, *The Republic of Plato*, trans. Allan Bloom (New York: Basic Book, 1968), 543a–580c.

28. Patrick J. Deneen, *Why Liberalism Failed* (New Haven and London: 2018), 23. In this, Deneen agrees with Leo Strauss and other commentators who regard some of the key texts of modern political philosophy to involve an author's dissimulation that conceals new content with old language. See Leo Strauss, "Persecution and the Art of Writing," *Social Research* 8, no. 1 (1941): 488–504.

29. Robert Bellah, Richard Madsen, William M. Sullivan, Ann Swidler, and Steven M. Tipton, *Habits of the Heart: Individualism and Commitment in American Life* (Berkeley: University of California Press, 2008), 48.

30. Peter J. Stanlis, *Edmund Burke and the Natural Law* (Shreveport, LA: Huntington House, 1986), 131.

31. A helpful summary of Jean-Jacques Rousseau's thought on human freedom appears in Carl Trueman, *The Rise and Triumph of the Modern Self: Cultural Amnesia, Expressive Individualism, and the Road to Sexual Revolution* (Wheaton, IL: Crossway Books, 2020), 105–128.

32. The National Assembly, from June 1789 to September 1791, consisted initially of the representatives of the Third Estate (commoners), which was the initial revolutionary assembly, and was followed by the Legislative Assembly.

33. Pierre Manent, *An Intellectual History of Liberalism*, trans. Rebecca Balinski (Princeton, NJ: Princeton University Press, 1995), 77. Emphasis in original.

34. What is sometimes regarded as an artifact of post-Nietzschean French thought therefore is best understood as beginning in Rousseau's Romantic turn. Many of the famous names of contemporary French thought—Jean-Paul Sartre, Michel Foucault, Jacques Derrida—stand not only in Nietzsche's but also in Rousseau's long shadow. "The destiny of man is placed within himself," said Sartre, because "life is nothing until it is lived." After all, "it is feeling that counts." For Sartre, all people have "free choice," but the person who disagrees with that free choice does not have the choice so to disagree; such a person deceives themself and should be condemned as having abdicated "complete liberty."

35. As Deneen observes, thinkers such as Rousseau as well as contemporary thinkers like him

> increasingly approve nearly any technical means of liberating humans from the biological nature of our own bodies. . . . Under liberalism, human beings increasingly live in a condition of autonomy in which the threatened anarchy of our purportedly natural condition is controlled and suppressed through the imposition of laws and the corresponding

growth of the state. With humanity liberated from constitutive communities (leaving only loose connections) and nature harnessed and controlled, the constructed sphere of autonomous liberty expands seemingly without limit.

See Deneen, *The End of Liberalism*, 37-38. This is related to, if not exactly the same as, the argument presented by Alexis de Tocqueville that democratic culture is effectively interchangeable with the concentration of state power due to a rudimentary democratic sense of fairness that militates against variety: If we are all equal in our pursuit of liberty, why should we not all be subject to the same laws emanating from a central, distant political capital? See Alexis de Tocqueville, *Democracy in America*, trans. Harvey C. Mansfield and Delba Winthrop (Chicago: University of Chicago Press, 2000), 639-650 [II.4.1-4].

Something similar is argued in Michael J. Sandel, "The Procedural Republic and the Unencumbered Self," *Political Theory* 12, no. 1 (1984): 93-94:

> Where liberty in the early republic was understood as a function of democratic institutions and dispersed power, liberty in the procedural republic is defined in opposition to democracy, as an individual's guarantee against what the majority might will. I am free insofar as I am the bearer of rights, where rights are trumps. Unlike the liberty of the early republic, the modern version permits—in fact even requires—concentrated power. This has to do with the universalizing logic of rights. Insofar as I have a right, whether to free speech or a minimum income, its provision cannot be left to the vagaries of local preferences but must be assured at the most comprehensive level of political association.

36. Planned Parenthood of Southeastern Pennsylvania v. Casey, 505 U.S. 833 (1992).

37. Obergefell v. Hodges, 576 U.S. 644 (2015).

38. Obergefell v. Hodges, 576 U.S. 644 (2015).

39. Dobbs v. Jackson Women's Health Organization, 597 U.S. (2022); the Supreme Court earlier affirmed "ordered liberty" in Palko v. Connecticut, 302 U.S. 319 (1937).

40. Quoted in Greg Weiner, *Old Whigs: Burke, Lincoln and the Politics of Prudence* (New York: Encounter Books, 2019), 102.

41. The most well-known presentation of the thesis that Burke's opposition to natural right shows a relativistic reliance on historical tradition appears in Leo Strauss, *Natural Right and History* (Chicago: University of Chicago Press, 1965), 294-323; Strauss emphasized Burke's reliance on history and tradition and suggested that Burke did not see in reason the ability to appeal to some theoretical principle that could guide the development of that tradition. Similarly, Richard Weaver argued that Burke spurned theory and used only "argument from circumstance"; see Richard M. Weaver, *The Ethics of Rhetoric* (Chicago: Regnery, 1953), 57. Similarly, Morton J. Frisch argued that Burke believed that reason was neither necessary nor competent to guide to politics; see Morton J. Frisch, "Burke on Theory," *The Cambridge Journal* 7, no. 5, (1954):

3-8; and Morton J. Frisch, "Rational Planning Versus Unplanned Becoming," *The Classical Journal* 47, no. 7 (1952): 288-290.

However, Steven J. Lenzner argues persuasively that Strauss's treatment of Burke in *Natural Right and History* is not what it at first seems. According to Lenzner, Strauss was writing his book for a semigeneral readership and when read carefully, the book shows that Strauss did in fact think that Burke did have a solid, rational, and theoretical basis for judging the development of history but that he made it seem as if he did not, since he did not think that Burke was the best source on which to rely for "staving off the crisis of the west"; see Steven J. Lenzner, "Strauss's Three Burkes: The Problem of Edmund Burke in Natural Right and History," *Political Theory* 19, no. 3 (1991): 377. Assuming this to be an accurate exposition of Strauss's commentary on Burke, then Strauss effectively sided with Peter Stanlis in arguing that Burke was in fact an exponent of traditional law rooted in reason and universal moral truths and a fierce critic of modern natural right, which he regarded as little more than a restatement of ancient philosophic hedonism rooted in individual will; see Stanlis, *Edmund Burke and the Natural Law*; and Peter J. Stanlis, "The Basis of Burke's Political Conservatism," *Modern Age* 5, no. 3 (Summer 1961): 263-274. This is also the view in Weiner, *Old Whigs*.

42. Burke, *Reflections on the Revolution in France*, 154.

43. Burke, *Burke's Politics*, 58.

44. Burke, *Reflections on the Revolution in France*, 150.

45. Russell Kirk, *The Conservative Mind: From Burke to Eliot*, 7th rev. ed. (New York: Gateway Editions, 2014), 48.

46. Mary Ann Glendon, *Rights Talk: The Impoverishment of Political Discourse* (New York: Free Press, 1993).

47. Quoted in Weiner, *Old Whigs*, 96.

48. Burke, *Reflections on the Revolution in France*, 153.

49. Burke, *Reflections on the Revolution in France*, 152.

50. Jean-Jacques Rousseau, *Basic Political Writings* (Indianapolis: Hackett, 1987), 141. These are the famous opening words of Rousseau's *On the Social Contract*.

51. Jean-Jacques Rousseau, *Discourse on the Origin of Inequality* in *The Basic Political Writings*, trans. Donald A. Cress (Indianapolis and Cambridge: Hackett Publishing, 1987), 38.

52. Thomas Hobbes, *The Leviathan* (Penguin Books, 1985), chap. 13 [186].

53. Rousseau, *Discourse on the Origin of Inequality*, part 1, 40.

54. Rousseau, *Discourse on the Origin of Inequality*, part 1, 45.

55. Rousseau, *Discourse on the Origin of Inequality*, part 1, 47, 52.

56. Rousseau, *Discourse on the Origin of Inequality*, part 1, 53.

57. Rousseau, *Discourse on the Origin of Inequality*, part 1, 53-55.

58. Rousseau, *Discourse on the Origin of Inequality*, part 2, 60: "The first person who, having enclosed a plot of land, took it into his head to say *this is mine* and found people simple enough to believe him, was the true founder of society."

59. Trueman, *Rise and Triumph of the Modern Self*, 107-128.

60. Eric Voegelin, in his seminal essay "Ersatz Religion," argues that such indictment of the structure of the world and acquittal of human nature is

inherent in modern radical political movements that (attempt to) serve the function of a religion for people who have jettisoned religion. See Eric Voegelin, *Science, Politics and Gnosticism* (Wilmington, DE: ISI Books, 2004), 64-65.

61. Edmund Burke, "Tracts on the Popery Laws," quoted in Kirk, *The Conservative Mind*, 36.

62. Quoted in Daniel J. Mahony, *Aleksandr Solzhenitsyn: Ascent from Ideology* (Lanham, MD: Rowman & Littlefield, 2001), 50.

63. Burke, *Reflections on the Revolution in France*, 136

64. Levin, "Edmund Burke's Economics of Flourishing," 87.

65. As just a few examples of the literature on this topic, see Charles Murray, *Coming Apart: The State of White America, 1960–2010* (New York: Crown Forum, 2013), 153-171; Nick Schulz, *Home Economics: The Consequences of Changing Family Structure* (Washington, DC: AEI Press, 2013); and James Q. Wilson, *The Marriage Problem: How Our Culture Has Weakened Families* (New York: Harper, 2003).

66. Burke, *Reflections on the Revolution in France*, 136-137.

67. Burke, *Reflections on the Revolution in France*, 307.

68. Burke, *Reflections on the Revolution in France*, 147

69. Burke, *Burke's Politics*, 387.

70. For an informative account of Rousseau's life and work, see Paul Johnson, *Intellectuals* (New York: Harper & Row, 1988), 1-27; cf. Burke, *Burke's Politics*, 387.

71. Burke, *Reflections on the Revolution in France*, 171

72. Weiner writes that "the moral imagination is among the most complicated ideas in the Burkean corpus. It refers partly to a capacity to project oneself into the sufferings and situations of others, but it is far richer than empathy. Its association with mystery is suggested by the fact that it supplies a 'decent drapery of life,' one that covers the sharper edges of political and social life and is to be 'torn off' by the harsh edges of rationalism. . . . The key feature of moral imagination was that, especially as reason underlay it, drew people closer together, whereas speculative politics led to abstractions that caused people not only to spurn sympathy but actively to turn on one another"; see Weiner, *Old Whigs*, 68. One could think of any number of examples in modern political life.

73. Burke, *Reflections on the Revolution in France*, 181.

74. Burke, *Burke's Politics*, 279.

75. Weiner, *Old Whigs*, 11-12.

76. Quoted in Weiner, *Old Whigs*, 5.

77. Burke, *Reflections on the Revolution in France*, 182.

78. Edmund Burke, *Miscellaneous Writings*, vol. 4 of *Select Works of Edmund Burke*, ed. with foreword and select bibliography by Francis Canavan (Indianapolis: Liberty Fund, 1999), 21.

79. Burke, *Reflections on the Revolution in France*, 193.

80. Burke, *Reflections on the Revolution in France*, 192-193.

81. Burke, *Reflections on the Revolution in France*, 115.

82. Quoted in Stanlis, *Burke and the Natural Law*, 128.

83. As Weiner shows, Burke did appeal to natural justice, which he argued could be seen in the despoiling of property and in the repugnance that blatant

acts of tyranny present to human moral sensibility in the case of Warren Hastings's treatment of Indians; see Weiner, *Old Whigs*, 107–110.

84. Quoted in Weiner, *Old Whigs*, 105
85. Burke, *Reflections on the Revolution in France*, 143.
86. Burke, *Burke's Politics*, 280.
87. Weiner, *Old Whigs*, 1–10.

3. Alexis de Tocqueville and the Meaning of Equality

1. Alexis de Tocqueville, *Democracy in America*, trans. Harvey C. Mansfield and Delba Winthrop (Chicago: University of Chicago Press, 2000), 414 [II.1.3].
2. Tocqueville, *Democracy in America,*, 414 [II.1.3]. Tocqueville observed that American writers may often wish to distinguish themselves from the vulgar, but they scarcely succeed, their prose consisting of "a sort of aristocratic jargon that is scarcely less distant from beautiful language than the patois of the people"; see Tocqueville, *Democracy in America*, 447 [II.1.13].
3. Tocqueville, *Democracy in America*, 454–457 [II.1.16].
4. Tocqueville, *Democracy in America*, 447–449 [II.1.13].
5. Tocqueville, *Democracy in America*, 535 [II.3.1].
6. Tocqueville, *Democracy in America*, 411–415 [II.1.3].
7. Tocqueville, *Democracy in America*, 538 [II.3.1].
8. Tocqueville, *Democracy in America*, 513–514 [II.2.13].
9. Harvey C. Mansfield and Delba Winthrop, eds., editor's introduction to Tocqueville, *Democracy in America*, xvii.
10. Among the voluminous material available on the life and thought of Tocqueville, I suggest as an enjoyable, brief intellectual biography: Joseph Epstein, *Alexis de Tocqueville: Democracy's Guide* (New York: Harper Perennial, 2009). For a lengthy, scholarly account of Tocqueville's life, although one that in my estimation does not always capture the power and subtlety of Tocqueville's thought, see Hugh Brogan, *Alexis de Tocqueville: A Life* (New Haven, CT: Yale University Press, 2007). For a well-respected treatment of Tocqueville's magnum opus, see James T. Schleifer, *The Making of Tocqueville's "Democracy in America"* (Indianapolis: Liberty Fund Press, 2000). For a very dense but rewarding examination of Tocqueville's understanding of modern democracy, see Pierre Manent, *Tocqueville and the Nature of Democracy*, trans. John Waggoner (Lanham, MD: Rowman & Littlefield, 1996).
11. Tocqueville, *Democracy in America*, 3 ["Introduction"].
12. See, e.g., Tocqueville's discussion of the introduction of slavery into the English colony of Virginia in the early seventeenth century. Unlike the spirit of local self-government that appeared from the beginning at Plymouth and spread from New England throughout the Anglo-American colonies, the introduction of slavery in Virginia spread to a great extent but never became part of the law and spirit of the rest of America. For Tocqueville, America began in 1620 at Plymouth and not with Virginian slavery in 1619. See Tocqueville, *Democracy in America*, 30–31 [I.1.2].
13. Tocqueville, *Democracy in America*, 3–5 ["Introduction"].
14. Tocqueville, *Democracy in America*, 6 ["Introduction"].

15. Tocqueville, *Democracy in America*, 7 ["Introduction"].
16. The sociologist Raymond Aron noted that it was largely Tocqueville's more accurate and persuasive description of the modern world that accounted for the rediscovery and resurgence of Tocqueville scholarship during the Cold War; see Raymond Aron, "Tocqueville Retrouvé," *The Tocqueville Review* 1, no. 1 (1979): 8–23, https://doi.org/10.3138/ttr.1.1.8.
17. Tocqueville, *Democracy in America*, 666 [II.4.7].
18. Tocqueville, *Democracy in America*, 6 ["Introduction"].
19. Tocqueville, *Democracy in America*, 7 ["Introduction"].
20. Tocqueville, *Democracy in America*, 482, 482–484 [II.2.2].
21. Tocqueville, *Democracy in America*, 480–481 [II.2.1]; cf. 57 [I.1.5]. To better understand the claim that one more easily perceives the benefits of equality than of freedom, it may be helpful to turn briefly to another nineteenth-century French thinker who made a similar point by providing a more concrete example. In Frederic Bastiat's "What Is Seen and What Is Not Seen," the author explained a broken window's impact on economic well-being. If one breaks a window, it is easy to see that a glassmaker gets more work. This means that breaking a window is good, right? War, then, which involves breaking a good many windows, must be particularly good for poor people looking for work. On the contrary, Bastiat invited us to look not only at "what is seen"—the broken window—but also what is unseen. The glassmaker got a job, but the window-owner lost money fixing the window and now has less money to spend on various other things that will help him and many others in need of work. One must look not only at the obvious but also at the less obvious and less immediate. At the most basic level of public policy, one might think of minimum wage laws as a practical manifestation of Bastiat's illustration. These laws achieve greater equality, right? Well, sort of. Certain people end up getting more money for their labor. However, nearly all economists regardless of ideological commitment agree that the chief result of increasing the minimum wage is a corresponding increase in unemployment. Why? Because minimum wage laws effectively make it illegal to hire people whose labor is worth less than the minimum wage. Moreover, most businesses do not have significant excess profits; they are not paying workers more because they cannot, not because they are greedy. When the price goes up, more workers lose jobs than get raises. One could find any number of additional policy examples to illustrate this point. See Frederic Bastiat, *Economic Sophisms and "What Is Seen and What Is Not Seen"* (Indianapolis: Liberty Fund, 2016), 405–407.
22. Tocqueville, *Democracy in America*, 52 [I.1.3].
23. Tocqueville, *Democracy in America*, 52 [I.1.3].
24. Tocqueville, *Democracy in America*, 481 [II.2.1].
25. Tocqueville, *Democracy in America*, 6 ["Introduction"].
26. For a good discussion of the relationship between liberty and Christian anthropology, see Samuel Gregg, *Reason, Faith, and the Struggle for Western Civilization* (Washington, DC: Regnery Gateway, 2019), 23–51.
27. Tocqueville, *Democracy in America*, 11 ["Introduction"].
28. Tocqueville, *Democracy in America*, 673–675 [II.4.8].

29. Jean Pierre Royer-Collard, one of Tocqueville's contemporaries, remarked after reading *Democracy in America* that "to find a work to compare it with, you have to go back to Aristotle's *Politics*"; see Mansfield and Winthrop, editor's introduction to *Democracy in America*, xxxiii.

30. Aristotle, *The Politics*, trans. Carnes Lord (Chicago: University of Chicago Press, 1984), 1313a–1313b.

31. Herodotus, *The Histories*, trans. George Rawlinson, in *Great Books of the Western World*, vol. 6, *Herodotus, Thucydides* (Chicago: Encyclopedia Britannica, 1952), 179 [V.92].

32. Tocqueville, *Democracy in America*, 482 [II.2.2].

33. Tocqueville, *Democracy in America*, 413 [II.1.3], 483 [II.2.2], and 490 [II.2.5].

34. Tocqueville, *Democracy in America*, 485 [II.2.4].

35. Alexis de Tocqueville, *The Recollections of Alexis de Tocqueville*, ed. J. P. Mayer, trans. Alexander Teizeira de Mattos (London: Harvill Press, 1948), chap. 2.

36. Tocqueville, *Democracy in America*, 507 [II.2.10]. Tocqueville helpfully observed on a number of occasions that one of the primary reasons for this was the equality-inducing change in estate and inheritance law in the modern democratic world. Wealth is much more likely to flow between families when wealth is not bound up in the land or in land-related social statuses.

37. Aristotle, *The Politics*, 1314a15–23.

38. Tocqueville, *Democracy in America*, 601 [II.3.19].

39. Tocqueville, *Democracy in America*, 509 [II.2.11].

40. Tocqueville, *Democracy in America*, 511–514 [II.2.13].

41. Tocqueville, *Democracy in America*, 519 [II.2.15].

42. Tocqueville, *Democracy in America*, 282 [I.2.9].

43. Tocqueville, *Democracy in America*, 521 [II.2.15].

44. James Bryce, *The Predictions of Hamilton and Tocqueville* (Baltimore: Johns Hopkins University Press, 1887).

45. Theodore Roosevelt, "Introduction," in *Majority Rule and the Judiciary: An Examination of Current Proposals for Constitutional Change Affecting the Reflections of Courts to Legislation* (New York: Scribner's, 1912), 21–22.

46. Tocqueville, *Democracy in America*, 240 [I.2.7].

47. Tocqueville, *Democracy in America*, 454–457 [II.1.16].

48. Tocqueville, *Democracy in America*, 244 [I.2.7].

49. Tocqueville, *Democracy in America*, 236–237 [I.2.7]

50. Immanuel Kant, "What Is Enlightenment?," in *The Portable Enlightenment Reader*, ed. Isaac Kramnick (London: Penguin Classics, 1995), 1.

51. Tocqueville, *Democracy in America*, 409 [II.1.2].

52. Tocqueville, *Democracy in America*, 409 [II.1.2]. To understand Tocqueville's teaching on the tyranny of the majority completely, one must consult not only the portions from volume 1 on that topic but also those from volume 2, part 1, which is titled "Influence of Democracy on Intellectual Movement in the United States," and from which this extended block quote is taken.

53. Tocqueville, *Democracy in America*, 237 [I.2.7].

54. Consider, e.g., the following selections from Tocqueville, *Democracy in America*, 278–280 [II.2.9]: "It is permissible to think that a certain number of Americans follow their habits more than their convictions in the worship they

render to God"; "Among the Anglo-Americans, some profess Christian dogmas because they believe them, others because they are afraid of not looking like they believe them"; and "I do not know if all Americans have faith in their religion—for who can read to the bottom of hearts?—but I am sure that they believe it necessary to the maintenance of republican institutions." Later in the book, Tocqueville explained more plainly that "dogmatic beliefs are more or less numerous according to the times. They are born in different manners and can change form and object; but one cannot make it so that there are no dogmatic beliefs, that is, opinions men receive on trust without discussing them"; see Tocqueville, *Democracy in America*, 407 [II.1.2].

55. Tocqueville, *Democracy in America*, 250-251 [I.2.8].
56. Tocqueville, *Democracy in America*, 662-663 [II.4.6].
57. Tocqueville, *Democracy in America*, 644 [II.4.3].
58. Tocqueville, *Democracy in America*, 662-663 [II.4.6].
59. Tocqueville, *Democracy in America*, 663 [II.4.6].
60. This phenomenon was observed thoughtfully in Ben Sasse, *The Vanishing American Adult: Our Coming of Age Crisis and How to Rebuild a Culture of Self-Reliance* (New York: St. Martin's Press, 2017).
61. Tocqueville, *Democracy in America*, 88 [I.1.5].
62. See, e.g., Matthew Spalding, *We Still Hold These Truths: Rediscovering Our Principles, Reclaiming Our Future* (Wilmington, DE: ISI Books, 2009), 217-219; and Samuel Gregg, *Becoming Europe: Economic Decline, Culture, and How America Can Avoid a European Future* (New York: Encounter Books, 2013).
63. Alexis de Tocqueville, *"Memoirs on Pauperism" and Other Writings: Poverty, Public Welfare, and Inequality*, trans. Christine Dunn Henderson (South Bend, IN: University of Notre Dame Press, 2021), 18-20.
64. Tocqueville, *Democracy in America*, 645, 412-413.
65. Tocqueville, *Democracy in America*, 645 [II.4.3].
66. Tocqueville, *Democracy in America*, 489 [II.2.5].
67. Tocqueville, *Democracy in America*, 642 [II.4.2].
68. Tocqueville, *Democracy in America*, 652 [II.4.5].
69. Tocqueville, *Democracy in America*, 544 [II.3.4].
70. Tocqueville, *Democracy in America*, 666-673 [II 4.7].
71. Tocqueville, *Democracy in America*, 667-668 [II 4.7].
72. Tocqueville, *Democracy in America*, 666 [II.4.7].
73. Tocqueville, *Democracy in America*, 667 [II.4.7].
74. Tocqueville, *Democracy in America*, 667 [II.4.7].
75. Tocqueville, *Democracy in America*, 65 [I.1.5].
76. Tocqueville, *Democracy in America*, 665 [II.4.6].

4. Abraham Lincoln and the American Republic

1. Walter Berns, *Making Patriots* (Chicago: University of Chicago Press, 2001), 88.
2. Berns, *Making Patriots*, 89-90.
3. Stephen F. Knott, *The Lost Soul of the American Presidency: The Decline into Demagoguery and the Prospects for Renewal* (Lawrence: University Press of Kansas, 2019), 92.

4. Abraham Lincoln, "Speech at Peoria," in *The Language of Liberty: The Political Speeches and Writings of Abraham Lincoln*, ed. Joseph R. Fornieri (Washington, DC: Regnery, 2003), 153.

5. Abraham Lincoln, "Fifth Lincoln-Douglas Debate," in *The American Republic: Primary Sources*, ed. Bruce Frohnen (Indianapolis: Liberty Fund Press, 2002), 712.

6. Abraham Lincoln, "The Dred Scott Decision: Speech."

7. Abraham Lincoln, "Gettysburg Address," in *The American Nation: Primary Sources*, ed. Bruce Frohnen (Indianapolis: Liberty Fund Press, 2008), 56.

8. Abraham Lincoln, "Emancipation Proclamation," in *The American Nation*, 55.

9. Abraham Lincoln, "First Inaugural Address," in *The American Nation*, 38.

10. Abraham Lincoln, "Second Inaugural Address," in *The American Nation*, 82.

11. Alexander Stephens, "Cornerstone Speech," in *American Political Rhetoric: Essential Speeches and Writings*, 7th ed., ed. Peter Augustine Lawler and Robert Martin Schaefer (Lanham, MD: Rowman & Littlefield, 2015), 218.

12. Lincoln, "The Dred Scott Decision," 204.

13. Lincoln, "Speech at Peoria," 168. Emphasis in original.

14. Lincoln, "The Dred Scott Decision," 204-205. Emphasis in original.

15. Jason Jividen, *Claiming Lincoln: Progressivism, Equality, and the Battle for Lincoln's Legacy in Presidential Rhetoric* (DeKalb: Northern Illinois University Press, 2011), 3-32.

16. The seminal statement of this view appears in Willmoore Kendall and George W. Carey, *The Basic Symbols of the American Political Tradition* (Baton Rouge: Louisiana State University Press, 1970). For a helpful review of the literature and of the limits of this view, see Jividen, *Claiming Lincoln*, 3-32.

17. Lincoln, "First Inaugural Address."

18. Abraham Lincoln, "Speech in Reply to Douglas at Chicago, Illinois," in *The Language of Liberty*, 231.

19. Abraham Lincoln, "Gettysburg Address," in *The Language of Liberty*, 671.

20. Alexander Hamilton, "Federalist No. 1," in *The Federalist*, ed. Jacob E. Cooke (Hanover, NH: Wesleyan University Press, 1961), 3.

21. Lucas E. Morel, *Lincoln and the American Founding* (Carbondale: Southern Illinois University Press, 2020), 13.

22. Lincoln, "First Inaugural Address," 37-38.

23. Lincoln, "First Inaugural Address," 36.

24. Lincoln, "First Inaugural Address," 37.

25. Morel, *Lincoln and the American Founding*, 86.

26. Abraham Lincoln, "Message to Congress in Special Session," in *The American Nation*, 587-588.

27. Quoted in Greg Weiner, *Old Whigs*, 48.

28. Lincoln, "First Inaugural Address," 37.

29. Abraham Lincoln, "To George B. Ide, James R. Doolittle, and A. Hubbell," in *The Language of Liberty*, 790. Emphasis in original.

30. Lincoln, "Second Inaugural Address," 795. See also Abraham Lincoln, "Story Written for Noah Brooks," in *The American Nation*, 793: "I am not much of a judge of religion, but . . . in my opinion, the religion that sets men to rebel and fight against their government, because, as they think, that government

does not sufficiently help *some* men to eat their bread on the sweat of *other* men's faces, is not the sort of religion upon which people can get to heaven."

31. Abraham Lincoln, "Address to the Wisconsin State Agricultural Society," in *The American Republic*, 526.

32. Lincoln, "Speech in Reply to Douglas," 226.

33. Lincoln, "Speech in Reply to Douglas," 232.

34. Abraham Lincoln, "Speech at Cincinnati, Ohio," quoted in Greg Weiner, *Old Whigs: Burke, Lincoln & the Politics of Prudence* (New York: Encounter Books, 2019). 129.

35. Lincoln, "Message to Congress in Special Session," 46.

36. Abraham Lincoln, "Speech at New Haven," in *The Language of Liberty*, 770.

37. Lincoln, "Speech at New Haven," 771.

38. James Madison, Federalist No. 10, in *The Federalist*, 58.

39. Lincoln, "Speech at New Haven," 770.

40. Jividen, *Claiming Lincoln*, 23.

41. Jividen, *Claiming Lincoln*, 134–153.

42. As noted previously, the seminal statement of this view appears in Kendall and Carey, *The Basic Symbols of the American Political Tradition*. For a helpful review of the literature and of the limits of this view, see Jividen, *Claiming Lincoln*, 3–32.

43. See, e.g., Thomas J. DiLorenzo, *The Real Lincoln: A New Look at Abraham Lincoln, His Agenda, and an Unnecessary War* (New York: Three Rivers Press, 2003).

44. Abraham Lincoln, "Letter to Horace Greeley," in *The Language of Liberty*, 617. Emphasis in original

45. Lincoln, "Letter to Horace Greeley," 618. Emphasis in original.

46. Morel, *Lincoln and the American Founding*, 81.

47. James Oakes, *The Radical and the Republican: Frederick Douglass, Abraham Lincoln, and the Triumph of Antislavery Politics* (New York: Norton, 2007), 42; Abraham Lincoln, "Protest in Illinois Legislature on Slavery," in *The Language of Liberty*, 22.

48. Joseph R. Fornieri, ed., *The Language of Liberty: The Political Speeches and Writings of Abraham Lincoln* (Washington, DC: Regnery, 2003), 22; Lincoln, "Speech in Reply to Douglas," 224.

49. Morel, *Lincoln and the American Founding*, 81.

50. For helpful explanations of the virtue of prudence in Lincoln's statesmanship, see Jividen, *Claiming Lincoln*, 24–29; and Weiner, *Old Whigs*, 1–10, 31–51.

51. Lincoln, "Speech at Peoria," 158.

52. Weiner, *Old Whigs*, 32.

53. Weiner, *Old Whigs*, 43. Emphasis Lincoln's.

54. Frederick Douglass, "Oration in Memory of Abraham Lincoln," in *American Political Rhetoric: A Reader*, 5th ed., ed. Peter Augustine Lawler and Robert Martin Schaeffer (Lanham, MD: Rowman & Littlefield, 2005), 256–257.

55. Lincoln, "Speech at New Haven," 765.

56. Weiner also observes that Lincoln "sought to turn popular sovereignty against itself by showing that allowing some people to make slaves of others was not an exercise but rather a repudiation of popular sovereignty." See Weiner, *Old Whigs*, 126–127.

57. Abraham Lincoln, "The Repeal of the Missouri Compromise and the Propriety of Its Restoration: Speech at Peoria, Illinois, in Reply to Senator Douglas," in *The Language of Liberty*, 153. Emphasis in original.

58. Lincoln, "Speech in Reply to Douglas," 225.

59. Knott, *The Lost Soul of the American Presidency*, 78-79.

60. Lincoln, "Speech at Peoria," 153.

61. "Northwest Ordinance," in *The American Republic: Primary Sources*, ed. Bruce Frohnen (Indianapolis: Liberty Fund, 2002), 228.

62. Lincoln, "Address at Cooper Institute," 547.

63. Lincoln, "Address at Cooper Institute," 548-549.

64. Lincoln, "Address at Cooper Institute," 550.

65. Lincoln, "Speech at Peoria," 158.

66. Lincoln, "Speech at Peoria," 166.

67. Lincoln, "Speech at Peoria," 166-167.

68. This is Lincoln's almost exact rendering of Douglas's words from an 1858 speech in Memphis.

69. Lincoln, "Speech at New Haven," 766-767.

70. Lincoln, "Speech at Peoria," 167.

71. Weiner, *Old Whigs*, 118.

72. Lincoln, "Speech in Reply to Douglas," 231.

73. Lincoln, "Speech in Reply to Douglas," 231.

74. Lincoln, "Speech in Reply to Douglas," 231.

75. Lincoln, "Speech in Reply to Douglas," 232.

5. The Federalist Papers and the US Constitution

1. Sanford Levinson, *Our Undemocratic Constitution: Where the Constitution Goes Wrong (and How We the People Can Correct It)* (New York: Oxford University Press, 2008).

2. Levinson, *Our Undemocratic Constitution*, 6.

3. *The Federalist*, ed. Jacob E. Cooke (Hanover, NH: Wesleyan University Press, 1961), Federalist No. 1 [p. 3].

4. Matthew Spalding, *We Still Hold These Truths: Rediscovering Our Principles, Reclaiming Our Future* (Wilmington, DE: ISI Books, 2009), 148.

5. Randy E. Barnett, *Our Republican Constitution: Securing the Liberty and Sovereignty of We the People* (New York: Broadside Books, 2016), 70-71. Barnett points out that another member of the Committee of Detail, Edmund Randolph, successfully argued before the Supreme Court in 1793 in the case of Chisholm v. Georgia 2 U.S. 419 (1793) that citizens could sue state governments because sovereignty rests with the American people.

6. Barnett, *Our Republican Constitution*, 63-64. Barnett also helpfully observes that the language of the Tenth Amendment ("The powers not delegated to the United States by the Constitution, nor prohibited to it by the states, are reserved to the states respectively, or to the people") and the language of the Nineth Amendment ("Rights ... Retained by the People") assume popular sovereignty.

7. Joseph Story similarly observes that the Constitution may not be understood as a "compact" between "the distinct people of a *particular state* with the

people of the other states." Instead, "The language is, 'We, the people of the United States, do *ordain* and *establish* this *constitution* for the United States of America.'" See Joseph Story, *Commentaries on the Constitution of the United States: With a Preliminary Review of the Constitutional History of the Colonies and States, Before the Adoption of the Constitution*, vol. 2 (Boston: Hilliard, Gray, 1833), 118 [sec. 153].

8. Chisholm v. Georgia, 2 U.S. 419 (1793).
9. Federalist No. 37 [235].
10. Federalist No. 46 [315].
11. Federalist No. 78 [525].
12. Federalist No. 22 [146]; emphasis in original.
13. Federalist No. 1 [3]; emphasis mine; cf. Federalist No. 38 [239].
14. Federalist No. 33 [206].
15. This is a faithful summary of a somewhat tricky means of popular proposal and ratification of the US Constitution's Article V, which reads in part, "The Congress, whenever two thirds of both Houses shall deem it necessary, shall propose Amendments to this Constitution, or, on the Application of the Legislatures of two thirds of the several States, shall call a Convention for proposing Amendments, which, in either Case, shall be valid to all Intents and Purposes, as Part of this Constitution, when ratified by the Legislatures of three fourths of the several States, or by Conventions in three fourths thereof, as the one or the other Mode of Ratification may be proposed by the Congress."
16. Forrest McDonald observes that Beard himself stated publicly that the primary motivation for his book *An Economic Interpretation of the Constitution* was to contribute to the progressive movement, which generally viewed the Constitution as an obstacle to social and economic progress. See Forrest McDonald, *We the People: The Economic Origins of the Constitution* (London: Routledge, 2017), xxi–xxii.
17. Alan Gibson, *Interpreting the Founding: Guide to the Enduring Debates over the Origins and Foundations of the American Republic* (Lawrence: University Press of Kansas, 2010), 89.
18. McDonald, *We the People*.
19. Martin Diamond, "Democracy and *The Federalist*: A Reconsideration of the Framers' Intent," *American Political Science Review* 53, no. 1 (March 1959): 53–56.
20. Diamond, "Democracy and *The Federalist*," 56–57.
21. Gibson, *Interpreting the Founding*, 7–8.
22. See, e.g., Aristotle's *Ethics*, book 1.
23. Federalist No. 55 [374].
24. Federalist No. 51 [352]; Federalist No. 10 [58].
25. Reynolds v. Sims, 377 U.S. 533 (1964).
26. Federalist No. 10 [61].
27. Woodrow Wilson, *Congressional Government: A Study in American Politics* (Boston: Houghton Mifflin, 1885).
28. J. Allen Smith, *The Spirit of American Government: A Study of the Constitution: Its Origin, Influence and Relation to Democracy* (London: MacMillan, 1907), 9.
29. Federalist 47 [331]; Federalist No. 51; cf. Federalist No. 63 [430–431].

30. Federalist 51 [349].
31. Federalist 10 [61].
32. Federalist 10 [58].
33. Federalist 55 [378]; Federalist 10 [60–61].
34. Federalist 55 [374].
35. Federalist 10 [62].
36. Martin Diamond, "The Declaration and the Constitution," *The Public Interest*, no. 41 (Fall 1975): 52. Emphasis in original.
37. Federalist 48 [333–334].
38. Federalist 51 [350].
39. Federalist 51 [350].
40. Federalist 78 [525–527].
41. Federalist 63 [425].
42. Federalist 48 [333].
43. James Madison, "Vices of the Political System of the United States," in *The Founders' Constitution*, ed. Philip B. Kurland and Ralph Lerner (Indianapolis: Liberty Fund Press, 2000), chap. 5, doc. 16.
44. Greg Weiner, *Madison's Metronome: The Constitution, Majority Rule, and the Tempo of American Politics* (Lawrence: University Press of Kansas, 2012), 1.
45. Weiner, *Madison's Metronome*, 4.
46. Federalist No. 37 [235]; Federalist 10 [62]. It may be worth noting here that Madison's definition of the word *republic* was quite new. In most of the history of political thought, *republic* was somewhat ambiguous, only signifying some kind of government that was not ruled by a king, prince, or some executive howsoever titled. For a more microscopic look at the development of the word *republic* in the years of the American founding, see Donald S. Lutz, *Popular Consent and Popular Control: Whig Political Theory in the Early State Constitutions* (Baton Rouge: Louisiana State University Press, 1980), 1–22.
47. Federalist 10 [64].
48. Federalist 10 [57, 61].
49. Alexander Stephens, "Cornerstone Speech," in *American Political Rhetoric: Essential Speeches and Writings*, 7th ed., ed. Peter Augustine Lawler and Robert Martin Schaefer (Lanham, MD: Rowman & Littlefield, 2016), 218.
50. My evidence in this paragraph is indebted to Thomas G. West, *Vindicating the Founders: Race, Sex, Class and Justice in the Origins of America* (Lanham, MD: Rowman & Littlefield, 2001), 14–19.
51. Federalist 40 [262]; Federalist 39 [250]; Federalist 43 [298].
52. Federalist No. 42 [281–282].
53. Federalist No. 54 [367–368].
54. Jason Ross, "William Lloyd Garrison's Shattered Faith in Antislavery Constitutionalism: The Origins and Limits of the 'Garrisonian Critique,'" *American Political Thought* 9, no. 2 (Spring 2020), 225.
55. Ross, "William Lloyd Garrison's Shattered Faith."
56. Frederick Douglass, "The Constitution and Slavery," accessed March 17, 2025, https://teachingamericanhistory.org/library/document/the-constitution-and-slavery/.

57. Frederick Douglass, "The Constitution of the United States: Is It Pro-Slavery or Anti-Slavery?," in *Anti-Slavery Political Writings, 1833–1860: A Reader*, ed. C. Bradley Thompson (London: Routledge, 2003), 144–158.

58. Abraham Lincoln, *The Language of Liberty: The Political Speeches and Writings of Abraham Lincoln*, ed. Joseph R. Fornieri (Washington, DC: Regnery, 2003), 176.

59. Lincoln, *The Language of Liberty*, 558–574.

60. Spalding, *We Still Hold These Truths*, 131.

61. Story, *Commentaries on the Constitution*, 157 [sec. 210].

62. Lewis Carroll, *Through the Looking-Glass, and What Alice Found There* (London: MacMillan, 1872), 124.

63. E.g., Cooper v. Aaron, 358 U.S. 1 (1958): "[T]he interpretation of the Fourteenth Amendment enunciated by this Court in the Brown case is the supreme law of the land."

64. For an excellent treatment of the US Supreme Court in serving as a vanguard of historical progress while simultaneously overruling democratic majorities, see Bradley C. S. Watson, *Living Constitution, Dying Faith: Progressivism and the New Science of Jurisprudence* (Wilmington, DE: ISI Books, 2020).

65. Federalist No. 78 [525].

66. Federalist No. 78 [525].

67. Federalist No. 49 [339].

68. Watson, *Living Constitution, Dying Faith*, 112. Emphasis in original.

69. William J. Brennan, "Construing the Constitution," *University of California, Davis Law Review* 19, no. 2 (1985): 4.

70. Another reason why this view appears to be popular is that the claim that the Constitution means whatever the justices say that it means is a species of relativism that denies that there is any real distinction between legitimate and illegitimate interpretations of words. As one political scientist, Gary Glen, observes, this idea "resonates with ordinary citizens whose own less sophisticated relativism inclines them to regard such distinctions as just 'a matter of opinion,' i.e., not a matter of the truth. . . . [This] popular relativism may be as much an obstacle to persuading the people of the existence and harm of judicial usurpation as is intellectual class affection for the judiciary. Might not that popular relativism make the distinction between legitimate and illegitimate abuse too subtle for even intelligent and thoughtful citizens to understand?" See Gary D. Glenn, "The Venerable Argument Against Judicial Usurpation," in *The End of Democracy? II: A Crisis of Legitimacy*, ed. Mitchell S. Muncy (Dallas: Spence, 1999),112n9.

71. Brennan, "Construing the Constitution," 7.

72. Brennan, "Construing the Constitution," 12.

73. Brennan, "Construing the Constitution," 5–7.

74. Brennan, "Construing the Constitution," 6.

75. James Madison, "1791: Madison, Speech on the Bank Bill," accessed March 21, 2025, https://oll.libertyfund.org/page/1791-madison-speech-on-the-bank-bill.

76. Federalist No. 37 [238].

77. Federalist No. 37 [238–239].

78. Federalist No. 37 [232–233].

79. Federalist No. 37 [238].
80. Federalist No. 15 [88-89].
81. James W. Ceasar, *Presidential Selection* (Princeton, NJ: Princeton University Press, 1979).
82. Federalist No. 55 [378].
83. James Madison, "James Madison, Virginia Ratifying Convention," in *The Founders' Constitution*, vol.1, ed. Philip B. Kurland and Ralph Lerner (Indianapolis: Liberty Fund, 2001), chap. 13, doc. 36.
84. Federalist No. 33 [206].

6. George Washington and Religious Liberty

1. For helpful brief accounts of the life and statesmanship of George Washington, see Richard Brookhiser, *Founding Father: Rediscovering George Washington* (New York: Free Press, 1996); Stephen F. Knott, *The Lost Soul of the American Presidency: The Decline into Demagoguery and the Prospects for Renewal* (Lawrence: University Press of Kansas, 2019), 1-27; and Jeffry H. Morrison, *The Political Philosophy of George Washington* (Baltimore: Johns Hopkins University Press, 2009), 19-61. For an extensive biography, see Ron Chernow, *Washington: A Life* (New York: Penguin Books, 2011). For a helpful discussion of Washington's use of the vine and fig tree metaphor, see Daniel L. Dreisbach, *Reading the Bible with the Founding Fathers* (New York: Oxford University Press, 2017), 211-227.

2. Brookhiser, *Founding Father*, 103.

3. George Washington, "To Catherine Macaulay Graham," in *George Washington: A Collection*, ed. W. B. Allen (Indianapolis: Liberty Classics, 1988), 537.

4. George Washington, "To Colonel Lewis Nicola," in *George Washington: A Collection*, 203-204.

5. Morrison, *The Political Philosophy of George Washington*, 42.

6. Katherine Carté, *Religion and the American Revolution: An Imperial History* (Chapel Hill: University of North Carolina Press, 2021).

7. Quoted in Morrison, *The Political Philosophy of George Washington*, 135.

8. Vincent Phillip Muñoz, "Religion and the Common Good: George Washington on Church and State," in *The Founders on God and Government*, ed. Daniel L. Dreisbach, Mark D. Hall, and Jeffry H. Morrison (Lanham, MD: Rowman & Littlefield, 2004), 19.

9. Mark A. Noll, *Christians in the American Revolution* (Vancouver, British Columbia: Regent College, 2006).

10. James G. Leyburn, "Presbyterian Immigrants and the American Revolution," *Journal of Presbyterian History* 54, no. 1 (Spring 1976): 24.

11. Thomas J. Wertenbaker, *Early Scotch Contributions to the United States*, quoted in Leyburn, "Presbyterian Immigrants and the American Revolution," 29. For an informative cultural history of Irish Presbyterians in the early republic, see Peter E. Gilmore, *Irish Presbyterians and the Shaping of Western Pennsylvania, 1770-1830* (Pittsburgh: University of Pittsburgh Press, 2018).

12. Leonard J. Kramer, "Muskets in the Pulpit: 1776-1783," *Presbyterian Historical Society Journal* 31, no. 4 (1953): 229-244.

13. Muñoz, "Religion and the Common Good," 16.
14. Muñoz, "Religion and the Common Good," 17.
15. George Washington, "To the General Assembly of the Presbyterian Churches," in *George Washington: A Collection*, 533.
16. "Address of the Presbytery of the Eastward to George Washington," in *The Sacred Rights of Conscience: Selected Readings on Religious Liberty and Church-State Relations in the American Founding*, ed. Daniel L. Dreisbach and Mark David Hall (Indianapolis: Liberty Fund Press, 2009), 356; emphasis in original.
17. George Washington, "Letter from George Washington to the Presbyterian Ministers of Massachusetts and New Hampshire," in *The Sacred Rights of Conscience*, 358.
18. Muñoz, "Religion and the Common Good," 11.
19. Quoted in Morrison, *The Political Philosophy of George Washington*, 138.
20. For a helpful discussion of religious liberty's compatibility with the pursuit of truth, see Samuel Gregg, *Reason, Faith, and the Struggle for Western Civilization* (Washington, DC: Regnery Gateway, 2019).
21. Opposition to religious liberty is something that at the turn of the twenty-first century may have been associated with violent religious fundamentalism, but in more recent years, as secular opposition to the free exercise of religion has grown, a certain species of Roman Catholicism and evangelicalism has produced its own reaction against religious liberty and against political modernity more generally.
22. George Washington, "To the United Baptist Churches in Virginia," in *George Washington: A Collection*, 532; emphasis mine.
23. Robert Louis Wilken, *Liberty in the Things of God: The Christian Origins of Religious Freedom* (New Haven, CT: Yale University Press, 2019), 11.
24. Timothy Samuel Shah, "The Religious Roots of Religious Freedom in Early Christian Thought," in *Christianity and Freedom*, vol. 1, *Historical Perspectives*, ed. Timothy Samuel Shah and Allen D. Hertzke (New York: Cambridge University Press, 2016), 33–61.
25. Martin Luther, *Martin Luther: Selections from His Writings*, ed. John Dillenberger (New York: Anchor, 1958), 385.
26. Wilken, *Liberty in the Things of God*, 160. Owen may seem a strange authority on religious liberty insofar as he was personal chaplain to Oliver Cromwell, the Lord Protector of Britain, who perpetrated a vicious persecution against Roman Catholics during the Interregnum. It is sufficient to note here that John Owen was not Oliver Cromwell and that Owen distanced himself from Crowell's murderous actions against Roman Catholics and also from his political rule more generally, although Owen preached the eulogy at Cromwell's funeral. See Sinclair B. Ferguson, *The Trinitarian Devotion of John Owen* (Sanford, FL: Reformation Trust, 2014), 6–25.
27. Roger Williams, "The Bloudy Tenent, of Persecution, for Cause of Conscience (1644)," in *The Sacred Rights of Conscience*, 15.
28. David VanDrunen, *Politics After Christendom: Political Theology in a Fractured World* (Grand Rapids, MI: Zondervan Academic, 2020), 199. Emphasis in original.
29. Morrison, *The Political Philosophy of George Washington*, 162.

30. Washington, "To the Hebrew Congregation in Newport," in *George Washington: A Collection*, 548.

31. "Dutch West India Company Instructions, 1656," in *The Sacred Rights of Conscience*, 108.

32. "Petition for Equality by the Philadelphia Synagogue to Council of Censors of Pennsylvania," in *The Sacred Rights of Conscience*, 294–295.

33. Barack Obama, "Remarks by the President at National Prayer Breakfast," February 6, 2014, accessed March 17, 2025, https://obamawhitehouse.archives.gov/the-press-office/2014/02/06/remarks-president-national-prayer-breakfast.

34. James V. Schall, "Obama's 'Right to Worship' Ushers in New State Religion," *Crisis Magazine*, February 27, 2014, accessed March 17, 2025, https://www.crisismagazine.com/2014/obamas-right-to-worship-ushers-in-new-state-religion.

35. Philip Bump, "Where Justice Alito and Rep. Greene Overlap on Religious Liberty," *Washington Post*, July 29, 2022, accessed March 17, 2025, https://www.washingtonpost.com/politics/2022/07/29/where-justice-alito-rep-greene-overlap-religious-liberty/.

36. Washington, "To the Hebrew Congregation in Newport," in *George Washington: A Collection*, 548.

37. Micah 4:4.

38. Dreisbach, *Reading the Bible with the American Founders*, 225.

39. Morrison, *The Political Philosophy of George Washington*, 60.

40. "Fairfax County Resolves, 18 July 1774," in *The Founders' Constitution*, vol. 1, *Major Themes*, eds. Philip B. Kurland and Ralph Lerner (Indianapolis: Liberty Fund Press, 1987), 633–634.

41. Samuel Gregg, "Religious Liberty and Economic Freedom: Intellectual and Practical Paradoxes," in *One and Indivisible: The Relationship Between Religious and Economic Freedom*, ed. Kevin Schmiesing (Grand Rapids, MI: Acton Institute, 2016), 1–10.

42. George Washington, "Farewell Address," in *George Washington: A Collection*, ed. W. B. Allen (Indianapolis: Liberty Classics, 1988), 521.

43. Muñoz, "Religion and the Common Good," 4–5.

44. Muñoz, "Religion and the Common Good," 3.

45. Morrison, *The Political Philosophy of George Washington*, 139.

46. "The Declaratory Act," in *The American Republic: Primary Sources*, ed. Bruce Frohnen (Indianapolis: Liberty Fund Press, 2002), 135–136; emphasis in original.

47. John Adams, "To H. Niles, February 3, 1816," in *The Political Writings of John Adams*, ed. George W. Carey (Washington, DC: Regnery, 2000), 708.

7. Friedrich Hayek and the Free Market

1. Samuel Gregg, *The Next American Economy: Nation, State, and Markets in an Uncertain World* (New York: Encounter Books, 2022) 9–16.

2. Like so many intellectuals who experienced the Great War and its aftermath, Hayek was a socialist as a young man. But after learning more about economics, especially under the influence of the writing and teaching of

Austrian economist Ludwig von Mises, Hayek became a rigorous defender of the free market, and in the early part of his academic career, his technical economic writings distinguished him as a rising star in classical liberal economics. In the 1930s, he visited the London School of Economics, where he delivered a series of lectures in which he defended the claim that the best way to avoid recessions—and to escape from them when they happen—is to allow the market to operate freely so that prices could guide people into knowing what to buy and to invest in a way that reflected actual savings and demand for goods in a society. By contrast, he argued that governmental attempts to end recessions through artificial stimuli such as deficit spending had the effect of prolonging recessions. The result of Hayek's lectures was that he was invited to join the faculty of the London School of Economics so that he might be a voice in Great Britain to oppose John Maynard Keynes and the new economic orthodoxy of Keynesian thought that advocated government intervention to stimulate an economy into recovery by promoting increased demand for production of goods. After Hayek's move to England, he began to combine his interest in economics with a broader concern with political theory and with the conditions of a free society, a development that resulted in his popular book *The Road to Serfdom* as well as his two major works of political and economic liberty, *The Constitution of Liberty* and *Law, Legislation, and Liberty*.

3. Nicholas Wapshott, *Keynes Hayek: The Clash That Defined Modern Economics* (New York: Norton, 2011), 203, 253–255; and Lawrence H. White, "Hayek's *The Road to Serfdom*," in *Champions of Freedom: The Ludwig von Mises Lecture Series: Mises, Hayek, and the Austrian School*, vol. 45, ed. Gary Wolfram (Hillsdale, MI: Hillsdale College Press, 2017), 39.

4. F. A. Hayek, *The Road to Serfdom*, ed. Bruce Caldwell (Chicago: University of Chicago Press 2007), 59.

5. Hayek, *The Road to Serfdom*, 58.

6. Hayek, *The Road to Serfdom*, 58.

7. Hayek, *The Road to Serfdom*, 137.

8. Hayek refers to his way of thinking about humanity and society as the Anglican tradition of the Enlightenment, represented by thinkers such as John Locke, Adam Smith, and Charles de Montesquieu, and which was opposed to the more rationalist Gallican tradition of thinkers such as Thomas Hobbes and René Descartes. See Friedrich A. Hayek, *The Constitution of Liberty* (Chicago: University of Chicago Press, 1960), 55–70; and F. A. Hayek, *Individualism and Economic Order* (Chicago: University of Chicago Press, 1980), 1–32.

9. Roland Hill, *Lord Acton* (New Haven, CT: Yale University Press, 2000), 300.

10. See Jean-Jacques Rousseau, *Basic Political Writings of Jean-Jacques Rousseau*, trans. and ed. Donald A. Cress (Indianapolis: Hackett 1987), 60–81.

11. Hayek, *The Road to Serfdom*, 136.

12. John Locke, *Two Treatises of Government*, ed. Peter Laslett (Cambridge University Press: Cambridge and New York, 2003 [1960]), sec. 123.

13. Hayek, *The Road to Serfdom*, 136.

14. Hayek, *The Road to Serfdom*, 136.

15. Hayek, *The Road to Serfdom*, 87.

16. Milton Friedman, *Capitalism and Freedom* (Chicago: University of Chicago Press, 1962), 15.

17. Tom Bethell, *The Noblest Triumph: Property and Prosperity Through the Ages* (New York: St. Martin's Press, 1998), 17.

18. See Heritage Foundation, Index of Economic Freedom, 31st ed., accessed March 22, 2025, https://www.heritage.org/index/.

19. Those people friendly to socialism are quick to dispute this number, either on the grounds that twentieth-century socialism was not true socialism or else on the statistical grounds. My concern here is not to dig into the details of this debate. For a readable overview of this history that explains the plausibility of these figures through a discussion of the historical context, see Paul Johnson, *Modern Times: The World from the Twenties to the Nineties* (New York: Harper Perennial, 2001).

20. Bethell, *The Noblest Triumph*, 9.

21. Bethell, *The Noblest Triumph*, 17.

22. For more on Karl Marx's understanding of human nature and his understanding of his own radical political and economic experimentation, see Eric Voegelin, *Science, Politics, and Gnosticism* (Wilmington, DE: ISI Books, 2004), 17–31, 61–87.

23. One of the earliest advocates of this false notion of freedom was the English Social Darwinist T. H. Green, who wrote in the nineteenth century that freedom "does not mean merely freedom from restraint or compulsion" but instead means "a power which each man exercises through the help or security given him by his fellow men." See Green's lecture "Liberal Legislation and Freedom of Contract," in *Ideals and Ideologies: A Reader*, 10th ed., ed. Terence Ball, Richard Dagger, and Daniel I. O'Neill (New York: Routledge, 2017), 126–130.

24. Bernie Sanders, "On Democratic Socialism in the United States," in *Ideals and Ideologies: A Reader*, 11th ed., ed. Terence Ball, Richard Dagger, and Daniel I. O'Neill (New York: Routledge, 2019), 359.

25. Franklin Delano Roosevelt, "The Four Freedoms," in *American Political Thought: A Norton Anthology*, ed. Isaac Kramnick and Theodore J. Lowi (New York: Norton, 2009), 1189.

26. Franklin Delano Roosevelt, "A Second Bill of Rights," in *American Political Thought*, 1191.

27. Roosevelt, "A Second Bill of Rights," 1190–1191.

28. Hayek, *The Road to Serfdom*, 147.

29. Sanders, "On Democratic Socialism," 359.

30. Hayek, *The Road to Serfdom*, 132.

31. Hayek, *The Road to Serfdom*, 133.

32. Hayek, *The Road to Serfdom*, 78, 147.

33. H. G. Wells, *The Rights of Man* (New York: Vintage Classics, 2015 [1940]), 67–68.

34. Hayek, *The Road to Serfdom*, 121.

35. United Nations, Universal Declaration of Human Rights, accessed March 27, 2025, https://www.un.org/en/universal-declaration-human-rights/ (emphasis mine).

36. Hayek, *The Road to Serfdom*, 122.

37. Hayek, *The Road to Serfdom*, 76.
38. Hayek, *The Road to Serfdom*, 77.
39. Hayek, *The Constitution of Liberty*, 270.
40. Hayek wrote in the seminal essay "The Use of Knowledge in Society" that man "cannot know more than a tiny part of the whole of society," and "therefore all that can enter into his motives are the immediate effects which his actions will have in the sphere he knows." See Hayek, *Individualism and Economic Order*, 14.
41. Hayek, *Individualism and Economic Order*, 80.
42. Hayek, *The Constitution of Liberty*, 54–61; cf. Hayek, *Individualism and Economic Order*, 8, 14–15, 19.
43. Hayek, *The Constitution of Liberty*, 56–58.
44. Hayek, *Individualism and Economic Order*, 85.
45. Hayek, *Individualism and Economic Order*, 88; emphasis mine.
46. See Henry Hazlitt, *Economics in One Lesson* (New York: Three Rivers Press, 1979 [1946]), 103–109; and Thomas Sowell, *Basic Economics: A Common Sense Guide to the Economy*, 4th ed. (New York: Basic Books, 2011), 11–38.
47. See Thomas Sowell, *The Housing Boom and Bust*, rev. ed. (New York: Basic Books, 2010).
48. Higher mortgage interest rates are customarily given to people with weaker credit; in this way, the lending institutions increase the price of lending to the borrower, who pays more per month for their home. In addition, a sizable down payment for a home loan acts as the price of borrowing; government regulations that permit borrowing home loans at under 5 percent of the price of the home effectively lower the price that borrowers must pay in order to purchase a home.
49. George Leef, "One Bad Law Usually Leads to Others: The Housing Bubble and Dodd-Frank," Forbes.com, accessed March 22, 2025, https://www.forbes.com/sites/georgeleef/2014/01/10/one-bad-law-usually-leads-to-others-the-housing-bubble-and-dodd-frank/.
50. Hazlitt, *Economics in One Lesson*, 47.
51. Hayek, *The Road to Serfdom*, 117.
52. Hayek, *The Constitution of Liberty*, 142–143, 151–153.
53. Bruce Caldwell, *Hayek's Challenge: An Intellectual Biography of F. A. Hayek* (Chicago: University of Chicago Press, 2004), 290.
54. Hayek, *The Road to Serfdom*, 112–113.
55. Hayek, *The Road to Serfdom*, 114–115.
56. Hayek, *The Road to Serfdom*, 86; cf. Hayek, *The Constitution of Liberty*, 227–228.
57. Friedman, *Capitalism and Freedom*, 144–160.
58. Michael J. De La Merced, "GM Wins Final Approval of DIP Financing," NYTimes.com, June 25, 2009, accessed March 22, 2025, https://dealbook.nytimes.com/2009/06/25/gm-wins-final-approval-of-dip-financing/.
59. Congressional Budget Office, An Update to the Economic Outlook: 2015–2025, accessed March 22, 2025, https://www.cbo.gov/sites/default/files/114th-congress-2015-2016/reports/50724-BudEconOutlook-3.pdf.
60. Hayek, *The Road to Serfdom*, 117.
61. The full context of the quote is as follows: "If all men were completely equal in their gifts and inclinations, we should have to treat them differently in order to achieve any sort of social organization. Fortunately, they are not

equal; and it is only owing to this that the differentiation of functions need not be determined by the arbitrary decision of some organizing will but that, after creating formal equality of the rules applying in the same manner to all, we can leave each individual to find his own level. There is all the difference in the world between treating people equally and attempting to make them equal." See Hayek, *Individualism and Economic Order*, 15-16.

62. Hayek, *The Road to Serfdom*, 117, 150.
63. Hayek, *The Road to Serfdom*, 113, 141.
64. Hayek, *The Road to Serfdom*, 150; cf. Hayek, *The Constitution of Liberty*, 88-90, 95-100.
65. Hayek, *The Constitution of Liberty*, 95-97.
66. See Sowell, *Basic Economics*, 40-49, for a discussion of the economic consequences of rent control in cities such as New York and San Francisco. His discussion of agriculture subsidies appears at 58-63.
67. Hayek, *The Road to Serfdom*, 137, 151-152.
68. Hayek, *The Road to Serfdom*, 72.

8. Wilhelm Röpke and the Cultural Conditions of the Free Market

1. Wilhelm Röpke, *The Solution of the German Problem* (New York: Putnam's, 1947 [1946]), 6.
2. Röpke, *The Solution of the German Problem*, 60.
3. Samuel Gregg, *Wilhelm Röpke's Political Economy* (Cheltenham, UK: Edward Elgar, 2010), 1-2.
4. Röpke, *The Solution of the German Problem*, 6.
5. Wilhelm Röpke, *A Humane Economy: The Social Framework of the Free Market* (Wilmington, DE: ISI Books, 1998), 5.
6. Röpke, *A Humane Economy*, 6.
7. Deidre McCloskey is the best contemporary advocate of this thesis. See, e.g., Deirdre McCloskey, *The Bourgeois Virtues: Ethics for an Age of Commerce* (Chicago: University of Chicago Press, 2006); Deirdre McCloskey, "Avarice, Prudence, and the Bourgeois Virtues," in *Having: Property and Possession in Religious and Social Life*, ed. William Schweiker and Charles Mathews (Grand Rapids, MI: Eerdmans, 2004), 312-336; and Donald McCloskey, "Bourgeois Virtue," *American Scholar* 63, no. 2 (1994): 177-191.
8. McCloskey, "Bourgeois Virtue," 182.
9. Röpke, *A Humane Economy*, 121.
10. Röpke, *A Humane Economy*, 120.
11. Röpke, *A Humane Economy*, 98.
12. Röpke, *A Humane Economy*, 98.
13. Röpke, *A Humane Economy*, 3-4, 126. See Eric Voegelin, *Science, Politics, and Gnosticism* (Wilmington, DE: ISI Books, 2005) and *The New Science of Politics* (Chicago: University of Chicago Press, 1987).
14. Adam Smith, *An Inquiry into the Nature and Causes of the Wealth of Nations*, ed. Edwin Cannan (New York: Modern Library, 1937), 734-735 [V.1.3.2]:

> The man whose whole life is spent in performing a few simple operations, of which the effects too are, perhaps, always the same, or very

nearly the same, has no occasion to exert his understanding, or to exercise his invention in finding out expedients for removing difficulties which never occur. He naturally loses, therefore, the habit of such exertion, and generally becomes as stupid and ignorant as it is possible for a human creature to become. The torpor of his mind renders him, not only incapable of relishing or bearing a part in any rational conversation, but of conceiving any generous, noble, or tender sentiment, and consequently of forming any just judgment concerning many even of the ordinary duties of private life. Of the great and extensive interest of his country he is altogether incapable of judging; and unless very particular pains have been taken to render him otherwise, he is equally incapable of defending his country in war. . . . But in every improved and civilized society this is the state into which the laboring poor, that is, the great body of the people, must necessarily fall, unless government takes some pains to prevent it.

15. Röpke, *A Humane Economy*, 109.
16. John Zmirak, *Wilhelm Röpke: Swiss Localist, Global Economist* (Wilmington, DE: ISI Books, 2001).
17. Röpke, *A Humane Economy*, 219.
18. Alexis de Tocqueville, *The Recollections of Alexis de Tocqueville*, ed. with introduction by J. P. Mayer (London: Harvill Press, 1948).
19. Röpke, *A Humane Economy*, 6.
20. Röpke, *A Humane Economy*, 8.
21. Zmirak argues in his biography of Röpke that this is true of Röpke's mature writings. Earlier in his career, Röpke shared a broader Enlightenment view of the history of the West that saw rationalism and unaided human reason as the chief source of economic and political well-being.
22. Röpke, *A Humane Economy*, 9, 109; cf. 12, 70.
23. Röpke, *A Humane Economy*, 102, 108–109.
24. Röpke, *A Humane Economy*, 8.
25. Röpke, *A Humane Economy*, 107.
26. Gregg, *Wilhelm Röpke's Political Economy*, 119.
27. Röpke, *A Humane Economy*, 175.
28. Röpke, *A Humane Economy*, 163, 167, 177.
29. Röpke, *A Humane Economy*, 162.
30. Röpke, *A Humane Economy*, 164, 175.
31. Alexis de Tocqueville, *"Memoirs on Pauperism" and Other Writings: Poverty, Public Welfare, and Inequality*, trans. and ed. Christine Dunn Henderson (South Bend, IN: University of Notre Dame Press, 2001).
32. See, e.g., Nicolas Eberstadt, *The Great Society at Fifty: The Triumph and the Tragedy* (Washington, DC: American Enterprise Institute, 2014); Nicolas Eberstadt, *A Nation of Takers: America's Entitlement Epidemic* (West Conshohocken, PA: Templeton Press, 2012); and Marvin Olasky, *The Tragedy of American Compassion* (Washington, DC: Regnery, 1992).
33. Röpke, *The Solution of the German Problem*, 26: "The fact remains that that is the abyss in which we are inevitably plunged in the end if we once pursue the mistaken path of the biologism off which Darwin and his school laid the

foundation. The Nazi racial doctrine is the final putrid product of the decay of an intellectual process by which in the course of the nineteenth century man was degraded, with the zeal of a misunderstood science, to a subject of zoology and stud farming, but in this process all the principal countries of the West took part."

34. Wilhelm Röpke, *Welfare, Freedom, and Inflation* (London: Pall Mall Press, 1957), 22.

35. Röpke, *A Humane Economy*, 155.

36. Röpke, *A Humane Economy*, 158, 162; *Welfare, Freedom, and Inflation*, 27–28, 41.

37. Röpke, *Welfare, Freedom, and Inflation*, 21.

38. Röpke, *A Humane Economy*, 165.

39. Röpke, *A Humane Economy*, 166.

40. Röpke, *Welfare, Freedom, and Inflation*, 43.

41. Röpke, *A Humane Economy*, 137. Röpke was not original or unique in this, but his explanation and analysis of this feature of market societies is, I think, the most thoughtful that there is. For other treatments of this topic, see Michael J. Sandel, *What Money Can't Buy: The Moral Limits of Markets* (New York: Farrar, Straus & Giroux, 2012), 3–15; Gerson Moreno-Riano, "Democracy, Humane Economics, and a Culture of Enterprise," *Journal of Markets & Morality* 13, no. 1 (Spring 2010): 10–13; and *The Hedgehog Review*, 5, no. 2 (Summer 2003): 7–27.

42. Röpke, *A Humane Economy*, 138.

43. Röpke, *A Humane Economy*, 128.

44. Röpke, *A Humane Economy*, 128.

45. Röpke, *A Humane Economy*, 128.

46. Röpke, *A Humane Economy*, 148–149.

47. Röpke, *A Humane Economy*, 132–133.

48. Röpke, *A Humane Economy*, 130–131.

49. Röpke, *A Humane Economy*, 130–131. We must observe here that this is most true of his mature thought as expressed in *A Humane Economy*. At some points in Röpke's career, he actually seemed to be more open to the use of government intervention into the economy. At least in the 1940s, he seemed to be open to the possibility of expansion of property ownership even possibly through property redistribution, because he argued that land gives people security beyond that which one can achieve through wage-earning. At the same time, however, Röpke somewhat incoherently called for respect for private property ownership. His observation of the threat to liberty posed by the emergence of the modern welfare state in the 1950s and 1960s seems to have steered him toward a more consistently free market perspective. A less dangerous policy option that he advocated was the use of tax incentives for achieving a society that Röpke thought conducive to a healthy and sustainable culture. For reading on the tension between his desire for liberty and the free market on the one hand and, at least during the earlier portion of his career, an openness to government intervention on the other hand, see Gregg, *Wilhelm Röpke's Political Economy*, 135–140.

50. Gregg, *Wilhelm Röpke's Political Economy*, 133.

Conclusion

1. Quoted in Greg Weiner, *Old Whigs: Burke, Lincoln & the Politics of Prudence* (New York: Encounter Books, 2019), 102.
2. Edmund Burke, "Letter to Charles-Jean-Francois DePont," in Edmund Burke, *Further Reflections on the French Revolution*, ed. Daniel E. Ritchie (Indianapolis: Liberty Fund, 1992), 7.
3. Edmund Burke, *Select Works of Edmund Burke*, vol. 2, *Reflections on the Revolution in France* (Indianapolis: Liberty Fund, 1999), 152.
4. Friedrich A. Hayek, *The Constitution of Liberty* (Chicago: University of Chicago Press, 1960), 54-56.
5. F. A. Hayek, *Individualism and Economic Order* (Chicago: University of Chicago Press, 1996), 1-10.
6. Michael Anton, *The Stakes: America at the Point of No Return* (Washington, DC: Regnery, 2020); Kevin Slack, *War on the American Republic: How Liberalism Became Despotism* (New York: Encounter Books, 2023); and Stephen Wolfe, *The Case for Christian Nationalism* (Moscow, ID: Canon Press, 2022).
7. Chisholm v. Georgia 2 U.S. 419 (1793).
8. Federalist No. 46 [315], in *The Federalist*, ed. George W. Carey and James McClellan (Indianapolis: Liberty Fund Press, 2001).
9. Federalist No. 22 [146].
10. Federalist No. 37 [238].
11. Federalist No. 37 [232-233].
12. George Washington, "To the Hebrew Congregation in Newport," in *George Washington: A Collection*, ed. W. B. Allen (Indianapolis: Liberty Classics, 1988), 548.
13. See R. R. Reno, *Return of the Strong Gods: Nationalism, Populism, and the Future of the West* (Washington, DC: Regnery, 2021); and Various, "Against the Dead Consensus," *First Things*, March 21, 2019, accessed March 22, 2025, https://www.firstthings.com/web-exclusives/2019/03/against-the-dead-consensus.

Selected Bibliography

This bibliography lists many of the sources that were cited in the notes in this book, but the sources here are those that will be of most use to the reader. The primary sources below include most that were referenced in this book, and they will be of interest to those readers who may wish to read them for themselves. The list of secondary sources is more selective and includes only those which were particularly helpful to the author in understanding the political ideas in this book.

Primary Sources

Burke, Edmund. *Burke's Politics: Selected Writings and Speeches of Edmund Burke on Reform, Revolution, and War.* Edited by Ross J. S. Hoffman and Paul Levack. New York: Knopf, 1959.

Burke, Edmund. *Letters on a Regicide Peace.* Vol. 3 of *Select Works of Edmund Burke.* Foreword and biographical note by Francis Canavan. Indianapolis: Liberty Fund, 1999.

Burke, Edmund. *Miscellaneous Writings.* Vol. 4 of *Select Works of Edmund Burke.* Forward and select bibliography by Francis Canavan. Indianapolis, 1999.

Burke, Edmund. *Reflections on the Revolution in France.* Vol. 1 of *Select Works of Edmund Burke.* Foreword and introduction by E. J. Payne. Indianapolis: Liberty Fund, 1999.

Burke, Edmund. *Selected Writings of Edmund Burke.* Edited by W. J. Bate. New York: Modern Library, 1960.

Hamilton, Alexander, James Madison, and John Jay. *The Federalist.* Edited by Jacob E. Cooke. Hanover, NH: Wesleyan University Press, 1961.

Hayek, F. A. *Individualism and Economic Order.* Chicago: University of Chicago Press, 1980.

Hayek, F. A. *The Road to Serfdom.* Edited by Bruce Caldwell. Chicago: University of Chicago Press, 2007.

Hayek, Friedrich. *The Constitution of Liberty.* Chicago: University of Chicago Press, 1960.

Lincoln, Abraham. *The Language of Liberty: The Political Writings of Abraham Lincoln.* Edited by Joseph R. Fornieri. Washington, DC: Regnery, 2003.

Röpke, Wilhelm. *A Humane Economy: The Social Framework of the Free Market.* Wilmington, DE: ISI Books, 199.

Röpke, Wilhelm. *The Solution of the German Problem.* New York: Putnam's, 1947 [1946].

Röpke, Wilhelm. *Welfare, Freedom, and Inflation.* London: Pall Mall Press, 1957.

Tocqueville, Alexis de. *Democracy in America.* Translated by Harvey C. Mansfield and Delba Winthrop. Chicago: University of Chicago Press, 2000.

Tocqueville, Alexis de. *"Memoirs on Pauperism" and Other Writings: Poverty, Public Welfare, and Inequality.* Translated by Christine Dunn Henderson. South Bend, IN: University of Notre Dame Press, 2021.

Tocqueville, Alexis de. *The Recollections of Alexis de Tocqueville.* Edited with an introduction by J. P. Mayer. London: Harvill Press, 1948.

Washington, George. *George Washington: A Collection.* Edited by W. B. Allen. Indianapolis: Liberty Classics, 1988.

Secondary Sources

Barnett, Randy E. *Our Republican Constitution: Securing the Liberty and Sovereignty of We the People.* New York: Broadside Books, 2016.

Berns, Walter. *Making Patriots.* Chicago: University of Chicago Press, 2001.

Bethell, Tom. *The Noblest Triumph: Property and Prosperity Through the Ages.* New York: St. Martin's Press, 1998.

Brogan, Hugh. *Alexis de Tocqueville: A Life.* New Haven, CT: Yale University Press, 2008.

Brookhiser, Richard. *Founding Father: Rediscovering George Washington.* New York: Free Press, 1996.

Caldwell, Bruce. *Hayek's Challenge: An Intellectual Biography of F. A. Hayek.* Chicago: University of Chicago Press, 2004.

Chernow, Ron. *Alexander Hamilton.* New York: Penguin Books, 2004.

Chernow, Ron. *Washington: A Life.* New York: Penguin Books, 2011.

Den Hartog, Jonathan J. *Patriotism & Piety: Federalist Politics and Religious Struggle in the New American Nation.* Charlottesville: University of Virginia Press, 2015.

Diamond, Martin. "Democracy and the Federalist: A Reconsideration of the Framers' Intent." *American Political Science Review* 53, no. 1 (March 1959): 52–68.

Dreisbach, Daniel. *Reading the Bible with the Founding Fathers.* New York: Oxford University Press, 2016.

Dwan, David, and Christopher J. Insole, eds. *The Cambridge Companion to Edmund Burke.* New York: Cambridge University Press, 2012.

Epstein, Joseph. *Alexis de Tocqueville: Democracy's Guide.* New York: Eminent Lives, 2006.

Friedman, Milton. *Capitalism and Freedom.* Chicago: University of Chicago Press, 1962.

Gibson, Alan. *Interpreting the Founding: Guide to the Enduring Debates over the Origins and Foundations of the American Republic.* Lawrence: University Press of Kansas, 2010.

Gregg, Samuel. *The Next American Economy: Nation, State, and Markets in an Uncertain World.* New York: Encounter Books, 2022.

Gregg, Samuel. *Reason, Faith, and the Struggle for Western Civilization.* New York: Gateway Editions, 2019.
Gregg, Samuel. *Wilhelm Röpke's Political Economy.* Cheltenham, UK: Edward Elgar, 2010.
Guelzo, Allen C. *Abraham Lincoln: Redeemer President.* Grand Rapids, MI: Eerdmans, 1999.
Hazlitt, Henry. *Economics in One Lesson.* New York: Three Rivers Press, 1979.
Jividen, Jason. *Claiming Lincoln: Progressivism, Equality, and the Battle for Lincoln's Legacy in Presidential Rhetoric.* DeKalb: Northern Illinois University Press, 2011.
Kirk, Russell. *The American Cause.* Wilmington, DE: ISI Books, 2002.
Kirk, Russell. *The Conservative Mind: From Burke to Eliot.* 7th rev. ed. New York: Gateway Editions, 2014.
Knott, Stephen F. *The Lost Soul of the American Presidency: The Decline into Demagoguery and the Prospects for Renewal.* Lawrence: University Press of Kansas, 2019.
Levin, Yuval. "Edmund Burke's Economics of Flourishing." In *Economic Freedom and Human Flourishing: Perspectives from Political Philosophy*, edited by Michael R. Strain and Stan A. Veuger. Washington, DC: American Enterprise Institute. 2016.
Lilla, Mark. *The Reckless Mind.* New York: New York Review of Books, 2001.
Mahoney, Daniel J. *The Statesman as Thinker: Portraits of Greatness, Courage, and Moderation.* New York: Encounter Books, 2022.
Morel, Lucas E. *Lincoln and the American Founding.* Carbondale: Southern Illinois University Press, 2020.
Morrison, Jeffry H. *The Political Philosophy of George Washington.* Baltimore: Johns Hopkins University Press, 2009.
Oakes, James. *The Radical and the Republican: Frederick Douglass, Abraham Lincoln, and the Triumph of Antislavery Politics.* New York: Norton, 2007.
Shirer, William L. *The Rise and Fall of the Third Reich.* New York: Simon & Schuster, 1960.
Sowell, Thomas. *Basic Economics: A Common Sense Guide to the Economy.* 4th ed. New York: Basic Books, 2011.
Spalding, Matthew. *We Still Hold These Truths: Rediscovering Our Principles, Reclaiming Our Future.* Wilmington, DE: ISI Books, 2009.
Stanlis, Peter J. *Edmund Burke and the Natural Law.* Shreveport, LA: Huntington House, 1986.
Trueman, Carl. *The Rise and Triumph of the Modern Self: Cultural Amnesia, Expressive Individualism, and the Road to Sexual Revolution.* Wheaton, IL: Crossway, 2020.
VanDrunen, David. *Politics After Christendom: Political Theology in a Fractured World.* Grand Rapids, MI: Zondervan Academic, 2019.
Wapshott, Nicholas. *Keynes Hayek: The Clash That Defined Modern Economics.* New York: Norton, 2011.
Watson, Bradley C. S. *Living Constitution, Dying Faith: Progressivism and the New Science of Jurisprudence.* Wilmington, DE: ISI Books, 2020.
Weiner, Greg. *Madison's Metronome: The Constitution, Majority Rule, and the Tempo of American Politics.* Lawrence: University Press of Kansas, 2012.

Weiner, Greg. *Old Whigs: Burke, Lincoln & the Politics of Prudence.* New York: Encounter Books, 2019.

West, Thomas G. *Vindicating the Founders: Race, Sex, Class and Justice in the Origins of America.* Lanham, MD: Rowman & Littlefield, 2001.

Wilken, Robert Louis. *Liberty in the Things of God: The Christian Origins of Religious Freedom.* New Haven, CT: Yale University Press, 2019.

Williams, Tony. *Hamilton: An American Biography.* Lanham, MD: Rowman & Littlefield, 2018.

Wood, Gordon. *Revolutionary Characters: What Made the Founders Different.* New York: Penguin Books, 2006.

Zmirak, John. *Wilhelm Röpke: Swiss Localist, Global Economist.* Wilmington, DE: ISI Books, 2001.

INDEX

Adams, John, 30, 124
amendments to the Constitution, 72, 80–81, 86, 88–89, 103–109, 162
American Revolution, 25, 31, 108, 114, 119, 121, 124
Anglicanism. *See* Church of England
Anglo-American political tradition, 1–2, 22, 159–164
Anti-federalists, 108
Aristotle, 5–6, 53–54, 91
Articles of Confederation, 17, 79
associations. *See* local community
Austrian School of Economics, 22, 163

Baptist, 113, 120
Bastiat, Frederic, 177n21
Beard, Charles, 90
beauty, 27, 54, 67, 148, 154–155
Berns, Walter, 67
Bethell, Tom, 129
Bible, 21, 73–74, 110, 118–119, 121
Blackstone, William, 17
Brennan, William, 105–106
Bryce, James, 57
Burke, Edmund, 8–10, 31, 159–160
  on free enterprise, 35
  on Jean-Jacques Rousseau, 32

Catholicism, 9–10, 113, 119–120
Christianity and politics, 16, 51–52, 112–118, 129, 150, 155
churches, 26, 37, 56, 155–156
Churchill, Winston, 23, 125
Church of England, 9, 112–113, 124
Cicero, 21
civic education, 37, 108
civic virtue, 108, 115–116, 119, 146–147, 151–152
Civil War, 71–72, 98
Cold War, 2, 13, 125, 129
collectivism, 23, 146
Congress of the United States, 92, 94–95, 99, 101–102, 104, 109

consent, 84, 86, 88, 90, 92, 94, 124
conservatism, 2, 10, 125, 157, 161, 164
Constitution of Liberty, The (Hayek), 23
Constitution of the United States, 17, 31, 107
  Article I of, 19, 85, 89, 99
  Article II of 89
  Article IV of, 88, 99
  Article V of, 72, 88–89
  Article VI of, 88
  Article VII of, 17, 88–89
  as democratic and majoritarian, 86–88, 90, 92–95, 97, 108, 115
  criticisms of the, 85–87, 89–90, 92–93, 98, 102, 104, 107
  interpreted ultimately by the American people, 87, 102, 105
  Preamble to the, 85, 88, 90, 103
  Tocqueville on the framing of, 13
  as true, long-term will of the American people, 88, 93, 104, 107, 109
Constitutional Convention of 1787, 18–19, 21, 101, 107–108, 112
Continentalist, The (Hamilton), 18
"Cooper Union address" (Lincoln), 79–80, 101

Declaration of Independence, 68–69, 80–81, 83, 88, 90, 92, 115
  contrasted with the Confederacy, 98
Declaratory Act, 123
democracy, 31, 49, 92, 94, 97
democratic culture, 47, 56, 59–60
  aristocratic culture contrasted with, 48–49, 52, 54, 63–65
  commercial character of, 47, 55
  mediocrity of, 47, 51, 55
  preference for general ideas in, 62
Democracy in America (Tocqueville), 12, 49, 149
Diamond, Martin, 94

201

INDEX

Dickinson, John, 17
Discourse on the Origin of Inequality (Rousseau), 38
divided knowledge, 134–136, 138, 140
Douglas, Stephen, 4, 67, 74, 80
Douglass, Frederick, 3
   on Abraham Lincoln, 78
   on the Constitution, 80, 100–101
   on race and American identity, 69, 171n26
Dred Scott v. Sanford, 67–68, 73, 101

elections. *See* voting
Electoral College, 85–86
Emancipation Proclamation, 68, 76
equality
   of conditions, 49–50, 52–53, 56, 59, 63
   of humans, 50–52, 68–70, 74, 81, 83–84, 98, 152
   of outcome, 76, 139
   passion for, 4, 48–51, 59, 160
   rightly understood, 51–52
executive power, 77, 79, 92, 94–95, 105, 110–112
expressive individualism, 32–33

family, 39–40, 44, 60, 63, 134, 146, 152
   as "little platoon," 26, 37
Farewell Address (Washington), 21, 30, 111, 122
fascism, 23–24, 130
Federalist, The, 16, 19, 86, 161–162
   Federalist No. 1, 70, 89
   Federalist No. 2, 19
   Federalist No. 10, 75, 93, 97
   Federalist No. 22, 89, 161
   Federalist No. 37, 89, 107, 162
   Federalist No. 42, 100
   Federalist No. 46, 162
   Federalist No. 51, 93
   Federalist No. 54, 100
   Federalist No. 55, 91, 93, 108
   Federalist No. 78, 85, 103–104, 162
Fifteenth Amendment, 161
First Amendment, 4, 113, 120, 122
Fourteenth Amendment, 33, 161
Franklin, Benjamin, 80
freedom from want, 126, 130–132
freedom of religion. *See* religious liberty
freedom of speech, 6–7, 57–58
freedom of worship, 119–120
free enterprise, 35

free exercise of religion. *See* religious liberty
free market, 125–128, 140–151, 154–158
French and Indian War, 20
French Revolution, 3, 10–11, 25, 28, 32, 41–43, 45
Friedman, Milton, 129
fugitive slave clause, 99

Garrison, William Lloyd, 100
Gettysburg Address (Lincoln), 68, 70
Gibbon, Edward, 9
Great Depression, 126
Great Recession, 136–137
Great Society, 152
Great War, 22–23
Greeley, Horace, 76

Hamilton, Alexander, 4, 16–18, 70, 79–80, 85–86, 104, 111
Hayek, Friedrich, 22–23, 126, 163–164, 188n2
Hazlitt, Henry, 137
Herodotus, 53
Hitler, Adolf, 24
Hobbes, Thomas, 5, 36, 39, 44, 189n8
House of Representatives, 95
Humane Economy, A (Röpke), 24, 143–144, 156, 163
human nature, 56
   contrasted with animals, 5, 27, 29, 33–34, 60–62, 81–83, 152–153
   flaws in, 93, 128–129, 133–135, 138, 147
Hume, David, 17

impeachment, 92
individualism, 53, 59
intermediate institutions. *See* local community
Islam, 116, 122–123

Jay, John, 4, 16–17, 19–20, 86, 89
Jefferson, Thomas, 79–80, 87, 114
Johnson, Lyndon, 76
Johnson, Samuel, 9
Judaism, 113, 116, 118–120, 123
judicial review, 95, 104–106

Kansas-Nebraska Act of 1854, 16, 78–79, 81
Kant, Immanuel, 57–58
Keynes, John Maynard, 149, 151, 189n2
kingship. *See* monarchy
Kirk, Russell, 2, 26, 35–36

language, debate, and discourse, 5-6, 26, 39, 41, 47, 67, 111
  use and abuse of, 24-25, 31, 34-35, 67, 78, 103, 131-133
Law, Legislation, and Liberty (Hayek), 23
Letters on a Regicide Peace (Burke), 25, 29
liberal democracy, 6
libertarianism, 157
liberty
  absolute and unqualified, 26-33, 40-42, 78
  imprecise use of the concept, 25
  as inheritance, 26-27, 42-45, 108
  ordered, 26-32, 37, 40-41, 44-45, 56
Lincoln, Abraham, 14-16, 74-75, 77, 161
  on economic liberty, 68, 72-75, 84
  first inaugural, 68, 71, 73, 81, 105
  Lincoln-Douglas debates, 16
  second inaugural, 16, 68, 74
  opposition to slavery, 15-16, 34, 68, 76-79, 81-83
  criticism of, 76
local community, 64-65, 145-147, 152, 156
"little platoons," 26, 37-38, 40-43
local government, 65
Locke, John, 21, 36, 39, 43-44, 117, 128, 133
Louisiana Purchase, 80
Luther, Martin, 117
"Lyceum Address" (Lincoln), 15

Madison, James, 4, 16-19, 75, 86, 89, 91-95, 100, 123
Marcuse, Herbert, 7
Marx, Karl, 50, 130, 149
materialism, 148-150, 154-155, 164
Memoirs on Pauperism (Tocqueville), 61, 152
"Message to Congress in Special Session" (Lincoln), 75
Methodism, 113
Mill, John Stuart, 6, 30
minimum wage, 134, 140
Missouri Compromise, 79-80
moderation, 6, 11, 68, 149
monarchy, 22, 31, 42, 81, 84, 94, 110-111
Montesquieu, 11, 135, 189n8

National Socialism. *See* "Nazism"
natural law, 82, 137
natural rights. *See under* rights
Nazism, 23-24, 125-127, 141, 143-144, 149
Newburgh Conspiracy, 111-112
New Deal, 152

Nicola, Lewis, 111
Northwest Ordinance of 1787, 79, 102

occupational licensure, 138-139
Old Regime and the Revolution, The (Tocqueville), 14
ordoliberalism, 24, 163
Owen, John, 117

Pascal, Blaise, 11
patience and impatience, 6, 16, 96, 151
patriotism, 41-42, 44, 107, 112, 115, 119, 122
Plato, 31, 53
Plutarch, 18
popular sovereignty, 103
  and the Constitution of the United States, 4, 87-89, 182n6
  as right of states to choose slavery, 4, 67-69, 78-79, 81-82, 181n56
Presbyterianism, 112, 114-116
president of the United States. *See* executive power
presidential abuse of power, 109
prices, 133-137, 140-142
property, 53, 60, 73, 75, 121-122, 132, 138
  Burke on, 29, 44-45
  relation of political liberty to, 127-130
  Rousseau on, 39
prudence, 6, 10, 36-37, 43, 45, 77, 89, 108, 147

Quaker(ism), 9, 14

race and the American republic, 83-84, 112
Recollections (Tocqueville), 13
Records of the Federal Convention (Madison), 19
religion, 29, 116, 150
  social utility of, 37, 54-56, 63, 114, 122-123, 146, 155
religious liberty, 110, 112, 114-118, 120-124
religious toleration, 118-120, 124
Reagan, Ronald, 23, 125
Reflections on the Revolution in France (Burke), 10, 28, 37
rent control, 140-141
republican government, 67-70, 72, 74, 78, 81, 84, 110
  established by the United States Constitution, 86
  important of debate and persuasion in, 72

revolution, 5, 25, 36, 43, 65, 72, 149
   American. *See* American Revolution
   French. *See* French Revolution
Reynolds, Joshua, 9
rights, 69–70, 90, 93, 99, 121, 125, 131–132
   natural, 29, 34–35, 44, 75–76, 82, 116, 122–123
   Burke on, 26, 34–36, 173n41
   Hobbes on, 5
   Political debate and, 34–36
Road to Serfdom, The, 123, 125–127, 132, 137–138, 142
Robespierre, Maximilien, 11
Roman Catholicism. *See* Catholicism
Roosevelt, Franklin Delano, 76, 131
Röpke, Wilhelm, 23–24, 143, 163–164
   on asymmetry of the market, 154
   contrasted with Hayek, 157
   on culture, 144–145, 148–151, 155–158
   on freedom from want, 132
   and support for government intervention, 195n49
Rousseau, Jean-Jacques, 9, 32, 41–42, 128, 130, 135, 149
   on the meaning of freedom, 32, 38, 172n34
rule of law, 137–142

Sanders, Bernie, 131
Schmitt, Carl, 6
secession, 71–72
secondary institutions. *See* local community
Senate of the United States, 85–86, 95
separation of powers, 92–93, 95–96, 104
Seventeenth Amendment, 95
Sherman, Roger, 17
slavery, 49, 51, 56, 67–69, 73–74, 76, 80–81
   abolition of, 68–69, 72, 77–78, 102, 112
   injustice of, 81–84, 100
   and the Constitution, 67, 77, 79–81, 98–101
slave trade, 82, 99–100
Smith, Adam, 148, 155, 160
Smith, J. Allen, 92–93
social contract, 38–39, 44
Social Contract, On the (Rousseau), 38
Social Crisis of Our Time, The (Röpke), 24
socialism, 13, 125–131, 133, 141, 149, 151, 157
Socrates, 93
soft despotism, 59–66, 149

Solution of the German Problem, The (Röpke) 24, 144
Solzhenitsyn, Alexsandr, 40
Sowell, Thomas, 136
"speech at Cincinnati" (Lincoln), 75
"speech at New Haven" (Lincoln), 15, 82
"speech at Peoria" (Lincoln), 16, 67, 79–81, 83, 101
statesmanship, 36, 74, 77–78, 93, 111
Stephens, Alexander, 98
Story, Joseph, 102
Supreme Court of the United States, 20, 33, 67–68, 72–73, 87, 93, 102–106
   and constitutional interpretation, 105–107
   disagreement with, 73, 105

Taney, Roger, 68
temporal republicanism, 96–97
Tenth Amendment, 182n6
Tertullian, 117
Thatcher, Margaret, 125
theory and practice, 6, 70
   Burke on, 28–29, 34–36
   in *The Federalist*, 86–87, 91, 93, 95–97, 100
Third Reich, 6, 143
Thirteenth Amendment, 72, 101, 161
Thoughts on the Cause of the Present Discontents (Burke), 9
three-fifths clause, 99–100
Thucydides, 5–6
Tocqueville, Alexis de, 11–14, 135, 149, 160–161
toleration. *See* religious toleration
"To the General Assembly of the Presbyterian Churches" (Washington), 114
"To the German Congregation of New York" (Washington), 110
"To the Hebrew Congregation in Newport" (Washington), 116, 118, 121
"To the United Baptist Churches of Virginia" (Washington), 117
Tract Relative to the Laws Against Popery in Ireland (Burke), 10
tyranny, 86, 88, 94, 121, 128, 130, 141
   Burke on, 35, 45
   of caesars, 52–55, 59, 64–65, 67
   Lincoln on, 84
   of the majority, 56–59, 64
   Plato on, 31–32

United Nations Declaration of Human
   Rights, 132–133
"The Use of Knowledge in Society"
   (Hayek), 23, 134–135

veto, 85, 92, 95
Vindication of Natural Society (Burke), 9
Voegelin, Eric, 147
voting, 65–66, 72, 105, 109, 154

Warren, Mercy Otis, 30
Washington, George, 17–18, 20–22, 32,
   71, 110–112, 162–163
   in American Revolution, 1, 20,
      110–112, 114
   as political thinker, 20
   education of, 20, 110–111
   on freedom of speech, 7
   on French Revolution, 170n1
   military and political career of, 20–21
   as political thinker, 20
   on public support for religion, 122–123
   and slavery, 102
   Thanksgiving Proclamation, 122
   Tocqueville on, 13
Welfare, Freedom, and Inflation (Röpke),
   153–154
welfare state, 151–153
Wells, H.G., 132
Williams, Roger, 117
Wilson, James, 88
Wilson, Woodrow, 92
Witherspoon, John, 18, 114–115
World War II, 126, 143

www.ingramcontent.com/pod-product-compliance
Lightning Source LLC
Chambersburg PA
CBHW032214230426
43672CB00011B/2554